Sailing Away

Solo Sailing the Atlantic & Caribbean

A.J. McMahon

First published in 2020 by MCM Publications

Copyright © 2020 A.J. McMahon

All rights reserved.

No part of this publication may be reproduced, stored in a retrieval system, or in any form or by any means without the prior permission in writing of the copyright owner of this book.

ISBN: 979-8-5523-2985-4

I dedicate this book to
my Mum for my adventurous spirit,
to my Dad for my practical know how
and to my kids Kate and Sean.

Acknowledgements

Thank you to my family Sonya, Kate and Sean,
for enabling this adventure to happen
and to my brother Paul McMahon
for helping edit this book.

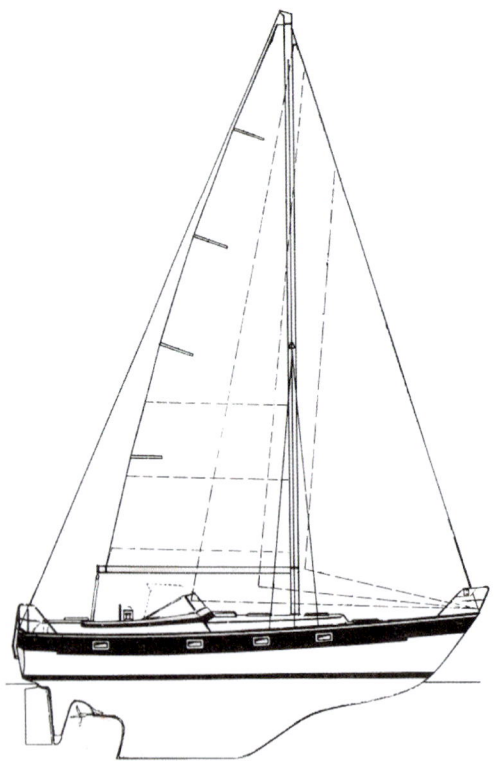

Contents

Introduction 1
   Sailing away 4
   Why sail now 7
   Finding the time away 9

Atlantic Preparations 16

Positioning to the start line 22

Lanzarote to Caribbean 36
   Bequia 75

Sailing the Caribbean 88
   Saint Vincent 88
   Saint Lucia 89
   Martinique 93
   Guadeloupe 99
   Montserrat 100

St. Barts (Saint-Barthelemy) 102

Saint Martin and back to St. Barts 103

Antigua 106

Les Saintes French Islands & Guadeloupe 107

Back to Europe 124

Shakedown Cruise 126

Caribbean to the Azores 132

Horta 164

Azores to Portugal mainland 176

Appendix 180

Hallberg Rassy 352 191

Sailing Glossary 192

About the Author 196

"It is good to have an end to journey toward,
but it is the journey that matters in the end."
Ernest Hemingway

Cruising Route 2018/19

Introduction

This adventure story is about breaking away from everyday life but not letting go completely. Breaking away from the shackles of the office to sail the Atlantic and explore the Caribbean while still officially working and getting paid. Breaking away from the family to take time out and to realise the importance of my role as the father to two teenage kids. It is a story born out of a deep desire to challenge myself by sailing the Atlantic single-handed, to prove if I had the 'right stuff'. It is a story of having it all, or at least trying too.

Why did I take on this adventure? Growing up I had no interest in sailing and was more interested in aeroplanes. My interests followed my father's, building aircraft models and radio-controlled aeroplanes, electronics and the dream of learning to fly. I certainly got my technical ability from my father; fiddling around with CB radio was a great background for future boat maintenance. In my teenage years, Richard Branson became my role model and my dream shifted from becoming the pilot to setting up and running my own business. At the age of sixteen I started MCM Productions with my father. We had the idea that a video showing everything that went on in the cockpit of an airliner would be a great product for aviation enthusiasts. To someone with little interest in aviation it made dull viewing but to aviation buffs this was pure magic. I contacted the marketing managers of all the European airlines to persuade them to grant us permission to film. Nobody realised they were negotiating with a teenager. In 1990 we produced our first video titled Capital 676 with Capital Airlines, filmed in a BAe 146 airliner from Dublin to London Luton. It was the first 'real time' cockpit film anywhere in the world. Over a number of years, we successfully produced and sold eleven aviation video titles. This was a business in line with my passion for aviation, so I decided to turn down a university place and concentrate full time on growing the business. While I enjoyed making aviation videos it was not what I really wanted to do. I wanted to be the pilot flying the aeroplane not the one doing the filming. This was the start of putting into action my dream to learn how to fly and to become an airline pilot.

I spent eight months in Australia learning to fly and obtained my Private Pilot Licence. I went on to complete the Airline Transport Pilot Licence exams and obtained the necessary flying experience for a Commercial Pilot License. The September 11 attacks in 2001 and a relationship breakup led me to put my pilot career on hold. My airline pilot dream never materialised so dreams do not always happen. I was still working in my own business, which had evolved from producing videos to publishing a construction trade directory. I needed to organise a house mortgage, which required taking a full-time steady income job. This led me to join a US multinational company based in Dublin. I planned to stay just six months in order to get the mortgage but twenty years later I am still working in the same company.

It was at work that I met my wife Sonya. We married in December 2002. She knew before we were married about my plans to fly around the world in a single-engine light aircraft with my friend Paul Ryan: World Flight 2003. I am not sure she realised what she was getting into and neither of us knew then that adventures were to be an ongoing theme in our lives. When I left to attempt the world circumnavigation, we were just 5 months married and Sonya was three months pregnant with my daughter Kate. The timing was not ideal but it was not something I could postpone as our plans were set. I had just completed the long bureaucratic process of getting approval for three months leave of absence from work.

The downside of adventures is the stress and worry it puts on family members back at home. I was so busy and focused on completing the trip that I was in my own bubble and did not see this. There is no doubt that my life was at considerable risk on this adventure but when you are young it does not sink in. We knew if the engine stopped there was no surviving the crash, as we had 150 gallons of fuel behind our heads. Especially difficult for my wife and father back home were the long fifteen- and eighteen-hour flights across the Atlantic and Pacific oceans. There was no way for them to contact us when flying or track the aircraft's position. All they could do is sit out and wait to see if we made it safely. At the age of 29, it was a great achievement to complete a circumnavigation of the world, arriving back at Shannon airport July 10th, 2003. Since 1924, there have been 106 flights round the world flights in single-engine aircraft. We were the 107th flight to circumnavigate and the first Irish pilots to do so.

My next few years were quieter in terms of adventuring. It was family time. I concentrated on building a family, working and renovating our home. We ended up with a gentleman's family, a girl and a boy, Kate and Sean. It was rewarding, simple fun with the kids. My project during this period in my life was to complete over four years, a part time Bachelor of Science degree in

Introduction

Psychology. I was also very busy with work as I held two jobs. For the day job I was in the office working in marketing for the US multinational company. In the evenings and on the weekends, I continued running my small publishing business from home. I had no free time for hobbies like sailing. The upside was that the day job paid our living expenses and bills while my second business allowed me to save money. It was these savings that later allowed me to buy the boat and consider sailing the Atlantic. But at this busy time in my life, boats, sailing and the Atlantic were not even ideas.

There came a point in my life where I asked myself: why am I working so hard and all the hours of the day, for what? I was in my mid-thirties and starting to feel bored. I wanted to feel some excitement. My house was near the sea and on my walks down Dun Laoghaire Pier, I would see the magnificent sight of boats of all sizes sailing in the bay. I had a nagging feeling that I was missing out. Was sailing something I should try? I needed a new challenge since I had put flying aeroplanes on the back burner. I tried crewing on a racing yacht but I did not really enjoy the racing aspect. I was asked to play the 'gorilla', the big guy who is asked to sit on the side of the boat with his legs dangling over the water to help flatten the boat when it is healing. Shouting skippers did not appeal to me. I decided I wanted command of my own boat.

Sailing away

In 2007, at the not so young age of 34, I bought a small 19-foot daysailer yacht. My Dad and I would go out into the bay and figure out sailing, by trial and error - there was plenty of error. I was bitten by the bug and soon decided I needed a bigger, more seaworthy boat. In the back of my head there was the idea to have a boat that would safely bring me across the Irish Sea, the 55 miles to Wales. It was the autonomy and freedom of the boat that really appealed; it would allow me to sail around Ireland, Wales, the Isle of Man and maybe even venture to Scotland. It seems simple now, but then I considered it a real achievement to sail seven miles offshore to the Kish Lighthouse in Dublin bay. The Irish Sea was a huge challenge for my abilities. I bought Charisma, a 25-foot Westerly Tiger, which was a solid English built boat and lovely to sail. To prepare for the Irish Sea adventure, I enrolled in a Yachtmaster Coastal Skipper course. That summer I sailed to Wales across the Irish Sea. It was one small step but a key building block to my future Atlantic ambitions.

During the winter months I built on my sailing theory by completing the Yachtmaster Offshore course. I read every sailing adventure book that I could get my hands on. I was particularly interested in exploits of sailing the Atlantic or round the world. Joshua Slocum's book resonated with me, Sailing Alone Around the World, the first person to sail around the world single-handed in

1895. I admired the challenge of being solo at sea with no one else to rely on but yourself. It seemed the ultimate test of one's mental and physical abilities: you either complete the trip single-handed or you fail, you either love it or hate it. In addition, the majority of sailing plans never happen. Boats never leave the marina because they can't arrange crew at the right time. Going alone solves this problem and gives much more opportunity for sailing.

The time felt right to buy a bigger boat, a 'go anywhere' type of yacht, an ocean-going vessel. My plan was to explore with the family Brittany and Galicia and that meant I needed a bigger, more comfortable boat. If I was trading up to the next level of boat, why not get the ultimate boat that would allow me to take on any future adventure? In the back of my head after reading all the sailing stories was an unframed idea of making a transatlantic voyage. It is in the buying and selling of boats - like houses - that you lose money. My theory was to spend more money now and get the boat I really wanted, so I would not be looking to change the boat again in five years.

I spent a year and a half and a fair bit of money travelling to look at boats in Ireland, Wales, England, Spain and the Netherlands. My requirements were ocean-going certification, an aft cabin to give me privacy from the crew, in-mast furling so the mainsail could be easily furled or rolled away into the mast from the safety of the cockpit, and an easy boat to sail single-handed. It came down to an English built Moody 37 or a Swedish built Hallberg Rassy 352. Hallberg Rassy is the Rolls Royce of boats, expensive but with a good resale value and built for ocean voyages. I sailed the Moody twice in Southampton but I was undecided. I felt the cabin was too wide with very few grab handles to hold onto in big seas.

I found online a Hallberg Rasy 352 for sale in Bruinisse, Netherlands. She was called Esperanza, which is Spanish for 'hope' - you can't get a better name than that. She was built in 1988. The previous owners had put a lot of money into the boat adding a new Yanmar engine, new teak deck, new upholstery, new sails and new nearly everything. I booked flights to view the boat but before I could get there, she was sold. I was very disappointed. As I had the flights booked so I went anyway to the Netherlands and viewed another boat. While I was there by pure luck or maybe it was fate, I got a call from the broker to say the buyer of Esperanza had finance problems, was I still interested? As it happened, I was just 20 minutes away. Once I saw Esperanza, I knew she was the boat for me. It was a big financial decision to move up to the Hallberg Rassy level of boat but I grabbed the opportunity knowing she would be easy to sell again if it did not work out. 15th May 2014 I now owned an ocean-going vessel, my sailing dreams were starting to become a reality.

Esperanza at 35 feet (10.5 metres in length) was a bigger boat to what I was used to, so I decided I needed to upgrade my skills. I took sailing lessons to prepare for my Yachtmaster Offshore test, which I completed October 2014.

Introduction

This was a gruelling practical test of seamanship over 13 hours, spanning day and night. It was hugely satisfying to know I had the skills to make the grade. And I did it on my own boat. I was now Yachtmaster Offshore certified. Over a number of seasons I became more familiar with Esperanza, sailing to England, Scotland, France, Galicia in Spain and completing an around Ireland sail. My experience of long voyages grew as I took on the Bay of Biscay, sailing across first with crew and then making the return trip home single-handed. Each winter I upgraded the boat to add redundancy with the idea of the Atlantic now clearly formed in my mind. It was a goal that I wanted to achieve but I had no idea when or how to get the time away from work and my family to make this possible. My thinking was, since I now had the boat, the next step was to get the boat ready and upgraded for a possible transatlantic, the rest would fall into place.

The idea appealed to me of sailing the Atlantic Ocean on my own single-handed. I wondered if I would be able to do this. To understand more I read every book I could find about solo sailing. It was reassuring that I had made many single-handed short trips and one long trip across the Bay of Biscay and I enjoyed it. Was it beginner's luck? Even the day before I was due to leave the Canaries for the Caribbean, I was not at all sure I could sail myself across the Atlantic. Doubt starts to creep in, like it did just before we set off to fly around-the-world in 2003. All sorts of reasons appear as to why it would be a good idea to delay the trip another few days, or a few weeks... or why not leave it entirely until next year? There is fear of the unknown, the possible danger that lies ahead, but you just have to get on with it and push the fear to the back of your mind. During World Flight 2003 in India I was asked by officials at the airport 'what is your mission'. I thought this an odd word to use - mission - and it stuck with me ever since. Mission is a very good word to describe adventures that have a defined goal and endpoint: fly around-the-world or sail your boat to Caribbean and back single-handed. All you need to do is fix your sights on the mission and say 'this is my job now, let's get it done'. No matter what challenges lie ahead, I must achieve the mission.

One question I am often asked is how will you deal with being alone for up to four weeks at sea with no other human contact, other than the odd email and satellite phone call home. The psychologist Carl Jung suggested that isolation over weeks at sea causes the unconscious mind and the conscious mind to blur. Messages from the unconsciousness come to the surface, voices are often heard. When sailing the Bay of Biscay solo I heard whispering voices. I could never make out exactly what was being said, maybe just as well. It feels like ghosts are onboard but they seem friendly spirits. It must from the sounds of water and air on the hull. Our brains are pattern recognition machines, we can't stop ourselves from trying to make sense of what we experience in the world around us. When we step into isolation, our mind occupies the gaps from the missing everyday interaction with other people. Solo sailors don't often mention the common occurrence of 'hearing voices' as people might think we are crazy. Many people already think solo sailors are crazy for wanting to sail oceans alone.

It does make me wonder if today we are afraid to spend time alone. Afraid to break away from everyday life as society tells us we will be lonely. I think time alone to one's self in solitude might be valuable, allowing meaning and insight from our unconsciousness to surface that would otherwise not. The longest time I had spent at sea alone before the Atlantic was 5-days crossing Biscay and I never felt lonely. Yes, of course I missed home, family and friends but I never found it an unpleasant experience, rather I found living in the simplicity of nature invigorating. For the Atlantic trip I needed to extend my isolation experience to at least 23-days, maybe more. It will be a self-experiment in isolation.

Why sail now

The reason I decided to make this trip in 2018, was that my father passed away. I had less commitments as both my parents had passed on. My Dad was diagnosed with cancer only a few months before. While I was sailing around Ireland in Esperanza, I got a call to say he was in hospital. He had gone to A&E on his own and had been admitted. We thought it was just a small growth in his bowel, to be fixed with a minor operation. The situation became more serious as the diagnosis showed the tumour was cancerous. This was a shock to me, as my mother died of cancer when I was 18. I thought my Dad would be the last person to get cancer as he never drank or smoked and was not overweight. Without an operation to remove the tumour the consultant said he had about a year to live. The consultant said he just wanted to save his life but Dad's motto was it was better to go quick than have a gradual, painful, undignified decline and become a burden on others.

A week later I had to bring Dad back to the hospital as he was in pain and looking much weaker. During his first hospital stay he made friends and had great chats. He had more social company in the hospital over a week than he had in the year before. Living alone was lonely. This time in the hospital the patients were older, sicker and not chatty. He was in the hospital just 5-days when he called me and said "get me out of here, the hospital is doing my head in". Dad was very down and miserable. Looking back, leaving the hospital was a turning point for him, as he had decided to go it alone and die in his own way.

At home that night he told me they did a higher resolution scan and the tumour was much bigger and now also attached to the bladder. The Urologist said it was likely he would lose his bladder and bowel after the operation. The cancer was so advanced it was unlikely they would find it all. The operation may buy a year or two but at what cost to his quality of life. Dad said he was not going

Introduction

to lose control and get drawn into the medical system with one operation after another to prolong his life for a little extra time. Dad was an engineer and he said he evaluated his situation like any other engineering problem. There was no escaping the reality. We talked in his house until late that evening and he seemed resolved to his fate. He described his life as complicated but he felt he had a good innings. His attitude was that we all have to die sometime. He had plenty of hobbies like Amateur Radio, classical music and HiFi but the cancer left him so weak and tired he was no longer able to enjoy them. Of course he would have liked another ten years but not if he lost his autonomy. That was the last big chat we had. I assumed we had a year to deal with things. I was wrong.

He became weaker and took to bed for the last time. I should have spent more time with him but I was so busy with work and the kids. I had planned to set up a bed in the family home as he was going to need care. I had no issue with the thoughts of caring for him. It actually felt good, like it was my duty and I wanted to do it. The next morning I arrived at my Dad's house and he looked very bad. He was shaking, not really conscious, he could not speak. The week before he had said to me that he did not want to go back into hospital and in no circumstance was I to call an ambulance. His eyes were dilated and fixed in the distance, he looked to be in a lot of pain and to me he was dying in front of me, there and then. I was alone and did not know what to do. I called my brother Paul and Sonya to discuss what I should do. Do I obey his wishes or do I get help? What a dilemma, a real moral maze. I couldn't leave him like this as I was out of my depth. I called 999 and the ambulance arrived and we went on blue lights to the hospital. En route they upgraded the call as they fought to keep him alive.

Later in the hospital he was conscious again after fluids, pain relief and antibiotics. He had Septicaemia, blood poisoning. The A&E duty doctor took me aside that night and said he is dying; no more can be done and it is only a matter of time. I was in shock and numbed hearing this, I didn't really take it in. The doctor said to get my brother on a flight right now as my Dad may go at any time. My brother lives in New York and booked the first flight to arrive at 7am the next morning.

That was the start of a long week in the hospital where my Dad at one point actually perked up a little. We had some good conversations in the hospital. The palliative care team took over and spoke with my Dad to be sure what he wanted. It was 5 more exhausting days in the hospital before his heart gave up. It was special that my brother and I were there the whole time. The moral of this story is to get regular medical check-ups. We put our car through rigorous annual checks so why do we give our bodies any less attention? If my father's tumour had been spotted earlier, it would have required a routine operation with a high success rate. He would have got his 10 extra years. My Dad said himself that he had been a bit too stoic. He endured pain for too long, when he should have gone to the hospital. My Dad died on the 29th September 2017, at the age of 74. Just like that I was in the position of no longer having parents. It is the oddest feeling not to have a parent to turn to for advice. Suddenly there is no one calling you every day on the phone. As an adult orphan it all goes very quiet. Just like that I was top of the family tree.

Out of the sadness emerges positivity, energy and new opportunities. I had a realisation that anything might now be possible and maybe this was my time. There was nothing stopping me now, I was unshackled from the historic parent-child relationship that had kept me close to home. I had a sense of newfound freedom and a boat ready to sail to new horizons. Up to now sailing the Atlantic was just a dream, now it felt like the time was right to grab this opportunity and set sail on my adventure. At the same time this might be just what I need to help me through the grieving process. The death of a loved one makes you realise that we do not know how much time we have left in this world, there is so much more to do and experience. Seize the day and launch your dreams, do not push those dreams too far into an uncertain future. My own personal sailing adventure across the Atlantic to the Caribbean had started.

Finding the time away

The Atlantic sailing circuit is from the Canaries across the Atlantic to the Caribbean where boats explore the islands before sailing on to the Azores and then back to Europe. It takes around eight months and you still have to add in the time to get the boat from Ireland to the Canaries, 1,700 miles. The question was how to get the time off work and be away from the family to make my Atlantic dream possible. I could not afford to leave my job; I had a family to support. My wife was working in a new job and could not consider taking a leave of absence. The kids were in secondary school so taking a year out was not an option. Teenagers are less interested in becoming liveaboard sailors. The only plan that seemed to work was if I went alone.

It became obvious that being away from my family for up to six months was increasingly impractical. My wife and I discussed how we could make this work. The plan we reached was for me to fly home from the Caribbean twice. I flew home for three weeks in February and for five weeks in April for Easter. The maximum time I was away from the kids in any one stretch was 8 weeks. Getting home twice over six months, we thought, would be enough to allow me to stay connected with family life. Flying back and forth between the Caribbean and Ireland required lots of planning. There was the complexity of deciding in advance which islands were best to leave the boat unattended, reserving marina berths and booking return flights from the Caribbean to Dublin. I figured out

Introduction

that the best value flights were from the French islands Martinique and Guadeloupe. The French islands were therefore the best option to base the boat for the weeks I was back home.

During my Atlantic adventure I was in the unusual situation of leading two completely different lives. I had my Caribbean life as a liveaboard sailor with a new circle of sailor friends. My home was the boat and it actually did feel like my home. My other life was the stability of family life back in Dublin. It took time to adjust between moving between the two very different lives. Like a commercial sailor by the time I had adjusted to being back at home, it was time to think about reverting back to my Caribbean life as a sailor. I enjoyed the experience of moving between Dublin and the Caribbean. It felt I had it all.

The downside was that I missed many big family events while I was sailing; Christmas, my son's birthday, St Patrick's Day, Father's Day, a family wedding and my brother in law and family who visited from Florida. It was the small stuff of family life that I really missed when I was at sea. The walks with the kids in the evenings, buying them a 99-ice-cream on the seafront, grabbing lunch in the local cafe, the family chats we would have in between the day's activities. I even missed chauffeuring the kids around to their activities. Ironically, it was this time apart from the kids that made me realize how important they are to me and that I love them very much.

I admire my family for allowing me the freedom to chase my sailing dream. They knew like World Flight, once I had the idea I could not let go. I also hoped my adventure would act as an inspiration to my kids to show them that anything is possible if you put your mind to it. I now had a plan agreed with the family but what about time off work?

I was 18 years working for the same US multinational company. I held many different positions in the company over the years from marketing to I.T. My role allowed me to work remotely from home which gave me freedom that other jobs couldn't offer. I lived my life not through my work but through my hobbies and passions. I always expected, when the time was right to move back into self-employment and put my passion and determination into building my own business. I did it before and will do it again. Though I knew if I was working in my own business it would be unlikely that I would have the time for adventures. The 9-5pm corporate job was the perfect complement to planning and implementing thrill-seeking adventures.

To make the Atlantic trip I calculated that I needed at least six months off work. A career break after 18 years in the same company was exactly what I needed. It would allow me the time to recharge my batteries and return to a tenured job. My employer did offer leave of absence programs up to a maximum of 6 months. But the reality of applying and being accepted is a very different matter and there is no guarantee you will return to the same role in the company. The other possibility was redundancy. Redundancy, I felt, was the answer as I was ready to move on to new opportunities. It would give me the time for my Atlantic adventure while giving me the money cushion for a twelve-month break. But you can't just march in to work, demand to be made redundant and please can I have a nice redundancy package? There are ways and means to position an exit but it was not working in my favour.

I concluded the only option was to go ahead and apply for a leave of absence and take the financial hit of zero income for six months. I was waiting for the last moment to apply when Murphy's law struck: 'anything that can go wrong will go wrong'. Overnight I got promoted to management. I was suddenly a manager of a team of eight people. This had been rumoured for some months but I hoped it would not happen until the following year as it would screw up my sailing plans. To turn down the promotion would not look good and certainly lead to a career dead end. It was a new exciting role for me and an opportunity I did not want to miss. A leave of absence request from a newly appointed manager would never be approved. It looked like the door had closed on my sailing aspirations, or so it seemed.

A friend suggested why don't I sail the Atlantic using my earned vacation time and work remotely from the Caribbean. Did I need a leave of absence at all? Working remotely was certainly possible as my daily work was based around email and conference calls. In Dublin I already worked 4-days from home and one day in the office. I was planning to fly home twice from the Caribbean to see my family so I could also go into the office when I was back in Dublin to show my face and remind people I still worked in the company. Could I pull this off, I wondered, sail the Atlantic and live in the Caribbean without taking a leave of absence? It got me thinking and mapping out my vacation time and what was possible. By buying an additional 5-days of holidays and carrying 5-days over from last year, I had a total of 36-days' vacation time. I had just enough time to sail the boat from Dublin to Lanzarote (working remotely when in port) and complete the sail across the Atlantic. Working remotely from the Caribbean also looked possible as the team I manage were based around-the-world and my manager was based in America. The question was where to get the additional 22-days leave to sail home from the Caribbean to Europe. As it worked out the return trip was in the next year 2019, so that leg of the trip would come from my next year's vacation allowance. It was all looking plausible. I was excited this new plan was coming together.

The next step was to inform my manager and work colleagues of my plan and I hoped they would support me in my adventure. But a sailing friend of mine, who was a retired astute business executive, suggested not telling anyone at work about my plans. His view was that once I told them that I would be working

Introduction

remotely from the Caribbean, their perception of me would change. They would see me as being on one long extended holiday at the company's expense. Any issues at work would be blamed on me not being fully committed to my work. He made a valid point, why risk telling then. I decided to go incognito and tell nobody at work.

But what would happen if I was in the Caribbean and there was a meeting request to attend the Dublin or London office. This was not unusual. I would either have to spend a lot of money and buy a flight back home at short notice, find an excuse of why I could not attend, or try to engineer for the meeting to be changed to the dates I had already planned to be back in Dublin. It was a bit cheeky and optimistic to expect meetings could be arranged around my schedule but madder things have happened. This did actually happen. My boss in the US wanted to meet me in Dublin but I was in the Caribbean, so what was I to do? I came up with a reason for why the dates my boss proposed to travel were not so ideal. We were able to reschedule the meeting a couple of weeks later when I would be in Dublin. As it turned out, the same day my boss landed in Dublin airport, I also arrived from Guadeloupe. Monday morning was comical as we were both jetlagged by midday. It all worked out well in the end and just shows anything is possible.

The second practical detail of working from the Caribbean was how to deal with the five-hour time zone difference between Dublin and the Caribbean. Everyone at work thinks I am in Dublin but I am in reality five hours behind. For me to attend a 9am conference-call scheduled on UK/Irish time, I would need to wake up at 4am in the Caribbean. This did not sound fun or even likely. Luckily many of my calls were arranged during US working hours, which was conveniently during the morning in the Caribbean. My promotion to manager became useful as I was able to move my own team calls to the morning time in the Caribbean. I would wake up at 7am in the Caribbean which was midday in Ireland and work until 12.30pm Irish time which was 5.30pm in Ireland when everyone expected me to log off at the end of the working day. Any additional work I needed to catch up on I would do at Night-time. I had the afternoons free each day for exploring the Caribbean islands which was a huge benefit. Working remotely did not really impact on me enjoying my Caribbean experience. Of course it would have been nicer not to have work to do but as I was alone on the boat so it was also ok to have conference calls and chats with the team to keep me busy and socially connected.

The nightmare scenario I faced was how to deal with a broken work laptop, or if it fell in the sea or even if it was stolen. I had no solution for this. I can't just buy a new laptop, as I must use the one issued by my company to access the corporate network. I would need to physically visit the Dublin office to pick up my replacement, but that would mean an 8,000-mile round trip.

As I sailed around the Caribbean islands, I was one of the few people working at the same time and being paid. It was nice to know my family at home were financially comfortable. I had no nagging worries about making sure the bills were being paid. In comparison, other sailors were burning through their savings and on tight budgets. Those who had not retired had left their jobs and many were worrying about what they would do when they returned home after their Atlantic adventure. I had no worries at all.

I wrote this story during the Covid-19 pandemic in 2020 which has had consequences for the sailing community worldwide. My Dutch friend Dennis from yacht Mach3, who features in my story, was in lockdown at anchor in the Galapagos islands. He was only allowed ashore to buy food supplies and medicine and then straight back to the boat. He told me that after 52-days at anchor he saw nothing of the Galapagos. He then missed the weather window to continue across the Pacific to French Polynesia. He had no option but to sail back to Panama to wait out hurricane season. Hundreds of cruising yachts are stuck in lockdown in the Caribbean with the approach of the hurricane season. To sail back to Europe is no longer straightforward as ports are closed. In addition the world's oceans in 2020 are recording record high temperatures and predicting a very active hurricane season. If I had delayed my trip by one year, which I was considering, I would now be in lockdown in the Caribbean. My sailing adventure would have turned into a nightmare. More than ever, this shows the importance of seizing opportunities when they emerge. If we procrastinate and delay it is very likely we lose our window of opportunity. Timing is everything. As this virus shows life is unpredictable.

The story that follows is written in diary format with a day by day account of my experience of being alone at sea. It is a truthful and honest account of a single-handed sailor's life crossing the Atlantic and his adventure in the Caribbean.

On ocean passages the expression 'we' is used which relates to the author and Esperanza, the boat. After spending so much time on Esperanza, she embodies a person that you trust your life to when at sea.

Distances are shown as nautical miles. The commonly used mile is the statute mile (1 nautical mile = 1.151 statute mile or 1.852 Kilometre).

Introduction

CHAPTER 1

Atlantic Preparations

The boat Esperanza is a Hallberg Rassy 352. 802 boats of this type were built in Sweden between 1978 -1991. She is a 35-foot boat with an aft-cabin, elegant lines and excellent sailing qualities. A true offshore capable vessel. The first bit of advice you are given before undertaking an Atlantic crossing is know your boat. After sailing the boat for three and a half years I felt I knew her well. The next piece of advice is that you need lots and lots of spare parts when sailing offshore. My view is it makes more sense to put the new parts on the boat now and keep the used parts as the spares. I started this process in 2016, going through every bit of the boat and replacing anything I was unsure of. It is well worth the effort than finding a problem mid Atlantic which could really ruin the voyage.

Paul Heiney who sailed the Atlantic said there are just two things you need to do in order to successfully sail the Atlantic: first is to stay on the boat and don't fall in; second is to keep the mast upright and don't break it. Once the sails and rudder work you will cross the Atlantic at some stage. To make sure the mast stayed up I had all the standing rigging wires that support the mast changed for new in 2016. That was a big but essential job.

12th February 2018 - *New self-feathering propeller*
I changed the propeller on the boat to a new Darglow self-feathering propeller. A beautiful piece of English engineering. My previous propeller had fixed blades, which meant when I was sailing with the engine off, the propeller would continue to turn causing drag and slowing the boat down. This new self-feathering propeller adjusts the blade angle for least drag. When sailing I can expect to gain up to an extra knot in speed. I can also now stop the new propeller and the gearbox from spinning when under sail - this saves on wear and tear.

With 6,000 miles to sail across the Atlantic and back, it seemed madness to expose the gearbox to this amount of wear. A gearbox is an expensive item to replace so this is how I justified buying the new propeller. Boat maintenance is like standing in a cold shower tearing up hundred Euro notes.

With the old propeller I could not stop it spinning when sailing. This was to lead to an incident in September 2017, when the lifeboat was called to assist Esperanza, off the coast of Anglesey, Wales. I was sailing single-handed to Holyhead and the weather was deteriorating fast. Winds had risen to Force 7 with rough seas around Anglesey. It was 10pm and dark when I prepared to turn for the safety of Holyhead harbour that I realised I could not bring in the front jib sail. The furling system had broken at the top of the mast. The jib was flapping wildly and then wrapped around the forestay. A rope snapped and went overboard into water. I went to bow and managed to untangle the mess and manually wind in the sail and secure it. A dangerous task in rough seas at night. The waves were big and breaking as the wind was directly against the oncoming tide. In the meantime the rope that went into the water had been sucked into the rotating propeller which was turning even with the engine off. The rope had tangled around the propeller disabling it. I had no engine and no jib sail. The forecast was for increasing gale to strong gale force winds.

I was sailing at 3 knots on mainsail but it was difficult with the wind and tide to maintain my direction and I was concerned about being blown towards the cliffs. I decided as a precaution to inform the Holyhead coastguard of my situation. At least then they could keep an eye on my progress. I did not feel I needed assistance at this stage. With the weather taking a turn for the worse, Holyhead coastguard launched the lifeboat Christopher Pearce. On reaching Esperanza, a safe tow was made back to the Holyhead marina, arriving at 2am. Unfortunately it was rough and gusty in the harbour. Esperanza and the lifeboat were bouncing together in close quarters. The lifeboat impacted me hard on the starboard side and a crash was heard. The result of the collision was I was left with a repair bill of €3,538 for the replacement of the teak toe rail. At least I was safe and sound. I was able to continue on my journey home to Ireland the next day. My new propeller would reduce the likelihood of ropes wrapping around the propeller if they fell in the water, as it would not be spinning when sailing.

14th February 2018 - *New engine water pump and propeller shaft seal*

I fitted a new engine water pump and kept the old one as a spare. The new water pump means engine cooling should be one less issue I could face in the Atlantic. Why wait for problems with the pump and then have to fit the spare in a rough sea when I can do it now as a preventative measure. In this way I am reducing risks. A bigger job was to replace the propeller shaft rubber seal. This is a critical seal where the shaft of the propeller enters the boat and connects to

Atlantic Preparations

the engine. If the rubber seal fails, water will flood into the boat very fast and you will sink in less than 20 minutes (a 5cm hole below the water line will leak three hundred litres per minute). I can't take a chance with this seal. Even the smallest drips would cause me nightmares of what might happen next. It is not worth losing sleep over, so I bite the bullet and get the seal changed.

The difficulty was to get access to the shaft seal. I had to first remove many pipes and parts of the engine and gearbox to allow the mechanic to climb in over the engine. The next stage is to pull the propeller shaft away from the engine coupling. This is no easy feat as the shaft is designed not to come loose and it has had 10 years to get very stuck inside the engine. With boat projects you never know the problems that can unfold even with the simplest jobs, suddenly a small job can turn into a nightmare requiring wheelbarrows of cash and days of work. I am hoping it will be a straightforward job. I have ordered a new 'PSS fit & forget' shaft seal for the mechanic to fit when it arrives.

18th February 2018 - *Am I able for this trip?*

Grief is a strange process. Many times I forget completely about my Dad but then wham bam something hits and reminds me. In my everyday life I feel I try to avoid grief by keeping busy but the sadness is always lurking. The main effect on me of my Dad's death is that I feel overloaded with the smallest things. I just can't deal with problems, hassle or complications. This is not the mindset to be in for preparing for the Atlantic. Grief is like you have woken into another dimension where you feel unsure of yourself, your plans and actions. I lack motivation and my usual drive to get on with things. At times like this my dream of sailing the Atlantic, feels just that - a dream that may just stay that way for a while longer. "Am I able for this trip?", I wonder.

I told only the people close to me about my planned voyage in case I decide to postpone it. The more people you tell the more you feel you have to go through with it. If I feel I am not ready I will delay the trip. The first step to see if I am ready is the sail across the Bay of Biscay single-handed. It will be a test of my mental state for a 23-days Atlantic trip in isolation. Who knows, this time I may hate being alone and decide this is not for me. I can always postpone and think about an Atlantic trip another year. Best to keep things loose and fluid, all options are open. I feel I have aged 10 years after my Dad's death… mentally and physically. I hope the Biscay sail will kick me back into gear. The challenge is just what I need.

25th February 2018 - *New anchor chain arrives*

The new anchor chain that I ordered arrived today on a pallet to the boat yard. I now have 50 metres of certified Grade 4 8mm chain, spliced to 50m of 14mm nylon rope. I would have preferred heavier 10mm chain but that would have meant changing my anchor Windlass electric motor. With my 100 metres of anchor chain and rope it means I can safely anchor in 12m of water at max scope of 8 times, which is recommended for storm conditions. In the Caribbean, anchor depths are deep, commonly 12 metres or more. The reason I changed the old chain was I found some rusty chain links that must be 30 years old. Chain is only as strong as the weakest link, as they say. Last year, I upgraded my anchor to a Spade high performance anchor which digs in rapidly to the seabed with excellent holding. This anchor and my new chain will help me sleep better when on anchor, which will be 90% of the time in the Caribbean.

Other small jobs completed, where adding two new lee-cloths to the bunks in the cabin to stop myself rolling out of the bunk onto the floor in rough seas. I also resealed the engine lid in the cockpit to make sure there will be no leaks in the engine from waves breaking into the cockpit.

16th March 2018 - *climbing the mast 60 foot high*

I am losing sleep over the jib sail Furlex installation as it is only 4 weeks before the boat launches and it is still not installed. The Furlex is the forward jib sail roller mechanism that allows me to roll in or out the jib sail. The existing Furlex is 30 years old and I had three instances last summer where it broke and I had to climb the mast. I lost faith in it and decided to bite the bullet and fork out €2,000 for a new system to have peace of mind for the Atlantic. When single-handed you can't have if's and but's, things need to work reliably. I got a call from the rigger to say he could not install the Furlex as he is undergoing cancer treatment and can't climb masts. There was no one else to turn to. I wanted to be sure a professional rigger installed it, as you only have one chance to get it right. A compromise was reached: I would climb the mast and take the Furlex down, the rigger would build the new Furlex to the same length and I will put it back up.

I asked a climber I know to help me spec professional climbing equipment that would allow me to climb Esperanza's mast on my own. The mast is 60-foot high above the water. I must be able to climb the mast alone in case I have to fix a problem at sea. Hopefully I never have to do it. But having the ability to go up the mast on my own on the marina without having to find two burley guys to winch me up is fantastic. My self-climbing gear includes an Ascender, Grigri breaking device and a climbing harness.

While I was up the mast, I changed the mooring light bulb to a low energy LED. I had been meaning to do this for years, twice I tried but I had the wrong bulb fitting each time. The old bulb used 10 watts of power while the new LED version uses just 3.2 watts. For a month at anchor that equates to 400 watts of power that I am saving. Conserving energy is key in the Caribbean as I will be on anchor most of the time. An added benefit is the new LED anchor light is much brighter.

Atlantic Preparations

18th March 2018 - *tying everything down to make it secure in rough weather*

Today's job was to secure the boat's old CQR anchor snugly into the cockpit locker so it can't be thrown around in high seas. I am keeping the old anchor onboard as a spare in case my new anchor gets stuck on a rock and I need to leave it there. I added tie-down points to the locker floor for the three 20 litre jerry cans of diesel. Nothing can be allowed to move around at sea as the boat could go inverted if rolled by a breaking wave. Can you imagine a 20kg unsecured anchor flying around in the locker, it would quickly punch a hole in the boat.

One of the more common points of failure on boats crossing the Atlantic is the gooseneck fitting, which is where the boom connects to the mast. I decided to buy a brand-new gooseneck fitting made from solid stainless steel and fitted it, keeping the old one, which is in good condition as the spare.

I also added tie-downs for the portable Honda EA10i generator which I bought on eBay for £250. This generator was from the UK Ministry of Defence, which I am not sure is a good or bad thing. It has probably seen duty in Iraq or Afghanistan. The seller assures me it has been serviced and is in perfect working order. My plan is to keep this in the cockpit locker and I can use it as a standby power source if the engine fails. It might also be useful to supply power when at anchor. It will run for 3 hours on just 1 litre of petrol. The generator uses petrol and not diesel so this is another type of fuel I need to bring but I was bringing some petrol anyway for the outboard engine on the dinghy.

Preparations complete - *launch day for Esperanza*

Esperanza launched at the Royal Saint George Yacht Club, Dun Laoghaire 14th April 2018. All the big jobs were complete. I had until June to finish the small jobs and carry out a shakedown cruise. I set the date of June 2nd to set sail for the Canaries, the starting point for the Caribbean.

My Dad would have thought sailing the Atlantic single-handed was madness. He knew the risks involved since he had worked for the Commissioners of Irish Lights, servicing lighthouses around the Irish coast. He had seen how unforgiving the Atlantic could be. It feels like the Atlantic challenge will as they say make a man out of me or else it will finish me. I will take things in stages, small steps. First, I will sail across the Bay of Biscay and then decide to continue or delay the Atlantic dream. Next I will sail to Vigo and then Lisbon. I can then decide to continue to the Canaries where I have a final chance to delay the trip. I feel comfortable with this plan. Donald Crowhurst committed everything he had to the round the world Golden Globe yacht race in 1968, but it left him with no way to climb down from the plan. He went ahead and sailed when he knew he was not ready and he shouldn't have. He died at sea to save his pride. It is always wise to have an escape route, a way to climb down from our plans.

Bags packed; on my way to join Esperanza on her mooring in Dun Laoghaire harbour, Dublin. I am ready to sail Biscay.
Below: Arrival party La Coruna, Spain with crew of Adrigole, Skipper Shay Quinn in the middle.

CHAPTER 2

Positioning to the start line

19th June 2018 - *my second single-handed Biscay sail completed*

I am sitting in Esperanza, at the Real Club Nautico marina in Vigo, northwest Spain. Dennis Woods joined me in La Coruna a week ago and we sailed down the coast to Vigo. Dennis is in his seventies and spritely for his age. It was an enjoyable trip.

As planned, I left Dun Laoghaire, my home port in Dublin, on the 2nd of June 2018. I completed my second single-handed Biscay crossing. It took 5-days to cross the Bay of Biscay to La Coruna in Galicia, North West Spain. The Biscay waters can be treacherous in bad weather. It is known as one of the worst bits of ocean in the world, but for my crossing I had fine weather. I had to run the engine for 42 hours over the 5-days but I was determined to sail as much as possible. I wanted to get some light wind sailing practice as on the Atlantic voyage I will not have the fuel reserves to turn on the engine every time the wind drops. I started the Biscay crossing feeling a bit lonely and then tiredness hit. But, by day three I was happy and comfortable with life at sea. Good quality food was important to lift the mood. I went up-market to treat myself and brought a selection of homemade pre-cooked meals from my local store, Cavistons Food Emporium. I had tasty dinners of Thai Green Curry, Quiche and Shepherd's Pie. It made a huge difference compared to the packet pasta and processed foods that I normally have onboard. Being alone, I was busy on the trip. I heard no voices this time other than the sound of the water sloshing against the hull. An enjoyable trip that did not put me off the Atlantic challenge.

Shay Quinn in Adrigole arrived a few hours later with his two crew. The two boats, Adrigole and Esperanza left Dun Laoghaire together but within 24 hours we were separated and out of radio contact. It was great fun planning the trip together and we had celebration drinks on arrival in La Coruna. Cruising in company is fun and I would like to do more of it. It brings a nice social aspect to sailing.

In Baiona, I met a boat from Dun Laoghaire, my home port. They were off to the Azores, 800 miles away and 7-days sailing. We wished them luck on their passage. The next day they arrived back at the marina. They had found diesel in the bilge and also encountered big seas. They were unsure where the diesel in the bilge was coming from. The boat had been lifted out in Vigo for the winter and had travelled the short distance from Vigo to Baiona since it launched, so it had not had a shakedown cruise to test if everything was working correctly. This was a good lesson, not to set sail for the Atlantic without a proper shakedown sail to test the boat. You don't want to find problems when you are halfway across the Atlantic. My shakedown sail is this trip down to the Canaries, any problems with the boat can be fixed in Lanzarote.

What separates coastal day sailors from offshore ocean sailors is one key thing, the ability to troubleshoot and fix problems at sea to ensure the boat keeps going. Unfortunately, every boat has problems of one sort or another. The more experienced the sailor, the more they can work through the problems. To continue sailing while fixing problems is most rewarding, it is the feeling of satisfaction at realising you are capable of being self-sufficient. Of course it is the foolish sailor that continues with a problem that they realise is above and beyond them. The key is to know your own abilities and admit your own limitations.

21st August 2018 - *sailing into the Atlantic to Madeira*

I am in Cascais, Lisbon with new crew members Bernadette Fox and Heather King, who have just joined the boat. They are friends from Dublin. The next leg of the trip is to sail 4-days to Madeira and then continue south to Lanzarote. In Cascais, the first problem emerged when I was carrying out engine checks. I noticed the hydraulic fluid in the gearbox was a strawberry milkshake colour indicating water was getting into the gearbox, not a good sign. I had a technician look at it who thought the strawberry milkshake in my gearbox was just lovely and no problem at all. Really? This was reassuring but my gut feeling was this is not right. As a precaution I changed the hydraulic fluid and cleaned the filter. We decided we were ok to sail. Lanzarote was the best place to sort this out.

We left Cascais and had a pleasant sail. I had just bought a second-hand cruising chute and we got to try it out. The cruising chute is a bigger and lighter genoa/jib sail. It is made out of nylon, lightweight like a parachute. It is designed to catch the very light winds. It was doing the job nicely by moving the boat in 8-10 knots of wind at 6 knots. We heard on the radio a yacht was on fire with three people onboard. They evacuated to their life raft and a cargo ship diverted to rescue them. A Navy ship was also on the way. This resulted in lots of excitement on Esperanza; we were glued to the radio for updates.

Positioning to the start line

On this passage I was trying everything I could as a mini test sail for the Atlantic. I tried the two poled out jibs. I ran the portable Honda generator to charge the batteries and found the best place to put it was on the starboard side at the stern. On this trip we spotted a whale and a number of turtles. After 431 miles and 4 days, we dropped anchor at the island of Porto Santo, 27 miles northeast of Madeira. This is a fantastic small Portuguese island with lovely sandy beaches. The marina was tiny and full, so we anchored off the beach in crystal clear blue water. I enjoyed climbing the highest point of the island Pico Castelo, where I had a 360-degree viewpoint. Keeping with Atlantic sailor traditions, I painted the name Esperanza and an Irish flag on the pier wall in Porto Santo to mark the start of my transatlantic sail. The pier wall was full of boat names and elaborate logos, some amazing artwork. The Atlantic was feeling ever more real, there was less of a chance to back out now as I had publicly declared my intentions. After a few leisurely days we sailed the short distance to Madeira and explored the capital Funchal.

29th August 2018 - *final leg of stage 1, to position the boat to Lanzarote which is the Atlantic start line*

We were off again on the final 3-day leg to Lanzarote. We left at night-time to avoid paying another night at the marina, which was expensive. It was windy, gusting 25 knots with a rough lumpy sea. We saw another whale just 150 metres off the starboard side and it gave us three blows of water from its spout. The seas were bigger on this leg of the trip. There were very few ships around, although we did pass the ferry to Tenerife. The fridge started to give problems with the compressor becoming red hot to touch. I switched the fridge off for the rest of the trip. That meant no more cold beer. I would have to get someone to look at the fridge in Lanzarote - I hope I do not need a new fridge as they are expensive and I am running out of time for a job like this before my Atlantic sailing date in December. The VHF radio jumped alive with a Pan Pan alert message from Las Palmas coast guard. A vessel was missing that was heading from Azores to the Canaries. Last known position 18 miles from Ponta Delgada, Azores, all vessels in the area to keep a lookout. That is a long way from us, I hope they are ok.

As we approach Lanzarote, we are a little concerned over the possibility of big waves as the sea is rough and the seabed depth goes from 1km deep to 100 metres in just 4 miles as we approach the coast. The waves may pile up here and grow in size. But it turned out fine and we arrived at 10.30am in Marina Lanzarote, Arrecife. I really liked it here. The marina is only 10 minutes in a taxi from the airport. It is a 20 minutes' walk to the beach or a 10-minute walk to the town with lovely local restaurants and bars. Unlike the rest of Lanzarote there are very few tourists here, just the locals and Spanish visitors from the mainland.

Arrecife has four marine supply chandleries, which I visited daily to buy bits and bobs. At the marina there are bars, restaurants and a super little coffee shop where I got my morning 'Leche Leche' coffee: a dollop of condensed milk at the bottom of the small glass; over which is poured the coffee and then the rest of the glass is filled with hot milk. The condensed milk stays at the bottom until you stir it. It looks great and tastes even better.

The boat will stay in Lanzarote for the next few months until I set sail for the Caribbean in December, date to be confirmed. I will fly home in a week. Beethoven's 7th symphony is playing today and it reminds me of my Dad. I am missing my Dad's regular phone calls when I arrived into a new port. He was always tracking the boat's position on marinetraffic.com.

I read a bereavement book that says the death of loved ones can make you go a little crazy and lead to a mid-life crisis. It is common for bereavement to bring about change, to allow the person left behind to see what is really important and find new paths in life. The downside of all this change is it can bring a wave of destruction and pain for the people around you. It is common for the bereaved to suddenly decide to quit their jobs, decide on career changes, have affairs or end long standing relationships. For me, it feels as if it is even more important to live my dreams now when I am still relatively young and in good health. We never know when we might be struck down with a debilitating illness that prevents us from doing the things we wanted to always do.

September to December 2018 - *back and forth to Lanzarote with more and more boat jobs to complete*

These were a busy few months flying back and forth from Dublin to Lanzarote to work on the boat. One job was to add an external satellite aerial for the Iridium Go satellite system. The Iridium Go is a portable satellite hotspot device designed to provide voice, text message, weather reports, basic email and Twitter connectivity. Adding the aerial was not an easy task, as I needed to find an aluminium pole to mount the aerial on and then attach it to the stern. I ran the satellite cable into the cabin and mounted the Iridium Go box by the navigation table. I fired it up and guess what? It worked, another job that I can cross off the list. Another job was to replace the leaking sea water pump in galley, which by luck the chandlery in Lanzarote had a spare pump in stock. I decided not to replace my short-range red rocket flares, which were out of date, but bought instead a new electronic battery red flare replacement.

I am now self-absorbed and completely obsessed with this trip. When out with family or friends I can't seem to talk about anything else so I must be boring people. Very selfish but probably necessary to ensure everything is planned for. My Night-time reading is all about sailing in Caribbean waters. The one worry is the security concerns I read about with robberies and attacks on sailors. There was a story of a boat wiring an electric fence around the deck to stop people trying to get onboard at night. In the old days it was to sprinkle tacks/nails on the deck for intruders to stand on. So in a fit of madness I compromised and bought on eBay two bright yellow plastic signs for farmyards, which said: 'Beware Electric Fence' in big bold black lettering. I can hang one sign on either side of the boat to scare away any undesirables. It sounded like a grand idea when sitting at home in front of the stove but when I was in the Caribbean it just looked very mad and not to mention unfriendly so I hid the signs and they were never used.

There is a real sense of excitement building when I look at the North Atlantic Ocean Passage Chart. It is so big it covers the entire kitchen table. It is also daunting to see on the chart the challenge ahead, I must sail 2,800 miles (5,100km) to reach the Caribbean.

22th November 2018 - *parachute anchor arrives*

The parachute anchor arrived; it was another second-hand purchase on eBay from a boat that circumnavigated the world but never had to use it. It is a heavy white cloth-like material that when opened forms a parachute under the water to slow the boat and keep the bow into the wind, just like if the boat was on a mooring. I will only deploy it for severe storms.

A news item today was an attempted boarding of a yacht off Western Sahara on the west African coast. I will be sailing not too far from this coastline when I leave the Canaries. It makes me worry about a pirate attack. I must try to keep well away from the African coast and head south west rather than direct south. I was surprised to see that Lanzarote is only 70 miles from the African coast. For boat defence I have been thinking of building a flamethrower as I have petrol onboard. I decided against it as I would more likely set Esperanza on fire than do any damage to the pirates.

25th November 2018 - *200 boasts leave for the Caribbean on the Atlantic Rally Cruise*

Today, boats from the Atlantic Rally Cruise (known as the ARC) left Las Palmas, Gran Canaria on their voyage to Saint Lucia. Over 200 boats left together to arrive for Christmas in the Caribbean. It is a nice idea to go as a group as there is safety in numbers, though within a couple of days you are out of sight of the other boats. I am opting for the 'NARC' cruise (Not the Atlantic Rally Cruise). This week I am researching the routing options for the transatlantic. I plan to take the traditional Columbus's route, sail south from the Canaries until my latitude drops to 20N, then pick up the trade winds blowing from the northeast and turn west for the Caribbean. If I turn west too early, I risk sailing into the mid-Atlantic high-pressure no wind zone.

30th November 2018 – *last day of Hurricane season*

I am back in sunny Lanzarote, 28 degrees. It is so nice to escape the cold wet Irish winter. The notice board at marina has many messages from people looking to join boats as crew across the Atlantic. The Atlantic crossing is certainly on many people's bucket list. Today is the last day of hurricane season, which runs from June 1st to November 30th. I am glad the hurricane season is over. I plan to leave in a couple of weeks and do not want a hurricane chasing me. I tested the EPIRB (emergency position-indicating radio beacon) today and the test sequence is correct (6 flashes equals all is ok). The EPIRB is my main way to raise help, with the pull of a switch I can activate a Mayday signal via satellite, which is sent to the coast guard. I spent a few hours rooting through the ever-growing medical box. I added the prescription medicines I brought with me from my doctor in Dublin.

This is my final trip to the boat before I leave for the Atlantic. I have been flat out busy with a never-ending list of jobs. It is now time to get back home to Dublin for some family time. My scheduled departure date is set for Monday, December 17th.

6th December 2018 - *satellite communications tested and working*

Back at home in Dublin, I tested the Iridium Go satellite device. I might as well play with all this technology now and not be on high seas trying it for the first time. There is no tech support in the middle of the Atlantic. I activated the Iridium Go satellite data card, which costs $150 per month for unlimited data. The low data bandwidth means it is not possible to browse websites or send big emails with pictures. For Iridium Go to connect to the satellites it needs a clear view of the sky. My back garden is in the suburbs surrounded by buildings so it was difficult to get a good signal. Instead I drove up nearby Killiney Hill where I had a clear sky view. I thought it funny to be sitting in my car downloading weather charts and very soon I would be doing the same in the Atlantic. All seems to be working fine. The download speed is slow, it takes 20-30 minutes to pull down the forecast files into the PredictWind app on my iPad. The result is a 5-day weather forecast of wind speed and direction.

The first Atlantic Rally Cruise boats are already reaching Saint Lucia after just 11 days. These first boats are the big professional racing yachts. I will be over twice as long in the range of 23-25-days, it all depends on the wind. At the same time in the Southern Ocean, the Golden Globe single-handed round the world race is on. Susie Goodall, an English sailor has been dismasted. Soon after this incident an Irish sailor Gregor McGuckin also lost his mast. A number of boats were caught in one of those big Southern Ocean storms. All were rescued safely but it makes you think of what can go wrong.

Positioning to the start line

13th December 2018 - *4-days before departure, bottom cleaning*

I am back in Lanzarote with Sonya to stock the boat with food and water. It is just 4-days before launch and there is so much to do. I also have to keep the day job running at the same time. I hired the local rigger, to fit a second swivel block at the top of the mast on the port side, so I could fly the cruising chute port or starboard. I also then had redundancy in case one spinnaker blog or rope halyard broke. At the same time I changed the bearings in the wind vane, which is the instrument that records wind direction and speed.

One vital task is bottom washing, not mine but Esperanza's as she has a dirty weedy bottom/hull. We motored over to the slip where a travel hoist crane lifted the boat out of the water for a couple of hours and she was power washed to a shiny green copper surface. To prevent seaweed and barnacles sticking to the hull of boats they usually have anti-foul painted on the hull each year. My boat doesn't use this system but has Coppercoat epoxied on the hull; which you apply every 10 years. It means you don't have the hassle of antifouling each year. The copper deters growth and has worked well for me. It is a similar system to the old sailing ships, which had their hulls sheathed with copper plates. Sonya cleaned the propeller to make it shiny and clean. It is very important to have a clean hull and a propeller or you lose speed. A 25-day crossing could become 30-days or more with weed and barnacles stuck to hull.

15th December 2018 - *shopping day*

Shopping day today. We have hired a car and drove to the local supermarket to do the giant shop in two runs. I need four weeks of food and water so that is a lot of trolleys to fill. The good news is the food is yummy in Lanzarote, lots of great Spanish chorizo and tortilla to keep me happy. So what did I buy, here is the list:

Breakfast: Weetabix (1), Muesli (1), UHT Long-Life Milk (5), Dried fruit (5 bags); Crunchy Nut cornflakes (1).

Lunch: Ham for first week (2 packs); Chorizo (6); Tinned soups (20); Cup A Soup (4); Juice boxes (5); Whole grain bread (1); Tortilla Wraps (5 packs as last long lasting and great for sandwiches); Peanut butter (3); Quiche for first couple of days.

Dinner: Lasagne, Thai Green curry sauce (5); Pasta sauce jars (5); Pizza base (1); Pasta (10); Pot Noodles (10); Baked Beans (10); Spaghetti in tin (4); Tins: Peas, Carrots, Sweetcorn, Tomatoes, Mushrooms, Green Beans, Lentils, Black Olives (5). Garlic powder; Salami (5), Chickpeas (1); Pesto (3); Curry Powder; Salt & Pepper.

Snacks: (very important to keep morale up): Biscuits (5); Crackers (5); Nuts mix (5); Coke 2 litres (5), Popcorn (1); Crisps (5); Muesli bar packs (5); Tins of fruit cocktail for deserts (10); Mini chocolate bars (30, 1 per day), Yogurts (18).

Vege/Fruit:
Lasts one week: Tomatoes (6); Salad mix (1); Bananas (2 bunches).
Lasts up to two weeks: Apples (30); Oranges (1); Lemons (4).
Lasts up to three weeks: Potatoes (20 spuds); Onions (20); Garlic (3 bunches); Carrots (4 bags, great to nibble on raw as a snack); Peppers (2).

Baking supplies: Dry Yeast (2); Castor Sugar (2); Wheat Flour (2); Thyme; Sesame seeds; Butter/Margarine (4); Baking Powder; Vanilla extract; Vegetable oil; coco; cooking salt; brown sugar; white Flour.

Water: 105 litres of bottled water (10 x 5 litre bottles + 42 x 2 litre bottles).

Miscellaneous: Coffee instant (2); Coffee decaf (1); Tea (1 box); Beer (30, 1 per day); Olive Oil (1); Mayonnaise (1); Balsamic Vinegar (1); Stock Cubes (1); Sugar Cubes (1); Evaporated Milk (1).

Non-food: Deodorant, Vitamin C; Kitchen roll (30, 1 per day); Toilet roll (15 rolls); Toothpaste; Washing Up liquid (2); Washing powder tablets for clothes (2); Measuring jug; Vaseline (1); Straws (1); Bin bags very strong (30); Sudocream for salt rashes; Hand cream; Matches (3) to light gas stove; Gas spark clickers (3). 30 bin liners, the strong outdoor type. Factor 50 sun cream and after sun. 48 batteries.

I wanted to buy the fruit and vegetables from a local market as it is meant to last longer than supermarket chilled fruit/veg, but we did not have this option, so just bought everything from the same supermarket. The boat is now stocked for 30-days at sea. What a job it was. Lugging trolleys and bags from the car to the boat. Thanks to Sonya for being here as it would have been much more difficult on my own. We removed all the cardboard packaging to reduce any risk of bugs like weevils. Weevils are disgusting bugs that actually live and feed on food like rice and pasta. They can be brought onto the boat in packaged foods. Once inside, a population can grow and expand if they are not controlled. I found them once in a bag of pasta on my old boat, yuck. I have lots of sealed plastic containers on this boat to store food.

The big problem was to find space for everything. I moved the mattresses from the bunks in the forward peak cabin and stored them in the aft cabin, which won't be used on the trip. This allowed me to add tie-down points and ratchet straps. The water was tied down so nothing could fly around. I also added 8 plastic sealed boxes to the port and starboard shelves and these were also tied down. These boxes were great for storing food. The forward cabin is now a storage room for sails, spare parts, food and water. Every cupboard is stocked to the brim.

My last night in Lanzarote was relaxing with lovely food and drinks. There is not a lot of wind forecast for the first few days so I will be motor sailing, but I need to get going. The weather will never be perfect but as long as there are no storms ahead, I am good to go. The boat and I are read

My office while on the boat, keeping the day job going.

Crew of Adrigole with Shay Quinn, Dave Coleman and Derek Gill from Dun Laoghaire Motor Yacht Club. Second from left (behind me) is Dennis Woods who joined Esperanza La Coruna to Vigo.

Family arrive to join the boat and sail from Vigo to Porto.

25th August 2018, Porto Santo island, in the Portuguese archipelago of Madeira.

Cascais, Lisbon with new crew members Bernadette Fox and Heather King.

As per tradition, I painted the boat name on the harbour wall in Porto Santo, my entrance point to the Atlantic.

Esperanza was based at Marina Lanzarote from 1st September 2018 until the Atlantic departure on 17th December. Time for final preparations.

The boat hull was washed and preparations completed. 15th December 2018, two days before departure the boat was loaded with food and water for 30 days at sea.

Santa wishing me luck.

Boat stocked, ready to go.

CHAPTER 3

Lanzarote to Caribbean

Day 1: 17th December 2018 - *After two years of planning Esperanza sets sail across the Atlantic*
N28 57 W13 32

Monday is departure day, finally the day has come. Sonya and I said our goodbyes, she has left for the airport. I am feeling nervous and a little anxious of what is to come. I am grabbing my last meal: a 'Leche Leche' coffee, toasted cheese sandwich and cake. I feel prepared. I have 390 litres of fuel onboard, 250 litres in the main fuel tanks and the remainder in seven jerry cans (three in the cockpit locker and four tied on the deck at the stern). I think I have plenty of fuel, I did the calculations many times. Allowing for charging batteries twice per day and 60 litres of reserve fuel, I have 60 hours of fuel for motoring. I also have 20 litres of petrol in a jerry can for the Honda generator as an emergency power source if the engine won't start. There are two full gas bottles onboard for the cooker and 30-days of food and water.

I motor out of Marina Lanzarote in the sunshine, leaving the capital, Arrecife behind me. So, I have finally left after two years of planning and preparation. It feels good to be moving, though a little unsettling as there is no real wind, just a light 5 knot breeze. I am motoring towards the island of Fuerteventura. My brother-in-law Paul Hogan is the Captain of the oil drilling ship, he and his ship also left the Canaries today for Guyana, South America.

It will take me a few days to settle into life at sea. I remind myself this is a marathon and not a race. I have a strong 5 bar signal on the Iridium Go satellite phone, which is reassuring so I can download the latest weather. The sea is lovely, flat calm as evening drifts in. Looking at the iPad there are very few ships around me. The marine VHF radio has gone quiet. I would like a little more wind but it is very peaceful motoring alone in the darkness. I have to stay awake during the night as I am near Fuerteventura and do not want to run into it. There goes an airplane above me landing at Fuerteventura so I am not totally alone.

I had a nice dinner, hot lasagne and pizza. The latest weather has downloaded. It shows 10-15 knots of wind from the east to northeast south of the Canaries islands, which would be perfect. The high-pressure system, which is bringing the slack winds, is expanding out towards Madeira. I need to get further south and away from the high-pressure. I am making great speed on the engine with the clean hull and in the flat calm sea. Tonight I am very tired so I am starting 20-minute cat naps in the starboard bunk. I won't sleep but I find closing my eyes for 20 minutes refreshes me. I am just 6 miles east of Fuerteventura travelling down the coast with mainsail and jib sails out opposite sides as there is a little wind behind me to help me along. This is called sailing goose winged (mainsail out one side and front jib sail out the other).

The plan is to try to get more west and away from Africa once I clear the island of Fuerteventura. I am very close to Africa at the moment, just 45 miles from Western Sahara. I can hear African fishing boats on the VHF radio. I do not want to encounter the pirates, who have operated in this area.

I am sitting in the dark in the cockpit of the boat, drinking coffee to stay awake and eating a Wispa chocolate bar. I am thinking everyone back in Dublin will all be fast asleep now in their beds, safe at home while I am awake on the ocean with just 2,819 miles to go… I am not feeling lonely but rather apprehensive of what is to come. I know the boat very well and she will look after me. Twitter is keeping me occupied as I am sending daily updates as tweets. To follow my trip, people can check the moving map on my blog, which updates the boat position every hour from the Iridium satellite system. It is reassuring to know family and friends can see at any time where I am.

3am: I was up on deck trying to put the pole out to stop the jib sail from flapping. The new bright deck light that I replaced for the trip is great for lighting up the deck. No sleep at all so far but I did move to 90-minute rest cycles, as there are no ships around and I am moving offshore away from the islands. Every 90 minutes I get up to look outside and to check if everything is ok. The Automatic Identification System (AIS) is installed on Esperanza, this transmits the position of my boat and receives the position of other boats. The positions of other vessels from AIS are overlaid on the electronic navigation charts on my iPad. I receive alerts if there are any vessels in the area but I can't rely on this as smaller fishing boats are unlikely to have AIS installed.

During the night I lost mobile phone coverage as I moved away from Canaries, that's it until the Caribbean.

Day 2: 18th December 2018 - *Uncomfortable sailing, lots of rolling side to side*
N27 52 W14 29

What a nice sunny morning. I just passed the southerly point of Fuerteventura - I am really now off into the deep ocean. Best I give George the autopilot a rest and I steer the boat for an hour. Skippers seem to name bits of their boat. All my autopilots have been called George for some reason. I have no idea why, the name just stuck. The engine is called Betsy. The wind has picked up nicely to 12 knots from the northeast. I am heading for an imaginary waypoint of 23N 30W, on the chart this is the recommended route for best winds to cross the Atlantic. I am settling into routines. 8am each morning I do a plot of my position on the paper chart. This is in case the electronics stop working so at least I know where I am, where I was and direction to go. It is reassuring to have a big picture view from the paper chart which spans the Atlantic, you don't get that from the electronic charts as the screen is too small on the iPad.

Last night the boat motion was uncomfortable, rolling from side to side with the sails set 'goose-winged', the mainsail and jib sail set on opposite sides of the boat. I am going to try a new sail configuration today. I will roll away the mainsail completely into the mast and raise the hank on jib sail. This sail is manually attached with brass hanks to a removable stay wire at the bow. The idea is to have two jibs flying from the bow, one either side to push the boat along when the boat is directly downwind. I hope this makes the boat more stable and will result in less rolling. Nothing beats a hot coffee in the morning when at sea, even instant coffee tastes so much better at sea. I am finding it a little difficult to get settled into a daily routine, I seem to be running from one thing to another. I need to slow down, relax and start to read some books. I can't find BBC on the radio so I am missing the comforting BBC voices. One of the nets I bought on Amazon that holds the fruit has split already, the first breakage of the trip.

All day I sailed nicely in a south west direction as the wind allowed, but as night fell the wind died. Frustrating. I had the cruising chute up early to catch the wind as it reduced. Tonight I am back to motoring. I am keeping the revs low at 1800RPM to save fuel. At this RPM I burn 2 litres per hour instead of the normal 3 litres at 2100 RPM, which is cruise power. Maybe I should actually have brought more fuel! The forecast ahead is looking good for more wind, as the high-pressure causing the slack winds is due to move away to the northwest. I should soon be getting east or northeast winds, Force 4 in strength increasing to Force 5 (12-20 knots). Wait, what's that in that water? I spotted something dark and floating. It was a big oil drum that must have fallen off a ship. I would not like to think what would happen if I hit this at 7kts, it would likely put a hole in the boat. You just can't worry about floating containers or debris or you would never sleep a wink.

6pm: Navtex warning received. A rowing boat is adrift position 27 07 N 18 57 W, this is a few hundred miles from me. Why is this adrift, I wonder, and where is the rower? I tuned in the BBC World Service on the HF long range radio. I installed this HF SSB radio in the boat for the Atlantic trip. It is the same radio we had in the aeroplane for talking to Air Traffic control when flying over the oceans on the World Flight 2003 trip. I liked the idea of using the same radio which has already been around the world in the boat. It is reassuring to have the BBC voices in the background, a little bit of home comfort. I am up to date on Brexit from the news.

As night falls and I am abeam Gran Canaria island, which seems to be always there when I look out. Once the island disappears from view, I will feel like I am making some progress. The wind is basically pushing the two sails and the boat along. We are now getting speed, so let's rock on. A bit scary as I am now only 80 miles off coast of Western Sahara, Africa, which has a high level of terrorism and known pirate attacks on yachts. I would like to get further west as I was advised to stay at least 100 miles off Africa. The wind is not playing ball though.

Later in the night I was sandwiched between two big ships overtaking me, High Efficiency and Rogaland. They can see Esperanza's position on AIS, and both ships altered their course to go around me. It feels good to have two huge ships change their course because of my little boat. During the night the wind increased, it was engine off and the boat speed picked up nicely to 6.5-7 knots. I am flying along. Good night all.

Day 3: 19th December 2018 - *Panic, rope in the water and around the propeller*
N26 41 W16 33

8am: I am awake on a lovely clear morning with a big sunrise. I am now 80 miles south west of Gran Canaria and 80 miles south of the other less well-known Canary island, La Gomera. In the last 24 hours I sailed 132 miles, which is averaging 5.5 knots. I am happy with that progress. Anything over 120 miles per day is good as it keeps the average speed over 5 knots. The north-easterly wind is back up at Force 4-5. The sea is becoming rougher with white horse waves all around the boat. The boat speed just hit 8 knots down a wave, good fun to be surfing the waves. The wind direction is allowing me to go more west so I am taking the opportunity to put some distance between Esperanza and Africa. At the same time it feels good to be making progress west towards the Caribbean.

It has been difficult to walk around the cabin today as the sea is choppy. Breakfast was a bowl of muesli and coffee. I got some sleep last night but I was often up to check that the sails were ok. I do feel more rested today but I would love a shower. I have to get used to my new home; I am not in the swing of being at sea yet. This morning my first job is to walk the deck and look for any ropes that may be chafing. On this trip of 2,800 miles, I will be putting the equivalent of many years of sailing on the boat in just a few weeks. Ropes and other bits and pieces around the boat can be expected to wear fast. I must be careful walking on deck as the boat is rolling side to side and it would be all too easy to end up overboard in the water. Note to self: remember to wear the safety harness and clip on to the boat when on deck.

Sitting at the navigation table in the cabin I am passing the time by searching the bands on the HF radio. I heard an English woman's voice broadcasting UK Royal Airforce weather reports. What a lovely accent to listen to. The aerial for the HF long-distance radio is the backstay wire that holds up the mast. It is a good radio setup and I can transmit as well if I need to. I feel more positive today as I got some rest last night. 2,641 miles to go, the miles are coming down slowly. I must remember to give George the autopilot a rest today; he has been working all night and will get angry if I forget about him.

11am: disaster strikes! Panic as the jib sheet rope came off the winch and flew into the water. I stupidly had no knot on the end because I was also changing the jib sheet ropes often with the regular sail changes. Now the rope is stuck on something under the water. It is either wrapped around the propeller or the rudder. I assume it is the propeller it was wrapped around. Bloody hell, this is exactly what happened to me last year off Wales, when the lifeboat had to come to my assistance. I am now shouting 'no no this can't be happening'. Maybe the engine is now out of action, so what do I do? I could turn around and go back to the Canaries but it would be difficult to sail into the wind or divert to Cape Verde islands, which is further south and sort the problem out there. Is this the end of the trip I wonder?

Thinking of what to do, I revert to doing nothing at all. There is a sailor saying that before making a big decision, first boil the kettle and make a cup of tea. This allows you time to assess the situation and not panic and jump to make the wrong decision. It is all too easy to make a bad situation worse by taking the wrong actions. The first step is to furl away the jib sail by pulling the furling rope in the cockpit and the sail rolls up onto the forestay. That is one thing safely out of the way and can't cause any more problems. It is out of the question to consider getting into the water as the sea is rough. I was able to walk the end of the rope down deck from the bow to the stern of the boat and get it around a winch. There was a strong pull on the rope, lots of force. By slowing the boat, the force on the rope reduced and somehow by pure luck I was able to yank it free and pull it back onboard. Oh my God, what relief and what a fright. I was so lucky. I must have a guardian angel looking out for me. What a scare and only day 3! Time for a glass of Coke and a Crunchie chocolate bar in the sunshine to recover from the drama of the day.

It is far too rough to be on deck today so I stay safe in the cockpit. I tell myself don't aim for perfection, stop constantly tweaking sails, if we are moving along at a nice speed then leave the boat alone. Relax and sit back with a book. Having too much anxiety can cause you to see problems everywhere which are not actually problems. You end up doing unnecessary tasks in an anxious state and are more likely to mess things up. Note to self: go slow be careful, double and triple check everything.

The weather on Navtex has come through and is showing not so good light variable winds south west of the island of El Hierro, where I am. El Hierro is another Canary island I had not heard of before this trip. I do not want these light variable winds as I will be stuck bobbing around going nowhere. I got a nice email from my daughter Kate today with all the news, our cat Ghibli still has bad breath. I called home last night on the satellite phone for the first time and it worked fine. Though we all sound drunk on the satellite phone as the low bandwidth has the effect to slur our voices.

Twice per day, in the morning and at night-time I download the 5-day weather forecast over satellite. I also receive Atlantic weather charts on HF radio, broadcast from US meteorological service NOAA (National Oceanic and Atmospheric Administration). I am receiving these black & white synoptic weather charts clearly. They give me the big picture view of the weather fronts and systems in the Atlantic. I like to see these as I can get the big picture view and see all the bad weather well north of me rolling towards Ireland. Dinner tonight is two cans of fried mushrooms with fresh garlic and two fried eggs on bread. Not bad but a bit dry. For dessert, it is a tin of fruit cocktail and a cup of tea. Lots of things are knocking around in the lockers in the cabin so I am trying to jam everything in to stop the annoying noises.

The batteries have dropped to 50% capacity so I need to start the engine and recharge. I will run the engine at low revs to save fuel and see how long it will take to bring the batteries up to 80% charge, which is my target. To look after the batteries, I am keeping them between 50 and 80% charge. Now that I am away from the Canaries, I am surprised there is nothing out here to be seen at all: no birds, no fish, no dolphins, no whales, no ships and no jet trails in the sky from airliners. Columbus said it feels like you are sailing to the end of the world and I can relate to that. I don't feel lonely in this isolation just in awe of the desolation. Tonight I am doing some star gazing. Feeling good tonight and settling into the voyage.

Day 4: 20th December 2018 - *Force 6 wind going downwind at 8 knots like a rocket* N25 43 W19 06

A daily routine is now established; I get up at 8am, write the log, download the weather, prepare breakfast and then I give George the autopilot a rest as I steer the boat for an hour. It is now 2,430 miles to the island of Saint Vincent in the Caribbean, 300 miles sailed. Writing the daily log is fun as you work out how many miles you sailed over the last 24 hours. It is like a competition to see how fast you went versus previous days. Amazingly, in the last 24 hours I sailed 161 miles, which is great progress and well over my 120 mile per day goal. Esperanza is not such a slow boat after all. At this speed I would arrive after just 17-days at sea on the 6th January, which is 6-days earlier than I expected, but I am sure this average speed won't hold up.

The autopilot's motor arm, which is under the bunk in the aft cabin, is getting hot with all the work it is doing. The big risk being single-handed is that the autopilot fails; I can't steer the boat myself 24 hours non-stop. There are two autopilot motor arms onboard. I modified them to make them fast to swap over by putting the power and control leads on plugs rather than having to unwire and rewire with a screwdriver (not easy to do in a rough sea). To give George the autopilot a rest and a chance to cool down, I must get stricter with myself and not forget to steer the boat an hour in the mornings and evenings. I have mastered being able to steer the boat lying down using my foot to turn the wheel while I relax in the cockpit. To save power I have turned off: the VHF radio; the AIS which transmits my position to other boats and receives positions of other vessels; and the navigation lights. Why have these switched on wasting power when there is nothing at all out here? Not even sea life.

Today I feel much more rested but I woke with a headache. The good news is that it is another sunny day and I have moved to wearing only shorts. It is getting warmer every day that I travel south. Last night was rough, with waves crashing at the stern, causing the boat to roll violently from one side to the other. The motion is so tiring, every muscle braces itself to counteract the rolling from side to side. During the night I felt that I had enough and wanted to get off the boat! After some hours during the early morning my body gave in and I fell asleep. Unusually, it is at night-time and not during the day when the wind seems to pick up and it gets noticeably rougher. The boat rolls shakes and shudders as waves smash into the hull. Bang, quiet for a while, then bang, crash, shudder. I find it difficult to relax and switch off at night. I am thinking the mast is going to fall down as it shudders and shakes every time a wave hits the boat. I am a little scared and wonder if the boat can take this punishment. I reassure myself that Esperanza is a Hallberg Rassy, a strongly built ocean yacht.

I am in a Force 6 wind going downwind like a rocket with the two jib sails poled out at the bow and no mainsail up. The boat is regularly seeing 8 knots surfing down waves. My worry is that I end up in a gale and the wind gets so strong that even with the main jib sail furled away, I am left stuck with the hank on jib flying. I can't reduce the hank on jib sail as it is either fully up or down, there is no way to reef or reduce the sail. The only way to reduce power further is to drop the hank on jib, which means going on deck to the bow in wild conditions to drop the sail. Going to the bow alone in a gale and rough seas is no joking matter, lots could go wrong. I am trying to work out in my head a procedure to do this.

The high-pressure system to the north has turned and is coming back down south. I don't want the High to move down on top of me as then I would be stuck in the no wind zone. This confirms I need to keep going south to keep out of the High's way. It is not yet time to turn west for the Caribbean. I changed my course to a more southerly heading and the boat is steadier with less banging into the waves, less like being in the washing machine, which describes last night. Now to sort out the pots and pans, which are banging around in the locker; I need to jam them with rolls of kitchen towel. I had stashed 15 bottles of water months ago in an empty void under the galley food locker. I decided to get these out today as they are older and should be drunk first. This means taking out all the plates and food from the locker and removing the locker floor. That will keep me busy and sweaty for an hour or so. That afternoon, I was not 100% happy that the engine regulator, which controls the voltage charge to the batteries, is set right. I spent an hour on the cabin floor with my head in the hot engine room investigating. It is hot inside the boat, which is likely why the regulator is not pumping out full power to charge the batteries.

7pm: darkness falls, that is the end of boat jobs for today. Night-time is simple, keep the boat moving at a steady pace but not too fast. It is not a time to be experimenting or fiddling with the boat. This usually means reducing sail to avoid any drama during the night. When things go wrong at night, danger looms larger than in the daytime. I can see lines of clouds ahead, organised like streets in the sky. This is a sign of trade winds, the prevailing winds that blow east to west between latitude 30N and 30S. In the northern hemisphere these winds blow from a northeast direction at Force 4-5. The trade winds have been used by sailing ships to cross the oceans for centuries. I am now at latitude 25N so I am in the trade wind belt. I can soon think about turning more west for the Caribbean.

11pm: the wind has risen to 20 knots. I have furled away the jib sail completely. I had to change my heading to 260 degrees to make for a more comfortable ride as the sea is wild tonight. I have a small bit of mainsail out and the full hank on jib sail flying. I am not messing around in the darkness on the slippery deck to drop the sail, it is too dangerous with the waves crashing over the bow. I will just ride out the night at this speed, 8 knots surfing down the waves. Hmm getting the hank on jib sail down in high winds is worrying me and something I need to plan for. Next time if wind hits 20 knots that's the limit, I must get the hank on jib sail down and switch to the traditional mainsail and jib sail. With traditional sails I can easily control from the safety of the cockpit how much sail is out.

Day 5: 21st December 2018 - *Violent rolling made the boat take a severe pounding*
N24 45 W21 45

8am: rough seas again this morning. The waves are not the big Atlantic rollers but short sloppy waves that push the stern of the boat one way and then the other, causing violent rolling of the boat from port to starboard. Last night was not pleasant at all as it was so rough. The violent rolling made the boat take a severe pounding. I kept rolling side to side in the bunk when trying to sleep so I grabbed every pillow I could find and extra duvets to pack myself into the bunk like I was in a coffin. In the end I got little sleep. I tried to slow the boat down to make it a bit more comfortable with little success. My brain felt it was rolling around in my head. I am glad that night is over. 151 miles in the last 24 hours. Woohoo I am 5-days at sea. Tomorrow is day 6, the longest time I have been at sea. Breakfast time: coffee, banana, orange and the last of the fresh bread. I need to focus on more sustained banana eating over the next couple of days as they all have ripened together.

The weather charts today show a nasty low-pressure system moving towards me but thank God the centre will remain north of me. I don't like the look of it. I can try to slip down below it and skirt the bottom of it. Time for a coffee and to think what is best. The forecast says moderate to rough conditions! The word 'rough' when in the middle of the Atlantic does not sound fun but I am here now and nowhere else to go. I downloaded the latest GRIB files from the Iridium satellite and looked at the four suggested routing models. Three of the models say go west while the European forecast model (ECMWF) says goes south. Hmmm what to do. You can never fully trust these models and need to make your own decision. Turning west would suit the current wind conditions but that nasty low is coming in from the east, so heading into it is not a good idea. I had enough rough seas last night to last me a while. The trick for using the routing models is not to use them to figure out where you should be tomorrow, but where the best winds are in 2-3 days' time and head for that position. I take the wheel and do some fun helming as we fly along in 6.7 knots in a north-easterly Force 4 gusting 5 wind. It is an exhilarating fast sail, which makes you feel alive and the master of your own destiny, as you steer a 9-tonne boat through the white horse waves. In these moments you feel totally alive, in the here and now, in flow.

3pm: the wind is increasing as the low-pressure is moving towards me so who knows what is coming. Let's get prepared and get this hank on jib down and back in its bag. I put the mainsail out and now I have full control over the sails from the cockpit. The rolling side to side has stopped on this sail angle. It is nice to experience a different motion. I am sitting in the cockpit taking a rest after the sail change, I am hot. I had a lovely cold glass of Coke, thank God for the fridge. I made my decision to keep going south west, rather than west. Options are still open to drop more south tomorrow to avoid the southerly end of the low-pressure system. The weather will probably have all changed tomorrow. The winds are gusty winds today with thunderstorms forecast. George the autopilot is making a whining noise at this sail angle as he fights to keep his course in the waves. I hope George is not going to give up the ghost. It looks like I will have wind in all directions for a while as the low-pressure front system passes. By Christmas day I will hopefully be back in the steady north-easterly trade winds.

Night-time brings a full moon, lighting up the way. There is a clear sky with twinkling stars. I am unsettled in my decision to go south west and questioning whether I should have gone more south for more wind. You never know if you are making the right choices as there is never one right way. The speed has fallen tonight, I am much slower. The sea has also calmed down, it was all breaking white water waves up to a few hours ago. So much for the high winds forecast, wrong again. What's that, my God I saw a bird! I am not alone in this world, life still exists. This is the first bit of wildlife in 5-days. I have music playing and as I listen and dance, I am steering the boat through this magical clear night. Music is so important at sea to boost your mood. I have a Spotify playlist for dance music, which keeps my mood up. In recent days the batteries are maintaining a high state of charge, which must be from all the sunshine at this latitude. The solar cells are generating electricity from the sun, and with much of my equipment turned off, I am drawing less power.

I enjoyed today very much but now tiredness is hitting me. I need to get to bed early and get a good rest while it is calmer. I recognise that I am over-tired, which is dangerous and probably why I am often questioning my decisions. I am hoping for a full night's sleep. There is nothing around so I see little chance of hitting anything while I sleep. George the autopilot will look after me.

Day 6: 22nd December 2018 - *Rowing boat on my portside!*
N23 47 W24 05

I woke to a cloudy day, how unusual compared to all the sunny days I have had up to now. On the weather chart, I can see the low-pressure and cold front ahead of me stretching down to latitude of 20N. There is also a low-pressure trough marked on the chart, which indicates thunderstorms. Sounds like ominous weather ahead. I am sure a cold front mid-Atlantic is much more severe than the fronts we experience when sailing near the coast. By 1pm the clouds ahead are very dark and the wind has dropped. Later that evening the wind dropped further to just 10 knots and the boat speed reduced to 5.7 knots, which is still an acceptable speed for a gentleman. I expect to be flying the cruising chute tomorrow as light winds are forecast. Dinner tonight is pizza and beer to wash it down. A beer in the evening is something to really look forward to. Pressure on the barometer continues to fall. I have that feeling of sailing into the unknown, let's see what will come from it. 2,165 miles to go, ETA (estimated time of arrival) has increased to the 8th January.

8pm: what the hell is that to port? A light is flashing, I am sure of it. I just spotted it as I looked around before going to bed. I turned on the AIS that picks up other boats positions and yes there is a vessel out there. My God, it is a rowing boat called 'The Kraken'. I did not expect to find a rowing boat out here. My VHF radio was even turned off as were the navigation lights as I thought no one was out here, oops. I turn on the nav lights and radio. I call up the rowing boat on the VHF on Channel 16 and chat to the rower, Tim Crockett, who is heading for Antigua. The boat name, Kraken, is a mythical sea creature that is believed to have immense power, enough to sink ships by wrapping its tentacles around the hull before dragging them down to the bottom of the ocean. I don't want to mess with this guy. He is doing the trip for Combat Stress charity. The creature symbolises his struggle with mental health issues and PTSD. Even more interesting, he is ex UK special forces from the Special Boat Service branch of the SAS. I would love to meet this guy for a beer, what stories he must have. He sounded groggy, tired and not too excited to talk to me so I expect I woke him up. My 6 knots boat speed sounds very impressive compared to his 2 knots. He will be another 40-days at least crossing the Atlantic where I have about 17-days to go. Good luck to him and lucky I did not run him down.

I also see two ships showing on AIS so there is lots of activity out here it turns out... Another lesson learnt; leave the radio on so ships can call me, leave the navigation lights on so I can be seen and leave the AIS on so I will be alerted if other vessels come within 3 miles of Esperanza. At least tonight I did not run anyone down. It was exciting to talk to another person. Now I know I am not the only fool out here, there is at least one other fool in the Atlantic. I could never cross an ocean in a rowing boat, imagine all the dampness and constant waves washing over you. I feel very sensible in my cosy yacht.

00.27: Beep Beep Beep Beep, the AIS alarm goes off and I jump out of bed from the deepest sleep of the trip yet. I am N23 07 W25 30. Another rowing boat has popped up called Boadicea from the UK doing just 1.7 knots. I can see from AIS it is 26 feet long with a 6 feet beam. These Atlantic rowing boats are not that small after all, just 9 feet shorter than Esperanza. Boadicea is 2 miles from me and has just turned 90 degrees as it is likely they see me coming at speed towards them and are avoiding any possible collision. Out of interest I turned the radar to see if it would pick up the rowing boat but it does not, they are too low in the water and hidden in the swell. I don't bother to call Boadicea as it is too late at night, they are more than likely asleep or have just been woken by their own AIS alarm triggered by Esperanza. An email from home confirms the Talisker Atlantic Rowing race is underway from Canaries to Antigua. I seem to be sailing through the fleet. Boadicea has a crew of two young women rowing for Cancer Research UK. They both took on the Atlantic challenge with zero rowing experience. In the end they ended up making it across the Atlantic to Antigua in 50 days, which was a world record for the fastest female crew in the race.

I stayed in the cockpit making sure I pass clear of Boadicea who's flashing white light I can see to starboard. I am under a blanket of stars on a super clear night. I see the Orion star constellation which looks like three bright stars together in a straight line. I have been listening to an audiobook biography of Winston Churchill: 'Walking with Destiny'. He describes using the Orion star system or Orion's Belt, a line of three bright stars to navigate safely across the desert when he ended up lost. The first star in the belt to rise and also set below the horizon is called Mintaka. It will always rise and set within one degree of true east and west wherever you are in the world. Orion's Belt in December/January in the northern hemisphere rises 8-9pm local time and climbs to the highest point in the sky around 1am local time. Reassuringly Orion's Belt is there every night. It is comforting to see and spotting them has become a nightly ritual for me.

Day 7: 23rd December 2018 - *Today is my longest time at sea*
N22 58 W26 07

I was woken at 5am as the wind dropped and the boat slowed to 3 knots. Time to put the engine on. At least when the engine is on the boat is stable and you can get more undisturbed sleep. It is very calm this morning, surprisingly calm with this frontal system ahead. I now am motor sailing on heading west to keep sails filled as there is only 6 knots of wind. This is my longest time at sea so it is a new milestone for me. Life at sea feels good, I am well settled into the trip. In only three days, on Boxing Day, I will be halfway to the Caribbean with 1,400 miles sailed. I am making real progress towards my goal of getting to the other side of the Atlantic. Breakfast time is my next trick, then I will try to put up the cruising chute and see if we can catch some breeze. The strong winds from the low-pressure system moved further north than forecast so they are gone and no longer a worry.

I decided to swap over the autopilot electric motor arm that moves the rudder. I was a little concerned about how hot the motor was to touch and the whining noise it made yesterday. I will switch to the spare as I do not want to burn out the motor. To do this I lift the bunk mattress in the aft cabin to get access. I remove the securing split pin, push the hinge pin out, disconnect two power plugs and the arm is off. In goes the spare one, plugs back in and within minutes we are back in action. I bought this spare Raymarine Type 1 linear arm second hand on eBay. It was described as never being used, as it was the spare on another boat. It looks new and is much smoother than the other one, so it is likely to draw less power, another plus. Job well done so coffee time and book reading. To keep any loneliness at bay, I usually have an audio book playing in the background with the reassuring tones of the narrator acting as my virtual crew on the voyage.

The big cruising chute is up and working well, boat speed is now 6.5 knots. I am not experienced with using this sail as I just bought it. I am always wary of it wrapping around the mast or getting jammed. It is just lightweight parachute style material and being light it can grab light winds and move the boat. The VHF marine radio comes alive "Marseille calling Lucy". A French woman is calling another yacht but I can't hear the other yacht as it is too far away. I don't see any boats on the horizon or on AIS. After lunch I have visitors. A pod of dolphins arrives to swim with the boat and I get a super GoPro video. Today is much warmer, 28 degrees inside the boat. The pressure continues to fall from 1019 to 1012 Millibars over 24hrs as low-pressure passes to the north. It looks like I may have missed the rain as the front has moved north. Today's weather chart shows the low-pressure scooting around the Azores high-pressure system and off to do battle across the Atlantic towards Ireland. I am glad I am not up there battling for survival in that weather.

Today's jobs included a nice bit of boat maintenance as the loudspeaker in the cockpit stopped working. After some examination I found a loose wire and fixed it. I also patched two small tears in the cruising chute with spinnaker tape. I passed close to a third rowing boat today from the Atlantic race. There are 28 rowing boats out here from the race. I spent the rest of the day looking at weather charts and routes to decide where it is best to be in 2-3-days' time to catch more wind. I will continue on this track until morning, heading northwest on 295 degrees, the only direction the wind allows at the moment. But I am now heading in the direction of New York. I will turn back south tomorrow morning as the wind is forecast to move around to the south east. By Christmas Day I should be back in the north-easterly trade winds.

I am an environmentally friendly boat. With the fridge, instruments, autopilot, VHF marine radio, Iridium Go satellite system and AIS, I am net positive in terms of electricity during daytime as the solar cells from the sun are producing enough electricity to power the boat. Nice to feel energy neutral. Dinner is pasta with sliced onion, fresh tomatoes, fresh garlic, tin of mushrooms and a jar of peppers. Very tasty, there is enough left for lunch tomorrow with added chorizo to spice it up. Just two very ripe bananas left; I am throwing the banana skins for the rowers. In 2-3 weeks the banana skins will have decomposed back to nature.

3am: I am in the cockpit as squall clouds are appearing on the horizon. Even in the darkness of night, I can see sheets of rain falling from the black squall clouds. These localised torrential downpours have so far missed me. I am wary of these squalls where wind gusts can reach up to 40 knots (Force 8).

5am: the sea is rough and the winds have increased back again to 20 knots. Esperanza has moved back into the rough angry Atlantic Ocean. I am helming on the wheel in the dark for another 30 minutes and then bed. There is a lot of cloud ahead so I may be coming to the edge of that frontal system. Behind me there is a super big moon lighting the path ahead. No other vessels or sea life around, all quiet this morning in the Atlantic.

Day 8: 24th December 2018 - *Christmas Eve middle of the Atlantic*
N23 05 W28 14

Christmas Eve and a very different Christmas Eve it will be. Due to the squalls last night I did not get much sleep. I am heading south trying to squeeze a little west at the same time. The sea conditions have changed as I am now punching into 20 knots of wind on the nose. Esperanza is pounding along on a tight beat into the waves. The wind is forecast to go northwest during the day, which will allow me back on course and back in trade winds for the next 10 days. The boat is healed well over on its side so it is not possible to use the stove and do any cooking at the moment. The pressure is back up to 1014 Millibars as the Low passes. 830 miles sailed and 1,980 miles to go so we have dropped below the 2000 mark. Time to get back into bed, it is 10am but I am tired from lack of rest last night with the constant squalls. I am going to get my head down for 2 hours.

At midday, I surfaced for coffee and the wind had shifted from its steady direction to being all over the place or, as the forecast describes, variable winds. I put the engine to charge the batteries so we will motor sail at the same time. On Christmas Eve I am listening to BBC World Service and Christmas Carols live from Kings College Cambridge! How cool is that, it is the same carol service that I would have playing in the background at home. As I listen, I am steering the boat this afternoon across the waves. Listening to Christmas carols mid-Atlantic makes me think of everyone at home wrapping presents. This is my first Christmas away from my family. At the moment I feel ok but tomorrow I expect I will be a sad to be alone on Christmas Day. I just know I have a job to do. I am holding onto my mission to get this boat to the Caribbean that is all I have to focus on. What is going on in the rest of the world has little impact on where I am now. I am alone in my own world with my boat, the sea and the ever-changing weather. This Christmas I miss my kids very much. I am missing the annual ritual of the Sandycove 40 Foot Christmas Day swim, which I normally partake for a quick dip. I will also miss the Guinness in my local pub Fitzgerald's where we often go on Christmas Eve to have a festive sing song.

Land of Hope and Glory is now playing on the radio, it sounds lovely. It makes me think of my Dad. If he was still here, he would be tracking my position every day and sending me emails. It would have been fun to be in contact with each other on the HF radio as he was a Radio Amateur enthusiast and had a radio station in his house. He would also now be listening to the same Carol service from Kings College. My brother Paul is up the Amazon in South America so our family is spread across the globe this Christmas. Christmas is a good time to ponder the past and consider the future…

Christmas Eve is a moonless night. I am wondering how Santa will drop off the presents on Esperanza, I will leave the hatch open, though it is open every night anyway as the nights are warm. Pressure is rising fast, which means wind. I had a big wash using some hot water heated from running the engine to charge the batteries. I decided I better have a little clean-up and look respectable for Christmas Day. I have given up worrying about water reserves for Christmas and washed my hair in hot water. I still have three quarters of water remaining in the boat's water tank. I was thinking today that the sea looks lovely for a swim but I remember watching a movie where the crew went for a swim and could not get back onto the boat. Looking at my fuel log, which I update every time I run the engine, I have burned 60 litres of fuel with 330 remaining. Plenty of fuel reserves at the moment, all is good. Tonight I am sailing west in the right direction towards the Caribbean at 6.2 knots. There are constant creaking noises from the boat and mast with all the slamming of the hull into the waves. I am amazed this boat stays together at all and does not just split apart. The Atlantic is at times so violent and fierce, then at other times so calm and gentle. Of course it is always bad at night.

It is late on Christmas Eve night and I am listening to two Amateur Radio guys chatting on the radio. I better get some rest as I am likely to be up during the night if the wind drops again. A full night's sleep would be heaven at this stage. This is the one thing I crave, uninterrupted sleep in a soft bed with big fluffy pillows. As I drift to sleep, I am wondering what I am going to have for Christmas dinner, it might be pizza and beer or fried wedges and beans. Shay from Adrigole emailed me to ask about my Christmas dinner and I said the Turkey was too big for my little oven and it would be more likely to be turtle soup out here. By the way all the bananas are gone, but the carrots are lasting very well and turning into the best snack food when eaten raw and peeled.

4am: bang, crash… What was that noise? Up I go into the cockpit and the davit pole on the stern of the boat, which holds the solar panel, has broken and is hanging off! It is about to fall into the sea. How do these things always happen at night? I put the head torch on and I grab a few big metal jubilee/hose clips, to see if I can make a temporary repair. Screwdriver in one hand, I climb out of the safety of the deep cockpit onto the deck to the stern of the boat. I have to be fast as the davit arm is swinging around and might do more damage taking out the GPS and Satellite aerials. The break was at the bracket. I managed to use a jubilee clip to hold the davit back in place. I am happy with the job but will have to get this fixed in Caribbean. It looks like metal fatigue caused the bracket to fail. The speed is up and down tonight, 3 knots then 7 knots when a wave picks me up and shoots the boat forward.

5am: I am still up and trying to get the boat moving as the speed keeps falling. In the last 24 hours I have only covered 122 miles so Esperanza is slowing. To allow me to go below and get some sleep, I put the engine on to keep the boat moving at a steady speed. I will motor a few hours until morning. I need sleep as I am exhausted. I drift off to sleep wondering how many more things are going to break on this trip. I make a mental note that the starboard winch is feeling rough to turn. I did service all the winches before I left the Canaries but it will need another strip down, clean and grease. Let's see what the journey brings next and I will just deal with what happens. I am asleep.

Day 9: 25th December 2018 - *Christmas Day; Santa brought presents*
N22 27 W30 04

I write in my logbook "Christmas morning, je suis tired, happy Christmas everyone from the middle of the Atlantic". I tweet my Christmas message to the world: "Happy Christmas everyone, off to work to put cruising chute up. No rest on the high seas, light winds today". Santa Claus arrived last night. There are wrapped presents to open. I open them and find a tin of biscuits, a Lindt Chocolate Bear, the DVD movie 'It's a Wonderful Life' and a pair of women's socks? What was Santa thinking, did he get the wrong boat with the girl's socks. I am looking forward to watching my favourite Christmas movie of all time, 'It's a Wonderful Life'. No decision yet on dinner, it may end up a pot noodle at this stage.

Yippie, the cruising chute sail is flying and nothing beats it in the right conditions. Esperanza is rocketing along at 7 knots. For Christmas Day the boat motion is comfortable and steady. Unfortunately from this morning's weather, it looks like later today the weather will change as I will sail into a low-pressure trough, which is extending from 40N to 22N where I am. I can expect changeable winds, squalls and thunderstorms. I will keep an eye out for cloud building up ahead. I plan to get the cruising chute down before dark, especially with the rough weather forecast. I had a nice rest in the bunk this afternoon as Christmas Day is all about lazing around. I heard the end of the Queen's speech on the BBC. She emphasised the importance of people with opposing views treating each other respectfully. I assume she has Brexit in mind when she says this. It is hot and pleasant to walk around the boat without the need for clothes.

Christmas dinner turns out to be an omelette with crisps while watching the movie 'It's a Wonderful Life'. I laughed when looking at my own Christmas dinner this year but it was tasty. I would love a slice of plumb pudding doused in whisky sauce and cream. I am feeling ok today but I am missing Kate and Sean opening their presents. I am looking forward to getting back to civilization in 10-days or so. I heard the weather in Dublin from RAF Volmet weather station: 9 degrees, clear skies and high-pressure. It is a nice day in Dublin for the Christmas traditional sea swim. Before dark I dropped the cruising, chute and switched to two poled out jib sails. I enjoyed watching 'It's a Wonderful Life', an old 1946 black and white movie full of deep themes: that life is all about true friendships; the value of duty and sacrifice; and that a sense of community and belonging is key for us to feel truly connected in society. I had a nice glass of Oban Scottish whiskey with the movie. Before bed I download the latest routing models, which suggest taking a direct westerly route to the Caribbean, except one model, which wants me to go south. I am being pushed south whether I like it or not but. I can change direction in the morning. It is cooler tonight with the northeast breeze. I am rolling about again with the boat but at least sails are fixed so no tweaking of sails tonight (I hope). I must try to experiment with sail size to see if I can reduce the rolling from side to side but that's for tomorrow.

3am and I am awake. The boat motion is very rolly and uncomfortable. I step into the cockpit in the dark and get the fright of my life! Looking at me is an eight-inch fish on the cockpit floor. I don't know how I did not stand on it. I let out a scream as I wasn't expecting to lock eyes with a fish. This wasn't a flying fish as I see no wings but looks like a wave dumped him into the cockpit. Back to the sea with you Mr Fishy.

Day 10: 26th December 2018 - *Creaking noise coming from the mast, should I be worried?*
N21 21 W32 06

7am: I woke to lots of rolling of the boat from one side to the other. I am trying a change to a setting on the autopilot to switch to wind vane mode where it follows a wind angle rather than holding an exact heading. Maybe this will give me a smoother ride. Very odd, this morning I can hear BBC Radio 4 on longwave radio (198kHz) loud and clear but I am a long way from the UK (4,200km from London). BBC World Service is broadcast on shortwave so the signal is designed to travel long distances, but the maximum distance of BBC Radio 4 on longwave is under 2,000km. It must be a propagation anomaly day. Fun to hear local BBC radio on St Stephen's/Boxing day. I have a sore shoulder from all the winching that I have been doing from the daily sail changes. I took two Ibuprofen for the pain.

Midday and a rain shower passed over the boat. I took the opportunity for a wash and dashed naked on deck with the shower gel and had a lovely freshwater wash. It felt like heaven to get the salt off my skin, very refreshing. I now smell nicely of the shower gel, like I am ready for a night out on the town. 155 miles covered in the last 24 hours; speed is picking up again. I am hitting 7 knots with the two jibs poled out either side. Distance to Caribbean has dropped to 1,680 miles with 1,000 miles sailed. In 300 miles, I should be at the halfway point. From then on, I will be nearer the Caribbean than Europe. Dark clouds and squalls are rolling through from the northeast. The squalls are like bombs around me. If I think one is coming for a direct hit on Esperanza, I reef away the bigger jib sail completely and continue just on the smaller fixed hank on jib. This helps de-power the boat as I can expect up to 40 knots of wind in a squall for 10-15 minutes. That is enough wind to rip the sails and cause damage if the boat is overpowered. On the wheel I am finding it very easy to steer the boat in these gusty rough conditions. It has been a great sailing day, fast, furious and fun.

For meals on this voyage I didn't make a schedule of what to eat each day. I just decide on the day depending on my mood and culinary urges or lack of them. The advantage of being alone is I usually have leftovers for lunch the next day. Today, it is fried rice with soya sauce and it is just what I am in the mood for. Only a few apples, oranges and carrots are left to eat. Sad to see the fruit and veg go.

The updated satellite weather is available from 6.30pm UTC each night and again in the morning at 7.30am UTC. Tonight's forecast shows a patch of calm wind ahead, so it looks like I will need another sail change tomorrow and back to the cruising chute. In 2-days I will be back to poled out jibs and the trade winds. It seems I need to keep going south to get more into the established trade winds as I am on the border of the steady winds and the calm winds of the high-pressure. The book says when trade winds are fully established, look for rows of small puffy clouds known as fair weather cumulus clouds. I am seeing fluffy little clouds so it looks like I have found the edge of the trades.

Time zone changes feel strange out here in the Atlantic as you decide yourself when to turn the clock back. I can decide what time I would like sunset to be. Do I want sunset at 7pm, 8pm or 9pm? It makes you ponder what time actually is. We are slaves to the clock at home but out here in the wilderness you don't bother too much about the actual time but work your day around the sunrise, midday when the sun is highest in the sky and dusk. The best practice is to turn your clock back 1 hour for every 15 degrees of latitude travelled west. When I reach 35W in 180 miles, I will move the clock back 1 more hour. It has to be done anyway or it starts to get darker earlier and earlier, which messes up dinner plans.

I have been hearing a creaking noise the last few nights and thought it was coming from the mast, which was a little worrying. With all the forces on the boat it is not uncommon for masts to snap and fall down. This is always a worry in the back of my head. After some investigation I found the noise was coming from the heads (the toilet compartment). I lifted the floorboards and found the spare pump mechanism for the toilet sliding around. Once secured the noise stopped so one less worry. Churchill's war speech is a rallying call for my transatlantic voyage 'Never give in. Never give in. Never, never, never, never—in nothing, great or small, large or petty—never give in, except to convictions of honour and good sense. Never yield to force. Never yield to the apparently overwhelming might of the enemy'. It resonates with me as I do battle with the Atlantic. I must complete my mission and sail this boat to the Caribbean. Night night all, the coffin bunk calls.

Day 11: 27th December 2018 - *Today I am truly remote working; from the middle of the Atlantic*
N20 00 W34 43

6.30am: I was rudely awoken by rain coming inside the cabin of the boat so I reluctantly had to get out of bed and put the washboard doors in to seal the boat. Outside it is torrential rain with 26 knots winds. Another squall scored a direct hit on Esperanza. In the cockpit I reefed the jib quickly to depower the boat. Speed hit 8.7 knots in the squall with just the small hank up jib flying. I should have reefed the jib sail last night before going to bed as I knew there were squalls around but it is tempting to keep the speed up. In hindsight, going slower at night is better as it means less interruptions which equals more sleep. After the squall the wind is all over the place and boat speed falls to 4 knots with the sails flapping and banging. 15 minutes later, we are back into the usual northeast wind and the speed returns to 6 knots. This drama has disturbed the deep sleep that I was in. Back to bed as Esperanza is stable and happy again. I did not wake again until 10am.

I could have stayed in bed longer but had to get up to download the weather forecast. Of the four weather models, two models called PWE and PWG are both agreeing on taking a more southerly route, so I will go with that. I will leave the hank on jib up, roll away the main jib and let out the mainsail to change sail angle to just off the wind on a broad reach. This all takes time and effort, I never expected to be changing sails so often on this trip. It is very tiring doing this alone. I turned on the Churchill audiobook, my friend on this voyage.

Today is Thursday, well I think it is. If it is, I must be available for work for my company today and tomorrow as my holidays officially only start close of business Friday. This is true remote working; you don't get more remote than the middle of the Atlantic. Work will be very quiet anyway as everyone is on Christmas holidays. Sonya at home in Dublin is helping me monitor work emails and Skype messenger. I cannot access the corporate network at sea as the bandwidth is too low using the satellite internet. Anything that I need to do she can relay to me via text message or email which I can download via Iridium satellite system.

There are many balls in the air at the same time to make this trip possible but it seems to be working out so far. Once I arrive in the sunny Caribbean, I will be remote working. I am unsure how successful this will be, as it all depends on finding reliable internet to allow me to make conference calls. The Caribbean is noted for dodgy 3G data signals so I will just have to hope it works out. To give me more options, I bought a Google phone that says it guarantees internet data in all the Caribbean islands (but it is not cheap as charges are per Megabyte of data used).

Reflecting today on single-handed sailing, it is similar to looking after a small baby. Like a baby, you think you have it settled and then it cries out for something to be done - change the sails, trim the sails or change the direction. Also, just like a small baby, you rarely ever get a full night's sleep as the boat relies on you so much. At times I wonder who is in charge, Esperanza or me. But I love being alone and in command of my own ship and destiny. I am very free out here. Even to the extent that my cockpit toilet is a 5-litre plastic coolant container, which is working out very well as the chamber pot. It is probably one of the most essential items onboard the boat and the lowest tech. It stops me from hanging overboard where I may fall in and making the trip to the heads (toilet) in the cabin can be a danger in itself in rough seas.

The weather routing software does not seem to factor in that my boat can go directly downwind so I am not sure I trust the routes suggested. I won't follow them exactly but I will do my own version, the Alan weather model. After lunch (ham and cheese wrap, coffee and fairy cake) another rain shower came over the boat, which allowed me to have a wash on deck. This time for a little luxury I also used hot water from the kettle in my wash. I have dropped below the latitude of 20N where it is noticeably warmer and humid. There are more squalls lurking around down here.

Small drama today as the jib sail sheet/rope slipped off the winch in the cockpit, releasing the jib sail which wrapped itself around the forestay wire. What could have turned into a disaster I was able to sort out by going to the bow. My skills are improving. This evening I started a new book, Charlotte Grey. I had a nice read in the cockpit with a beer. It is a lovely evening just before sunset. Dinner is already organised as it is last night's leftovers, veggie fried rice. Raw carrots are still a big hit, they are lasting weeks. Other key items have been baby wipes for removing the sun cream at the end of the day, kitchen roll, which is used for just about everything and digestive biscuits, which I find are the best biscuit on a boat (or ginger nuts but I could not find any of these in Lanzarote). I would like more crisps as I am running low and would willingly swap for chocolate as it is too hot for chocolate. More apples would be nice.

8pm: I just passed the latitude of 35W and that means it is time to turn the clock back another hour, so it is now 7pm. I was finding that I was eating my dinner in the dark so the clock change will move dinner hour 1 hour earlier and solve that problem. 1,500 miles to go, halfway tomorrow. ETA is 7th January, that would be a passage of 21 days. The speed is back up again at 6.7 knots and I am heading more south again, which I think is best. I have not yet decided which island to make my arrival in the Caribbean. It will be either the small island of Bequia or the larger island of Saint Vincent, which are both at a latitude of 13N. I am currently at 20N so I still have 420 miles more south to go.

Netflix time, and I have been looking forward to it all day. I am watching a series called 'Better Call Saul' and enjoying it. I find a TV series is a great way to stop the nagging twinge of loneliness you get each night when the darkness is surrounding the boat. It is the few hours after dinner and before bed, when you have less to do that you can feel alone in the big ocean. Though I am more worried about how I will feel when I arrive in the Caribbean, as nearly all the other boats will have crews to hang around with. I will be on my own. I hope I won't be too lonely when I go ashore. Maybe I will meet new sailor friends to hang out with. I am more of an introvert so I sometimes find it difficult to meet new people but I must force myself to make the effort.

Before bedtime I am reading up on Barbados, which is the first Caribbean island that I will pass, a full day before Saint Vincent. I am thinking maybe I should stop there. But my feeling at the moment is that with the limited time that I have in the Caribbean, I should aim to visit less islands and allow more time on the islands I choose to explore. This also means less officialdom from having to clear the boat in and out of customs and immigration, which I will have to do for every island I visit. The island of Bequia looks like my vision of a Caribbean island, so I am thinking I will go straight there and relax on its white sandy beach. Martinique, the French island seems the best for boat maintenance so I have booked the boat into marina Marin for a few weeks, while I will fly home to see the family. Another key factor in choosing which islands to visit, is that I need good internet phone coverage so I can connect my laptop for work. The thought of sandy beaches and warm 25-degree water is keeping me going.

Yawn, early bedtime tonight. It is just 9.30pm but this was 10.30 pm before I changed the clock today. As I close my eyes, I am thinking I must make Bermuda a stop on the way home across the Atlantic to Europe. Going direct from Caribbean to Azores is over 3 weeks and too much to be doing again within 12 months.

Day 12: 28th December 2018 - *During the night I saved a life!*
N18 39 W36 36

8.30am: time to get up after a rough and bouncy night. Once again, no real sleep. The bloody wind shifted during the night from northeast to east so I was kept busy adjusting the sails. I hit the halfway point this morning - 1,458 miles to go out of 2,830 miles, yippie. I should celebrate but I am too tired to get too excited. 149 miles travelled in the last 24 hours, a good result. I pat myself on the back for all the sail changes, which are paying off. The Churchill audiobook is coming to an end, what a life he led. Churchill had a number of lives in one life, he did so much.

To get the best performance from the boat I need to regularly trim the sails to ensure the mainsail behind the mast and the jib sail in front of the mast are balanced. If the boat is not in trim it will want to turn one way, like a car where the wheel tracking is out of alignment. To stay on a desired course the autopilot has to apply rudder, which causes additional drag and loss of speed. The big advantage of a boat with sails in balance is there is less strain on the autohelm so it draws less power from the batteries, an important factor on an ocean passage. Every time I take the wheel, I check the sail trim and rebalance.

4pm: it is pumping fuel time again. I am adding fuel from the jerry cans on the deck into the main fuel tank. I have only used 62 litres in 12 days, which is very good. I still have plenty of fuel left, over 300 litres. Today is engine checks day: coolant, oil and hydraulic fluid levels checked and all is ok. By the evening I am motor sailing on low revs. The battery capacity had dropped to 56% so the batteries needed to be charged anyway. 9pm engine off, three hours of charging but the battery level only rose to 67%. It must be the hotter conditions that means the batteries are charging more slowly. It is a gentle still night. I am on a broad reach with wind just off the stern on one side. No rolling motion at the moment. Tomorrow I expect back to the northeast trade winds and to my old reliable poled out jibs. At my current position the compass variation or error is large at 14 degrees. I need to make sure I take this into account in my navigation calculations or I might miss the Caribbean completely!

During the night I saved a life. A fish jumped aboard and was wriggling around on the deck gasping for air. I got a wooden spoon, picked him up and flung him back to the depths of the ocean. Pity I do not like to eat fish as they keep coming aboard and chunky ones too. Boat speed down to 4.7 knots. Worry about it tomorrow, I am off to bed, steady as she goes.

Day 13: 29th December 2018 - *Esperanza is sailing today nicely on the cruising chute*
N17 52 W38 52

What a great night's sleep for once! I slept 11 hours, amazing. I am still here and did not hit anything. I feel refreshed like a new man. I went to bed at 9pm and woke just once in the night at 3.30am to change the sail configuration to the poled-out jibs. Other than that I slept through the night until 11am. During the night there was a nice gentle motion but the flip side was that progress was reduced slightly. In the last 24 hours I have sailed 122 miles so I have slowed down. Breakfast was taken in the sunshine. I had cornflakes, coffee, yogurt, orange juice and a Berocca multivitamin tablet. Looking at the new weather I see hurricane force winds to the north of my position but they are well away from me. Another front is extending south to my position. I note the barometer reading every day as a drop-in pressure signals bad weather and oncoming wind. I need to monitor this hurricane force low in case it decides to move south. I will keep my heading direct west. There is endless bad weather to the north of me, I am glad I am well south of it. At the same time seeing this bad weather is making me nervous. How the hell am I going to get the boat home next year as I need to be up there in the weather to get to the Azores? Scary.

This afternoon the wind dropped to 4 knots and was non-existent at times. It has become hot outside with the lack of breeze. In the cabin it was 28 degrees. To cool down, the only solution is to dip a bucket on a rope into the sea and pour a bucket of cool seawater over my head. But even the sea water has become warm. I felt today I was burning in the sun, so I started putting on sun cream. I prefer to cover up from the sun with a long sleeve shirt as it means there is less scrubbing each evening with baby wipes to remove the sticky sun cream. I am getting a nice brown tan; red heads do tan it seems.

On the HF shortwave radio, I can hear airliners flying over the north Atlantic talking to Gander Air Traffic Control in Newfoundland. It is fun to listen to the different airlines checking in and passing position reports. Ominously, there are no aircraft overflying the area where I am. I am way off the grid down here, not even on the air routes between Europe and the Americas. From the other side of the Atlantic I heard Shanwick Air Traffic Control from Shannon, Ireland. Nice to hear the Clare accents, home of my mother's family. It reminded me of World Flight 2003 where we made our transatlantic crossing from St John's, Newfoundland to Shannon, Co Clare in one hop. On that flight I spoke to Gander and Shanwick air traffic control to pass our position reports. I vividly remember flying at 6,000 feet over the Atlantic in my survival suit and looking out the window of the Piper Cherokee. Through a break in the clouds I could see a rough angry ocean. The sea was white with breaking waves. I thought to myself thank God I am not down there in a boat in the Atlantic, much better up here flying over it. I never imagined I would be back in the middle of the Atlantic but this time in a yacht and alone. You never know what is coming next in life.

This afternoon I put up the cruising chute but I am not sure it is worth the effort. But later the wind picks up to 9 knots and Esperanza is sailing nicely on the cruising chute. I am making a gentlemanly 6 knots but in slightly the wrong direction. The forecast says squalls are expected tonight so should I drop the cruising chute for the night or do I risk leaving it up to maintain the speed? It is a lovely sunset evening in the cockpit with a beer in hand and the music blasting. Just me and the ocean, my favourite time of day, sunset. 8pm bang! The wind rose from 8 knots to 25 knots in seconds. I saw the squall coming. It was already dark but it was like a black hole was chasing the boat from behind. This cloud was as black as anything. Luckily, I got the cruising chute down minutes before the squall hit or it would have certainly ripped to pieces. A massive heavy rain shower followed the wind gust. The boat is soaking wet and the sky is dark and grey. Lesson learnt, don't leave the cruising chute up at night, which is the answer to the question I had earlier.

The Churchill audiobook is finished and I actually feel sad. I will miss the familiar narrator's voice who was my virtual crew member and companion. I had the audiobook playing every day over the last two weeks (51 hours of listening). A super book. Tonight I will get the laptop out and look at my work holiday plan, which I have mapped out in Excel. I am still working on how to maximise my holidays for next year to allow me to sail the boat back home.

Day 14: 30th December 2018 - *Spooky outside, a dark, cloudy and moody sky*
N17 37 W40 01

14-days at sea today, 2 weeks! I am enjoying it. 1,200 miles to go (about 9 days). It won't be long before I get under the psychological 1,000-mile mark. I am getting a little nervous about meeting land again as I have no idea what to expect in the Caribbean. I have never been there before. Is it as dangerous as they say? Will I be alone or will I meet new mates to hang out with? Will there be room to anchor in the anchorages? And many other questions. I have no big urge to go ashore to land at the moment as I am happy cocooned in my secluded and private sea home. I have my routines established, which will be broken once I reach the shore. I will then need to make new routines. My home has become the boat with a new view each day, while everything in the boat is in the same place and familiar. It will be odd to stop moving and switch to a new way of life at anchor and using the dinghy to go ashore.

Today for a change it is cloudy with a foreboding black sky. This is the cold front I saw yesterday on the weather chart. It is the real thing, a 3,000-mile Polar front stretching all the way from Iceland at 64N to near the west coast of Ireland and then down to 16N, near where I am. I am on the edge of the front. Worse than the weather, all the apples and oranges are gone. There are some onions, fresh garlic and a bag of spuds left from the fresh food. I am listening to a group of Amateur/Ham radio guys chatting and I can hear an Irish guy called Patrick from Mullingar.

134 miles travelled in the last 24 hours, happy with that. A very strange bird flew by the boat. I have not seen a bird in 10 days. This bird was Jurassic looking with a long tail sticking out from behind. It circled the boat. This bird is on its own just like me, we are two fellow solitary travellers. I haven't seen dolphins in a long time. I thought there would be more wildlife out here but this ocean is desolate. Today, I am starting a new audiobook, the novel 'Love is Blind' by my favourite author William Boyd. The narrator Roy McMillan will become my new

travelling companion for the remainder of the trip.

It just hit me tonight that I miss the very simple things of home like sitting down to a cup of tea watching TV with my family and of course the cat. Funny how these feelings just pop into your head from nowhere. It is ironic that when I am on adventures, I long for the mundane bits of everyday life and when I am back living my normal life, I long for adventure. I had the same feeling in 1999 when learning to fly in Australia. I was making my first long-distance flight in a single-engine Tobago light aircraft from Adelaide to Ayers Rock. I was nervous on this flight as I had just got my Private Pilot's Licence and I was relatively inexperienced. I was in sole command of an aircraft flying over the Australian outback hundreds of miles from civilization. My ex-fiancée at the time was my passenger, so it was not just my life at risk if I screwed up. I remember flying at 10,000 feet over the desert bush of Australia thinking of the mundane life I had back in Ireland, running a small publishing business and how good and safe that sounded versus in the air where I was then.

During that flight a helicopter also going to Ayers Rock had gone missing. I was called on the radio by Search and Rescue to make myself available in case I was needed to join in on the search for the helicopter. A number of other aircraft were already searching for the helicopter. We landed for the night as planned at Coober Pedy and stood by. Next morning, we heard they found the crashed helicopter burned out with the dead pilots still strapped into their seats. Aviation is not a forgiving hobby if things go wrong. With boats you have more leeway as you often have time on your side to figure out how to get out of a mess. In an aeroplane, or even worse a helicopter, you may only have seconds.

9pm: dinner was lovely. Thai Red Curry with fresh onion, garlic, nuts and for good measure a tin of corn, carrots and lentils. Served with rice. Very tasty if I may say so. At home I cook very little. I do not enjoy the hassle of making dinner whereas at sea I find it a pleasant distraction. The food has been good on this trip because there is very little processed food, it is all homemade concoctions. I listened to BBC tonight and there is no talk of Brexit so it must be a Brexit official break over Christmas. I am picking up BBC Africa so I am up to date on the African elections. It has been 7-days since I heard anyone on the VHF marine radio and 8-days since I saw my last vessel, the rowing boats.

It is a spooky night, pitch black, very cloudy and the sky looks moody. There are no stars at all showing. I don't have the comfort of seeing the Orion star system tonight. Best to hide below and put on Netflix with a cup of tea and a few digestive biscuits. I wear headphones watching Netflix to escape for an hour from the knowledge that I am at sea. I was laughing out loud at the series 'Better Call Saul'. It is important to have a distraction and downtime each day to take your mind away from running the boat. Before the trip I wasn't even sure I would bother to watch Netflix at sea. I thought I would focus on reading but Netflix has become a surprise highlight in the evenings and a simple pleasure. Tonight, the boat has the horrible icky damp feeling just like being back sailing in Scotland. The air is damp from the front. I have learnt my lesson, the cruising chute is down for the night, the two jib sails are left to power the boat. Making steady progress at 6 knots on 270 degrees, heading west as wind dictates.

Day 15: 31st December 2018 - *New Year's Eve 2018 - 'I did it My Way'*
N16 26 W43 14

New Year's Eve 2018 and my first New Year's Eve alone ever! I expected to feel sad or lonely but I feel ok. New Year is usually overrated anyway. I can't think of anywhere better to be than ringing in the New Year on the ocean. I will play my favourite New Year's song 'New York New York' by Frank Sinatra. Sonya will be going to a party at her friend's house tonight. I have sort of wished I was now flying home on arrival in the Caribbean to see the kids rather than staying another month before I go back home. It is a long time apart. This trip was all about sailing rather than exploring the Caribbean. But I am sure when I get there, I will enjoy my time. Anyway, I am not alone out here as on the chart I can see there is a navigation buoy called the mid-Atlantic Buoy 200 miles ahead. It is obviously unmanned but it is a reminder civilisation lies ahead. Today I moved to the other side of the Atlantic paper chart, a real sign of progress. I have 15 positions marked on the chart, one for each day from when I left the Canaries. On the chart I see that we are moving into the region of the Equatorial current, which should give me an extra 0.8-1.5 knots of speed. You would wonder how there is a current out in the middle of the Atlantic. But it is a nice surprise to get some free speed.

It is another cloudy day with squalls. I thought the Caribbean was a sunny place but as I get closer more and more clouds are appearing. I was sitting in the cockpit drinking my coffee after my lunch when I heard whizz and that bloody rope from the jib sail flew off the winch again. I had forgotten my new procedure to lock it off on a cleat! Into the water it went. The jib sail blew forward and wrapped around the forestay with some of it filling with the wind like a parachute on its side. Worse the rope is now in the water under the boat. The rope was stuck and would not pull in. I slowed the boat turned into wind to get the speed off completely. I was able to untie the rope from the jib sail clew and manually wind in the jib to take care of that problem. With the boat stopped I was able to pull the rope in. I was lucky again. The boat is back underway again, less drama please on New Year's Eve. It keeps slipping because the rope is only 8 millimetre and too small in diameter for the winch. I have to remember to lock the rope on the cleat beside the winch. The main consideration is not to let a situation like this create a bigger problem such as me falling into the water. I have stopped wearing a life jacket and harness as it is too hot so I am taking more risks. In all the drama my arms got sunburnt a little so on goes the long shirt.

The wind is all over the place so I had the engine on and off all day. I refuelled from another 20-litre jerry can. The freshwater tank is down to half full (150 litres). Dark dark clouds lie ahead from the weather front but I am ready with the shower gel if I get caught in another torrential rain shower. The forecast is showing lots of wind all the way to Caribbean in two days' time. Until then I may be motoring, which is ok as I have plenty of fuel. I am motoring along at 4.6-5.1 knots so we are slowing down. I have decided Bequia is to be my landfall in the Caribbean. I added its latitude and longitude to the boat GPS. Bequia was previously occupied by the Caribs tribe who were cannibals. Columbus on his first voyage gave the island a miss and sailed right by as I expect he did not want to be eaten. In 6 hours it will be under 1,000 miles to go. This is something to celebrate on New Year's Eve. Arriving in the Caribbean is getting real. I now can't wait to be at anchor, engine off with nothing to do but relax. I still expect to arrive on January 8th.

I am now in the GMT -2-hour time zone. I share this time zone with east Greenland and South Georgia at opposite ends of the world. I expect very few people live in this time zone. I feel exhausted tonight. New Year's Eve will be a quiet one with a wee dram of whisky to help me sleep. I would love to get a full night's sleep. Dinner was left over Thai green curry and for afters, yogurt and fruit salad from the tin. I will try to pop some popcorn tonight on the gas stove as an experiment. Popcorn and Netflix to celebrate New Year's. Midnight, I am in the cockpit with a glass of fine Oban whisky wearing my festive party tie. The clouds have cleared to give me a star show for New Year's. Playing in the background is Frank Sinatra's song 'I did it My Way' and I am singing along. I have always tried to do it my way, which I am not sure is always good for the people around me. New Year's resolution for 2019 is to have more stability in my life and move back to a normal year for me and the family. A bit of boredom sounds just right for 2019. Dolphins arrived to say Happy New Year's. 999 miles to Bequia, yippee.

Day 16: 1st January 2019 - *New Year's Day; dropped under 1000 miles to Caribbean*
N16 18 W44 59

Last night at 4am, it must have been from the Whiskey, but I woke from a nightmare thinking that my crew member had fallen off the boat. I actually jumped out of bed and ran to the cockpit to help. An odd dream to have when sailing alone and very vivid. 7am I awoke to no wind so I put the engine on. Back to bed and let 'Betsy' the engine do the work. Once the speed drops to under 4 knots I start the engine. I have fuel so I might as well use it and keep the average speed up. 134 miles in the last 24hrs. I am now at 45W latitude that is another 15 degrees sailed, so it is time to turn the clock back one more hour. The sea is calm at the moment so I took the opportunity to go on deck to the bow. I took the anchor out of the locker and put it on the bow roller ready to drop on arrival. I had it tied down in the anchor locker just in case a big wave broke it free and I ended up with the anchor crashing into the side of the boat. Next job is to pump another 40 litres of fuel from jerry cans into the main tank. Dolphins made a brief swim by the boat today but they did not stay long. They were a different kind of dolphin with smaller fins and bodies than the mid-Atlantic dolphins.

It is the first day of 2019 and I feel a little lost and lonely. I think it is also because I have the engine on all day. Motoring feels wrong and out of sync with a voyage that has been powered using wind and sails up to now. I am reading the sailing notes for the Caribbean. For some reason the navigation buoys in the Caribbean and the USA are the opposite colours to Europe. In Europe a green buoy marks the starboard or right side of a channel when coming into a harbour and a red buoy indicates the port or left side of the channel. This is reversed in the Caribbean; the red is on the starboard right side of the channel and green on the port left side. You wouldn't want to get that mixed up or you would end up outside the channel and could run aground. The good news is there are no real tides to worry about in the Caribbean. I plotted a route to the sheltered anchorage at Bequia through the channel between the island of Bequia and Saint Vincent. Just like flying an aeroplane, the most stressful part is arriving somewhere new and not knowing what to expect. I have no idea if there will be enough room in the anchorage for Esperanza.

New Year's Day dinner was different this year. I am used to the traditional turkey, ham and vegetables but today I had spinach pasta with tomato sauce, fresh onion, garlic, and a tin of corn and mushrooms. It was actually very nice, though mushrooms from the tin are rather tasteless. 6-days to go. I will be getting busier as I pass Barbados. I wonder what it will be like to see land again.

Day 17: 2nd January 2019 - *Felicity, a French yacht suddenly appeared behind me*
N15 38 W47 16

9am: what a great night's sleep. This morning I had a big surprise. When I looked outside there was a yacht behind me with a big colourful spinnaker sail flying! My God where did that come from? If they have wind then I should be able to sail as well. Looking up at the wind vane I see the wind is filling in from the northeast, back to trade wind sailing. On AIS I can see the boat's name is Felicity, a French 52-foot Jeanneau yacht. I called them on the radio and we had a great chat. There are three people onboard, a couple and their son. They were on their way to Brazil but the weather on route was not good so they switched their plans to sail to the Caribbean. They will make landfall at Barbados to drop their son off, he needs to fly home to New York to get back to work. It was exciting to talk to another boat. The last vessel I spoke to was the rowing boat

11-days ago, it was great to talk to another boat again. They left from the Cape Verde islands. Along the way they didn't realise their fuel gauge was broken; they thought they had lots of fuel when in reality they had not. They ran out of fuel completely. They will have to sail all the way to Barbados anchorage.

Esperanza is speeding up again, 142 miles in the last 24 hours, 803 miles to go. The cruising chute is back flying today as the wind is calm at 5 knots. It is lovely steady sailing. Felicity is on her spinnaker sailing dead downwind, which means she has to go more south. She is now a beam of Esperanza on the port side a few miles off. The news from BBC World service is bad as New Year started with global stock market falls due to weak manufacturing results from Asia. Is this the start of the next recession, I wonder? 33 degrees in the cabin today, it is hot and sweaty. I am drinking more and more water as the temperature rises.

As the boat is nice and steady, this is a good opportunity to try some baking. It would be a shame to arrive in the Caribbean and have not baked anything after all the baking supplies I bought. I am trying to bake muffin bread but I can't find any yeast. I only have baking soda and I am not sure if this is different to yeast. Anyway, some sort of bread mix is now cooking away in the Omnia oven on the gas stove. Elevenses time, I am having coffee and chocolate in the cockpit with jazz playing in the background. I am ready to do some duty time on the helm steering the boat and posing for the GoPro camera.

To get ready for night-time I lowered the cruising chute. Felicity is now 7 miles to port. She has tacked and is coming back to converge on my track. I am making a respectable 5 knots. The results of the baking were so-so. I ended up with a large 12-inch donut shaped thing. Is it a cake, is it bread? Whatever it is, it was not fully cooked in the middle. It also tasted of too much baking soda. My first attempt at baking cannot be called a success, much of it went overboard to feed the fish. Panic, the beer is running low, I may be forced to start beer rationing. I have started a new Hemingway book 'To Have and Have not'.

11pm: looking around the horizon I can see Felicity's navigation lights are visible on my port bow. I am going to call my brother on the Sat phone to wish him, Naomi and Dylan a Happy New Year. He is somewhere up the Amazon exploring with his family.

4am: I was woken by the increasing wind. It is raining outside. I have the iPad with me in the bunk to show the position of Felicity, as I don't want to collide with her when I am asleep. She is now 3 miles ahead of me and tacking up and down across my track. All that tacking back and forth seems like a lot of work. I am just pointing straight for Bequia with two jib sails set and no more work to do. I am gaining on 52-foot Felicity, at this rate I may overtake her during the night. I am keeping the speed down as I need to sleep and I don't want any drama tonight. I set the AIS alarm on the iPad for 1.5 miles, so if Felicity comes within that distance an alarm will sound and wake me up. Back to bed after munching on a digestive biscuit or two.

Day 18: 3rd January 2019 - *More damage, the jib sail ripped*
N15 21 W49 33

I woke up to a choppy sea but it's a nice sunny day after all the rain last night. 690 miles to go. No sign of Felicity at all, where did she go. I scan the horizon and check on AIS but nothing. I am lazing around in bed this morning. I didn't sleep well last night as the boat is back to its wild rolling. The boat has been so steady that it felt like I was not even moving. This was one of the slowest days with just 123 miles in the last 24 hours. The sea has gone from choppy to rough with white capped waves but I don't mind as the wind is back and the speed has picked up again. It is a late breakfast today, cornflakes with UHT milk and coffee. I am listening to Atlantic Air Traffic Control again. I heard a Ryanair aircraft talking to the Santa Maria radio in the Azores. Strange to hear Ryanair when I am so far out into the Atlantic. I passed the Middle Atlantic Buoy today but could not see it. The next buoy is the West Atlantic Buoy, 159 miles ahead. I finished the Hemingway book and I am starting 'Into the Water' by the author that wrote 'Girl from The Train'. I just found a hidden pack of Fairy Cakes I had forgotten about, a nice surprise to accompany my mug of coffee. Today, I am sailing through large patches of Sargasso seaweed.

This afternoon after checking around the boat I spotted a problem. The jib sail has ripped at the base near where it attaches to the furler on the deck. How did that happen? I went to the bow with the sewing kit but there was no way I could mend the rip as the sail material at this point was too thick to get a needle through. I decided to leave it alone and roll away just enough sail onto the furler so the tear is not exposed. I think it is ok but I must remember I can't unfurl the jib sail fully anymore. Another job to get fixed in Caribbean. I am admiring the flying fish which is the first time I have ever seen these odd creatures. At 4-6 inches long they pop out of the water and actually fly above the water. Their little wings mean they can glide above the waves before dropping back into the sea. They are half fish and half bird.

8pm: Felicity calls me on the radio. It is so nice to know there is another boat nearby thinking of you to make a radio call. She is 17 miles behind me so I did overtake them during the night. They are slower as they are tacking the spinnaker to keep direct downwind. Their 52-foot yacht is making less progress than my smaller 35-foot boat. I read in a sailing book to forget all this tacking back and forth when long-distance sailing. The quickest way to the destination is to find the sail solution that allows you to sail a direct course. This is working very well for me with my two poled out jib sails from the bow. It is such a simple low-tech solution. We agreed to talk in the morning. We exchanged emails as they have tips on the best islands to visit in the Caribbean.

The speed is back up at 7 knots. I just have tomorrow and the weekend at sea before I arrive, which is looking like Monday. I am settled into life at sea and one part of me does not want to stop. I could happily continue sailing further. On the other hand it will be so nice to be ashore on a sandy Caribbean beach looking at Esperanza anchored in the bay while sipping on a rum and Coke. Hemingway called those who like rum too much 'rummys'. I won't become a 'rummy' but it will be nice to have to spend time on the beach as a beach bum, kick back and relax, why not. I am already looking forward to the return trip to Europe in May. I feel I am becoming a real sailor now and it suits me.

9.30pm: it is a late dinner, pizza with chorizo. The good news is I found more beer in the cabin table hidey hole so I will make it to the Caribbean without rationing. I am up to two small beers per night in Esperanza's Netflix cinema. The speed is good tonight, long may it last. As per usual at 4am the boat calls me as wind has risen to 20 knots. The boat is turning into a rocket, 7 knots with waves crashing around the boat. I am a little concerned with the stresses on the boat at this speed so I reluctantly get up and reef way some more jib sail to slow the boat a little. When I was in the cockpit, I noticed the end of the spinnaker pole was bending upwards on gusts. This pole sticks out at right angles to the mast to hold the sail outwards and open. I do not like the pole flexing as it might break. On my previous boat, the Westerly Tiger, the spinnaker pole snapped in two. I need to figure out a solution tomorrow. It would be a real mess if this pole breaks as then I could not stop the hank on jib collapsing when the wind drops. The other big jib/genoa sail is held out using the boom which is much stronger.

4am: the usual shuffle around the boat to check all is ok. I noticed the battery charge is low at 56% charge; mental note to run the engine first thing in the morning. 590 miles to go, back to bed. There on AIS is Felicity doing 8 knots and flying along as well.

Day 19: 4th January 2019 - *During the night I was on deck doing the halyard dance to secure a loose rope*
N15 00 W51 47

153 miles in the last 24 hours. This morning I have been charging the batteries but I am struggling as the voltage seems to have reduced. After 2.5 hours the battery charge has only risen to 65% from 54%. It must be the heat. I lifted the mattress in the aft cabin, under which the batteries are located. I opened the battery box to allow as much air to circulate around the batteries for cooling. I have the Irish flag out from storage and ready to fly off the stern of the boat for arrival. The flag was very dirty so I gave it a wash. The flag is the first thing you look for on a boat to see what country they are from.

I had another chat with Felicity. Onboard is Pascal the skipper, his wife

Veronique and Aurelien their son who is 36. Pascal works remotely in IT security. Aurelien lives in Brooklyn and it turns out just a few blocks away from where my brother lives. They had lots of questions for me, wondering what a single-handed Irish sailor was doing out here. I asked for information about Bequia. Pascal said it was ok at night to go into the anchorage at Bequia if I have too. I am concerned that a night arrival is looking more likely, as boat speed has increased. I could slow the boat down but the wind might drop nearer Bequia so best to keep the speed up. I could sit offshore and wait for daylight as another option but if it is rough, I think it is better to seek shelter in Admiralty Bay. Their suggestion is to anchor off Princess Margaret beach.

Lots of crazy flying fish today, never seen anything like it, but lovely to watch at sunset. Today's forecast brings strong winds and squalls so I should prepare for heavy weather tonight. The boat today hit 8.6 knots in a gust. Just 470 miles to Bequia that is less distance than a sail across the Bay of Biscay. It is a bit of a shock to now be coming to the Caribbean. Dinner tonight is Tortilla Espanola, which lasts very well as it is vacuum packed. It goes very well with baked beans. I am enjoying the Netflix series Orange is the New Black. After Netflix and before bed I like to tune around on the Amateur/Ham Radio bands on the HF radio. Tonight I am listening to Albert in New York talking to a guy in Barcelona. The boat is going well so I am off to bed. The wind is steady at 20 knots. Every now and again there is a giant bang as a wave breaks on the side of the boat and kicks the boat over to one side in a vicious roll. Then she rolls back the other way - the Atlantic dance.

In the middle of the night a squall hit the boat. I said why not have a wash while I am up. I stand in the cockpit naked in the darkness and scrub myself with the soap and let the rain rinse me. It is pitch black out. I can't see the navigation lights of Felicity and there are no other boats on the horizon. While in the cockpit I noticed the cruising chute halyard line, the rope that pulls up the sail to top of the mast, had come loose and was swinging wildly over the deck. It was attached to the bottom of the mast but had unclipped itself. No time like the present so I went on deck to the mast and did the halyard dance. This is where I am trying to be in the right position to grab the halyard rope as it swings by. At least it was dark and no one could see the naked Irish man jumping around the deck. I grabbed the rope as it passed by and secured it back to the mast. I am now back in bed cleaner than when I got up. So nice to wash the salt off. Though the pillows are becoming embedded with salt and feel sharp and scratchy to lie on.

Day 20: 5th January 2019 - *43 knot squalls during the night, roughest seas of the voyage so far*
N14 32 W54 36

What a wild morning, there are lots of squalls, showers and towering cumulus clouds around. Last night was very rough, the wind speed was reading 43 knots in the passing squalls! The seas were scary with breaking waves surrounding the boat. It was my roughest night of the trip so far but at least we were moving fast in the right direction. 156 miles in the last 24 hours, my second fastest day of the trip. The fastest speed last night was 8.9 knots, that's fast for my boat. I am now speeding along at between 6 to 9 knots surfing down waves in the gusts. Sun cream is compulsory today as it is going to be a hot day. The batteries are charged to 76%, I am happy with that.

I had the idea to wire a light sensor switch to the anchor light so it would turn off the anchor light at dawn and then turn it back on at dusk. This will be very useful when I am off the boat ashore, as the anchor light will switch itself on in the evenings. It will also conserve power by switching off automatically at dawn; up to now it has stayed on until I get up to turn it off myself. Annoying, as I always felt I must get out of bed early to switch off the anchor light which disturbed my morning lie-in. Saving energy will mean that less engine or generator time is needed to charge the batteries. It was a job that I meant to do in Dublin but I never got around to it, today I took on the task. I wired the sensor in and it worked. It is satisfying when you take what starts as an idea and turn it into reality and it works.

I altered the course by 5 degrees to counteract some drift so I will pass safely clear of Barbados. ETA is now 1am Monday in 52 hours' time. I am a bit nervous about arriving in the dark so pondering options. It will depend on the weather and sea conditions on arrival. While pondering I baked some bread. It was better than last time but there was still too much baking soda. It is really too hot to be baking bread anyway. I am feeling a little run down today and low in mood. It must be the lack of proper sleep catching up on me. I took a multivitamin drink. I need to build in more time for afternoon naps. I am losing sleep during the night as the boat wakes me every night to do something. Looking out the window at the seaweed is getting thicker, like fields of grass floating by me.

I phoned home tonight and spoke to Kate and Sean; it was good to have a quick chat. I miss them a lot. Dinner is to be scrambled eggs and bread followed by a tin of peaches. While having a drink of water from the boat water tank, I notice black bits floating in the water. I examine them and it is not growth but must be carbon particles from the carbon filter. I have a spare filter and will change it tomorrow. I am not sure if drinking carbon would do me any harm. To be safe I am switching to bottled water. Another chat today with Felicity, they invited me onboard their boat in Bequia for French wine and cheese. From the rough seas last night Aurelien and Veronique are seasick and not able to talk on the radio. This is the last time we will talk on the radio as they are heading south of Barbados to get to the east side where I will be heading north of Barbados. On the radio tonight I heard a boat say 'As-salamu alaykum' (peace be upon you), and to you too.

Day 21: 6th January 2019 - *Just 110 miles to Barbados, I should see the lights of the island during the night*
N14 04 W56 58

Three weeks at sea today and the cornflakes have run out. For once I had a good sleep. The days are rolling by fast. It feels a little like being in prison but at least I have my release date when I reach the Caribbean. When you are in isolation to pass the time it is important to develop daily routines to give structure and meaning to the days. It has certainly helped to have the Sat phone, which has kept me in touch with family and allowed me to feel connected to the world through Twitter and email. Building regular routines means that no matter what happens the boat jobs get done, even if I am feeling down or lazy that day. I slowed down last night to sleep but I will let out more sail this morning. Two tanker ships passed me last night so shipping is around and I need to be watching out.

Lunch time now and I am having ham and cheese sandwich wraps with lashings of Hellmann's mustard. There is nothing but sports on BBC radio these days. It is just my luck that I only receive the BBC World Service for an hour per day and then they switch to another transmitter, which I can't hear. Unfortunately for the last few days it has been sports hour and I have no interest in sports. Today it is a Newport versus Leicester soccer match. The news is that the UK Prime Minister, Theresa May is still working on her Brexit deal, sounds like she may eventually get a deal done. Good on ya Theresa, let's get the deal, so we can all move on.

Midday, when I went to turn the engine on to charge the batteries, I felt lots of vibration on the propeller. Not good at all. The boat speed when motoring was slower than usual. Have I seaweed or something stuck around the propeller? I moved the throttle into reverse and ran the engine briefly in reverse and whatever was there was gone. Most likely seaweed from the Sargassum seaweed fields I have been sailing through. Easy fix and no problem. Nonetheless Esperanza is still one knot slower according to the GPS. This speed is calculated from GPS satellites and takes currents into account. It seems likely that the Equatorial current, which was assisting my speed going west is reducing as I get nearer the Caribbean. While doing my checks on the deck I found two fish, a tiny 2-inch fish and behind it a bigger 9-inch fish. From the crime scene I deduced the bigger fish was chasing the smaller one and both of them got flung onto the deck by a wave.

This afternoon I had a lovely sail, the wheel was so light I could steer with one finger. The skipper has trimmed Esperanza's sails perfectly today. Just 110 miles to Barbados. I will be passing in 18 hours around 10am tomorrow. I should see the lights of the island during the night. I am tempted to stop in Barbados but I would prefer to spend my time exploring a smaller island with a more rustic Caribbean vibe. I am sticking with my decision to continue one more day to Bequia. I am thinking ahead of what to expect for my arrival. It might get gusty and rough as I pass through the channel between Bequia and Saint Vincent. I think it will be best to drop the twin jib sails and switch to traditional sails. Then if I get into rough conditions, I can roll away the sails from the cockpit. Better to be prepared and safe.

It is the first time in three weeks that I pulled out my Dubarry sailing shoes to have them ready to wear for anchoring. I have been barefoot for the last three weeks or in socks at night. These new expensive Dubarry sailing shoes are not great at all; I find they are slippy on deck, which is dangerous. 29 degrees in the cabin, another hot day. I saw a turtle floating by from the porthole at the navigation table. Then I saw a swordfish jumping out of the water, a huge thing with its long sword nose. It happened so fast I wondered if I imagined it. Sea life is starting to appear as we get nearer the Caribbean.

Damn, I made a stupid mistake this afternoon and lost my new GoPro camera overboard. I had it secured around the front jib sail to get some wave action video from the bow. I forgot it was there and let out more sail and it spun off the bracket into the Atlantic. It floated away and was gone in seconds. Even worse, all my footage is gone. I have to remind myself I am tired and this is a warning to watch myself and double check what I am doing. At least it is the GoPro overboard and not me! I will look at this as a warning. The GoPro is waterproof, so it is going to wash up on a beach somewhere. Someone will find it and see a wild Irish man running around the deck and pouring buckets of water over his head. I hope whoever finds it enjoys the footage. I should have recorded my details on the GoPro and like a message in the bottle it might have found its way home to me.

For dinner tonight, the chief has prepared tomato and olive sauce pasta with fresh onion and garlic. Why does food taste so much better at sea? After dinner it is Netflix. I am continuing the series 'Orange is the New Black' and I am really enjoying it. Tonight, my ears and sinuses are feeling a little blocked. I don't want any risk of sinus infection developing so I will take an antihistamine before bed. I need to be wary of the antihistamine making me drowsy, in case I stay asleep and run into Barbados. I better get some sleep but I am excited as I am expecting to see the lights of Barbados at some stage during the night. I also need to watch out for fishing vessels as they are bound to be out here.

2am: Esperanza was hit by a squall. I have the radar on and can pick up the squall very clearly on radar. The rain is torrential. After the squall passes there is the wind dead zone, like a vacuum where the squall has sucked away all the air and wind, leaving the sails flogging and banging. I have to wait for the wind to settle back into the prevailing wind direction and then retrim the sails before I can go back to bed. But I can't sleep anyway when I really need to. Maybe the antihistamine has the opposite effect on me and causes insomnia! I am 50 miles from Barbados. The radar and AIS are both on as I get closer but there are no ships around. It is a humid night in the cockpit and visibility is not great due to lots of moisture in the air.

Day 22: 7th January 2019 - *Land ahoy! Barbados to port*
N13 33 W59 22

Monday morning and everyone at home is off to work but for me it is land ahoy! Yes, there is Barbados to port, 15 miles away. A big mountainous looking island. This is my first view of land in three weeks. It is a bit of a shock to emerge from the wilderness to the sight of land and civilisation. Columbus must have felt the same. Rather than feeling ecstatic at seeing land, I feel subdued. Of course, I am happy and excited but also a little sad to be ending my experience at sea. A real mix of emotions. Land means I am also arriving soon and I am getting more anxious as to what to expect on arrival in Bequia. Just one more day to go. I am listening to local radio from Barbados, they are discussing the cricket match playing in the Kensington Oval stadium. The Jaguars from Guyana are playing the Barbados Tridents. I am enjoying the Barbados guys discussing the cricket match, very cool to hear the Caribbean accent. Tuning around the local radio stations there is lots of reggae music playing, which makes me feel like I would like a rum and Coke right now. As I rework my ETA for Bequia at the navigation table I can see Barbados through the porthole. My ETA is now dawn, which is perfect as it will be daylight. 110 miles to go. I put up the Irish flag. It is flying from the stern to show the boat's nationality, which is required by maritime law. All quiet on the high seas, there are no boats on the horizon, not even fishing boats.

When I get ashore, I am looking forward to a very long hot shower with no anxiety over the water usage. My skin is dry and prickly after three 3 weeks in the saltwater atmosphere. I am using Aloe Vera and avocado after sun cream to moisturise my skin at night so at least I smell nice; well, I think I do and no one else is complaining. I moved the clock back for the final time by one more hour. I am now in the Caribbean time zone UTC/GMT -4 hours, (Ireland is 4 hours ahead). There is a strong current pushing me towards Barbados so I alter my heading to give Barbados some room. The sea is getting rougher as the day goes on and the pressure has fallen 3 millibars in 6 hours, a sign for more wind to come. It would be typical to arrive into the anchorage in a storm. Ok, let's get organised and drop the hank on jib sail and return to traditional sails.

I am getting excited to be arriving and achieving my mission of the transatlantic sail. I am ready now to be at anchor sipping a beer. Lots can still go wrong so I am on high alert. Dinner was last night's leftovers so I did not have to think about cooking, which allows more time to focus on navigation and seamanship. I have to mentally shift my attitude from offshore ocean sailing to coastal sailing. That means no more sleeping through the night but back to 90-minute naps and then shorter 20-minute micro naps as I get closer land. The new forecast shows the wind at 15 knots increasing to 20 knots. These higher winds will make it more difficult to get the anchor down but hopefully there is shelter in the anchorage. I am still a little worried that the channel between Bequia and Saint Vincent is going to be as rough as hell. In my experience any kind of channel between two bits of land is a trap for turbulent and rough seas.

Bye bye Barbados, it is strange to be sailing past a perfectly good island to go ashore. I make a mental note that on my next trip to the Caribbean I will stop at Barbados first. The next island is Saint Vincent. I can see the island of Mustique to port. Mustique is the private island where Princess Margaret, David Bowie, Mick Jagger, Bryan Adams, and Tommy Hilfiger owned homes. Leaving Barbados to stern I am off again out into the deep sea. 70 miles to the Bequia Channel. My ETA planning has gone a little screwy. I record my logbook in UTC/GMT and I notice that I worked out my ETA not in local time but in UTC/GMT, which is 4 hours ahead. My last calculation was that I would arrive around dawn in daylight, which was perfect but correcting this I am now due to arrive at 3am in the dark. It does not get bright here until 7am so that is a long wait to be hanging around offshore in rough seas to wait for daylight. I will keep going and see how I go but I don't like going into a port at night where I have never been before. I can always sit offshore if a night approach seems risky.

Looking at the chart, Admiralty Bay is a big anchorage so there should be plenty of room for Esperanza. The chart shows that the seabed is a mix of coral and sand. Dropping the anchor on coral means the anchor may not hold on the seabed or it could jam on the coral and not come back up to the surface again. So I hope I find a sandy patch. For my approach I don't see any obstacles or buoys on the chart to avoid. I will go into the bay very slowly on engine with the sails furled away. I am aiming to anchor off Princess Margaret Beach. Also known as 'fags & gin' beach, aptly nicknamed after Princess Margaret who used to visit from her home in Mustique.

Tonight I crossed 60W. I started in the Canaries at 13W so that is 47 degrees of longitude sailed, impressive. There is no moon tonight, it is pitch black, not a helpful start for my arrival. I brought the mainsail in as it was flogging. I am sailing downwind on just the jib sail, making 5.6 knots. The radar is on as I make my start for the channel. I think it is ok to go through the channel with just the jib sail. If a squall comes, I need to get the sail rolled away quickly and put the engine on. I am not messing around in the channel. The width of the channel between the islands is just 4.5 miles. Between islands you can get wind acceleration zones so it is wise to expect anything could happen. But if you are prepared usually nothing out of the ordinary happens.

Midnight and I am 12 miles from the island of Saint Vincent, the capital of Grenadines islands. To starboard, I can see the airport and the lights of the island. On the portside is Bequia, which does not have a single light showing. Bequia is so dark you wouldn't even know an island was there. It is odd that they do not have a lighthouse at the end of the island. The weather is good and the sea is reasonably calm. The radar is painting a clear picture of both islands and my route between them. I am staying in the centre of the channel where the water depth is 300 metres to avoid any nets or lobster pots. Close on my portside the water depth rises like a cliff to 60 metres. The next navigation mark is the lighthouse on Saint Vincent at Gunn Point, the light range is 14 miles and flashes every 4 seconds. No sign of it yet. I am dozing 20 minutes at a time in the cockpit. The cricket on the radio is helping. Just closing my eyes is refreshing. There is no chance I will drift off to sleep as I am too excited and the adrenaline is flowing with the night arrival.

Day 23: 8th January 2019 – *a true Caribbean island*
Arrival Bequia

1am: I am motor sailing along the coast of Saint Vincent, an ex-British colony. The engine is on because the speed dropped to 5.0 knots. I also want to charge batteries to get them well charged before I go on the anchorage, as I won't be in a marina for a number of weeks to avail of shore power. Here comes the rain, typically it starts just as I am in the channel. The speed is increasing so there must be a tide running. I am also getting pushed towards Bequia, I am compensating by heading more northwest. I throttled back as the boat speed hit 7 knots and the sea was becoming choppy. I am watching the drift carefully as I do not want to end up washed onto the cliffs of Bequia. I am listening to a local radio station playing 80s music. I can see Blue Lagoon marina on Saint Vincent in the distance.

2am: I cleared the channel and turned south to track down the west coast of Bequia towards Admiralty Bay. On AIS I can see many boats anchored in the bay. I now have a 1.5 knot tide against me and the wind against tide effect has created nasty breaking waves. The speed over the ground on the GPS has slowed to 5 knots. I decided there is no option but to go for the shelter of Admiralty Bay, as the sea is too rough to be hanging around for 5 hours waiting for dawn and I am very tired. As it is pitch black, my plan is to crawl into the bay to find shelter from the wind and drop the anchor in the first place that looks anyway ok. My goal is simple, to get the boat anchored and then to bed. Tomorrow in daylight, I can move the boat to a better spot closer to the shore. There are still no lights visible on Bequia, nobody must live on this side of the island. It is probably the exact same view Columbus had when he passed here on his third voyage. The next headland is Devil's Table; I will pass well clear as I have no desire to meet the devil.

2.30am: I am motoring very slowly into Admiralty Bay with the sails rolled away. I can't see much but I am heading for Princess Margaret Beach using a route I plotted on the iPad electronic chart. As I get closer to the shore, I can see some lights. It is much windier in the bay than I expected. I can see the light of what looks like a yacht anchored ahead. There looks to be a clear space to anchor between a giant motor cruiser vessel and the yacht ahead. I am always suspicious when I find a clear spot in an anchorage. Why has no one else taken this spot; is it because there are rocks below or an old shipwreck to snag your anchor. The charts show nothing untoward to be weary off. The seabed is marked as sand with coral patches. There is no point in indecision, just get the anchor down. Anchoring alone is less about perfection and more about getting the job done. Two people are ideal for anchoring, one on the wheel steering and controlling the boat, the second person deciding where and when it is best to drop the anchor. George the autopilot is steering as we continue into the bay. The wind has risen to 20 knots and even more in the gusts. These winds would make anchoring challenging even in the daytime so it is going to be even more stressful in the dark. I don't make things easy for myself.

I have my gloves on ready for releasing the anchor. Gloves are essential as it would be all too easy to lose a finger when letting the chain out. First, I need to go to the bow to prepare the anchor. The sea is choppy and the boat is rolling. I am crouching like a monkey to keep my centre of gravity low, in order not to get flung overboard as the boat rolls side to side. I don't want to be caught off guard and flung into the water while George the autopilot drives Esperanza up onto Princess Margaret Beach. I have the bright deck light switched on to put some light on the situation. To prepare the anchor for dropping untie the anchor safety line and use the anchor Windlass handle to open the locking mechanism. Now the anchor is loose on the bow roller and ready. The anchor goes down by gravity, it is only when raising it that you need to use the motor. I am ready to drop the hook.

Back in the cockpit I bring the boat in line with the stern of the anchored yacht ahead. I lock the wheel dead centre and put the engine into neutral. The boat is in 19 metres of water but the depth is reducing as I move into the anchorage. The speed is coming back 3 knots, 2 knots, 1 knot. I move to the bow and try to gauge the boat speed as I want to drop the anchor when the boat has stopped. Ready, steady, go! Down the anchor goes with the chain flying out of the anchor locker. I let out all 50 metres of chain. The boat drifts back and it looks like she is holding. I put the engine into slow reverse to help the anchor bite but it did not dig in, instead it dragged across the seabed which might be coral. I let the boat drop back further and the anchor bites. It looks like the anchor has dug into the sandy bottom.

With the strong wind there is a lot of force and pull on the anchor chain, it is bar tight. The chain is spliced to 50 metres of Nylon rope. I let out a further 10 metres of rope so I now have 60 metres of chain & rope. The Nylon rope is good to absorb snatching from the gusts. The depth gauge reads 13 metres. I have an anchor chain scope of 4:1; in other words the anchor chain length is four times the depth. The longer the anchor chain the greater the holding strength, which is what you need in high winds. I should really have a minimum of 5:1 scope but the boat is holding on station. I don't want to go messing further with the anchor in the dark and risk creating problems when I am tired. I will just leave things as they are until daylight and then reassess the situation.

3am: I am at anchor. Finally, the boat has stopped after 23-days at sea. I hoisted the Grenadines courtesy flag up the starboard side of the mast. The yellow Q flag is below it to signal I have just arrived and not yet cleared customs. It is a pitch-black night. I have no idea what this anchorage looks like or how many boats are here. I can make out a few boats around me but there doesn't seem to be that many boats. I can't make out anything ashore, just a few little lights in the distance.

I am too tired to think about anything or have a celebratory drink. I head down below to bed. Now that the sailing motion has stopped, I suddenly start to feel dizzy. How odd is that. It must be that my body was used to the constant motion of being at sea and that now since I come to a standstill my brain feels something is wrong. It will be exciting to wake up tomorrow and look out to see what this bay is like in daylight. As I drift off asleep my heart is pounding with the adrenaline from finally arriving. That's a wrap: 3,057 miles, 5,660 kilometres sailed in 23-days from Lanzarote to Bequia. I have done it, mission completed. Tomorrow, a whole new way of life starts in the Caribbean. I have also arrived on my son's birthday; he turns 13 today. Happy birthday Sean!

Bequia

Morning time; let's get upstairs into the cockpit to see what Bequia looks like. I am as excited as a kid to see outside; it feels like waking up Christmas morning to see what Santa Claus brought. I am amazed to see what looks like maybe a hundred boats in the anchorage. What a beautiful view to look at all these boats at anchor in Admiralty Bay. It is a postcard view on a sunny blue-sky day. I can see a white sandy beach with coconut trees - this must be Princess Margaret beach. The surrounding hills are dotted with wooden houses. The island is much

greener than I expected so it must get a lot of rain. The water looks amazing, it is so clear and inviting. I put my hand in the water and yes, it is warm.

I am anchored a long way from the town so I am using binoculars to spot a better location closer to the beach. It is still windy, 20 knots. I see a boat leaving from a spot closer to the shore. Ok, let's get in there before someone else snaps up that bit of water. Off I go to raise the anchor and reposition the boat, which again takes an hour or so. Now the boat is repositioned closer to the beach I am ready to go ashore. I have to untie and unwrap the dinghy, which is deflated and tied to the deck at the stern. It has to be pumped up and prepared for sea. The Honda 2.3 Horsepower engine is fuelled and started. I flustered around for ages wondering what I need to bring with me ashore in terms of clothes to wear. Do I need a spare change of clothes in case I find a shower? How much money do I need to bring? I have to bring the Ships Papers for customs, which I have put in the waterproof drybag.

It is already 2pm and I am only now ready to leave the boat. I step into the dinghy and motor towards the harbour. It feels odd to be leaving Esperanza and seeing her alone at anchor. I passed a floating bar in the middle of the bay, very cool. I will have to go there at some stage. You can dinghy up to the bar, tie up and step onto the floating bar and take a seat. I dock the dinghy at one of the many dinghy pontoons and lock it to the dock with a chain. Dinghy and engine thefts, I read are common in the Caribbean. I am ashore on land after three weeks. I don't feel dizzy or wobbly at all, isn't that odd. Back home I have often felt wobbly when stepping back on land, even after a short sail. I thought I would be swaying all over the place but, no, I am fine.

Bequia is a culture shock, and what a nice change. Everyone is black, the white folks stand out as sailors or tourists. My first task is to find customs and immigration, as legally all boats have to 'clear in' with authorities on arrival. In the office the officials are all wearing immaculate white uniforms. There are many forms to complete, all backed with carbon paper to make the copies. The customs official asked what was my last port of call. 'Lanzarote', I said and the customs official raised an eyebrow. Then the other eyebrow raised when he asked how many crew were onboard and I said just me. Lots of officialdom, paperwork and pomp. They wear their uniforms with pride as a sign of their status just like we saw when we were travelling through Africa on the World Flight. Clearing into Bequia was easier and quicker than I thought. I am also cleared to visit the island of Saint Vincent that I passed last night. Now I need cash to buy lunch and my celebratory drink of Caribbean rum. I exchanged US dollars for the local funny money currency called 'ECs' or the East Caribbean Dollar.

I spent the rest of the day walking around the harbour not knowing what to do with myself. I was completely at a loss of what I should be doing, I could not relax. I was rudderless as suddenly I had no jobs to do. Well there is one last job, to dispose of three big sacks of plastics from my trip. Disappointingly there are no recycling options on the island; you just put the plastic in the main refuse bin and who knows where it goes. My first impression is that the locals seem a little gruff or unfriendly. First impressions are often wrong so I will reserve judgement. I am enjoying the exercise of walking around the town. My red hair was a hit when a local girl came up to me and asked why was my hair so red?

I found a laundrette that will do my wash for $5 so that is a job ahead. In the local supermarket, which is tiny, I notice water is expensive: $5USD for a 5-litre bottle. My first drink is coconut water from a street seller; he takes a whole coconut and punches a hole in it for a straw. A tasty drink and very touristy but why not. I sat down at a little bar and had a Caribbean rum and Coke, watching the yacht crews in their dinghies coming and going. Each bar in the harbour has its own dinghy dock, which you can tie up too at no charge. It is very well organised. The locals have boats moving up and down the anchorage offering services: laundry, fuel, pizza, water, fruit. How handy is that, all the services you need at anchor. I have never seen this before anywhere else, a very enterprising idea. Happy hour I see is 5-7pm, I must remember that.

I walk around the bay to Princess Margaret beach and sit down to have a beer where I can see Esperanza safely at anchor. This now feels like the paradise I have been dreaming of. It starts to sink in that I have not flown here or arrived on a cruise ship. I have sailed myself across the Atlantic. Look, there is my boat at anchor in the bay to prove it! It is such a satisfying feeling.

Next day I feel like I am a resident as new boats arrive in the anchorage. My neighbours on the anchorage around me are from the UK, Australia, New Zealand, France, Canada and the US. On the dinghy ride ashore, I passed an Irish boat at anchor, a 38-foot Rival from Dingle, Kerry but there was no one onboard. This morning I did a food audit to see what is left and what I need to resupply. I have more food left than I thought, about two weeks of dinners but it is heavy food like pasta, which you don't want in this heat.

This week I am officially on holiday from work so it is time to explore the island. I walked around the headland in the afternoon and climbed the hill to find a fantastic postcard view of the Admiltery Harbour. It was so hot and humid. I am constantly sweating as my body tries to adjust to the humidity. To cool off the only option is to jump in the sea, which is crystal clear with colourful fish. You can stay in the water for ages as it is 25 degrees temperature. I saw a flat Ray fish swimming on the seabed below the boat. The sun is keeping my batteries charged as I have only the fridge running 24 hours per day. It is great that I am self-sufficient for energy on the anchorage. I can tilt the solar panels towards the sun for maximum power generation and turn them to follow the sun. Nice to know I am a green energy neutral boat.

I am starting to feel a little lonely as I have not had a face to face conversation with anyone for three weeks. I have a longing for human contact. They are right when they say, no man can live alone (or at anchor) for too long. The suggested social strategy for a sailor is simple; call over to the boats around you in your dinghy to say hello and introduce yourself. Try not to look too mad or too desperate. I find starting conversations difficult but once I get chatting, I am fine and can't be stopped. It is always making the effort and taking the first step that is difficult. After three weeks at sea, I have a wild untamed beard and a big mop of red hair. I fear I might look like a wild Viking and scare people away. I must go to the barber on the island for a haircut and a beard tidy up.

Thursday night I took the dinghy over to the floating bar in the middle of the anchorage. There are swings as seats set in a square around the bar. I say hi to the barman and take up my swing seat at the bar. A group of guys and girls are there that all seem to know each other so I say hello. One guy turns out to be Irish from Limerick and has just arrived in Bequia. He is an engineer working on charter yachts. Another girl is a Russian sailor who is stranded in the anchorage as her crew have left her. She was working out if she could continue sailing single-handed. Then there were the young English guys and girls who operate the charter boats. They were all fit and healthy looking from working all day in the sunshine. The charter boat people generally don't mix with the live-aboard sailors like me. They were all good fun but they did not stay long as they were just having a quick after work drink. The Irish guy told me where on the island I could get the davit bracket welded that broke on the Atlantic crossing. A very enjoyable evening.

It is time to go back to the boat for an early night to catch up on all that sleep I lost in the Atlantic. It is very dark at night so you need to watch carefully where you are going in the dinghy. When returning to the boat the problem is to find it amongst all the other boats. My solution is to use the Christmas lights I got from in my Christmas stocking. I have them hanging at the bow, stern and on the boom. They twinkle nicely making the boat stand out. I tie the dinghy to the floating boat bar and climb aboard.

The next day it still felt I had not had enough human contact. There was an Australian yacht MAC anchored just in front of me. I was watching the four-crew onboard while I was having my sundowner drink. The funny thing was that it turned out they were also watching me and wondering about me. They were asking themselves who was this wild Irish man on his own and nicknamed the boat Paddy Esperanza. I never got over to their boat to say hello, which I should have done, as I would have been welcomed with open arms. But as luck would have it, that night I met the crew in a local bar ashore and we had a great chat. Matt is the boat owner. He and his wife are in their thirties. They are on a multiyear trip, sailing the boat they bought in Greece back to their home in Australia. With them are their friends Jules and her Irish husband. Caroline and Reggie from a Danish boat and the skipper from a German boat then joined the group. We ended up with a group of 15 sailors having an international drinking session. I was 'machine gun' talking my way around the group to anyone who would listen to my stories. It was a great night out and just what I needed. Everyone was so friendly and welcoming. It was true, sailors are a community and bond like one big family to look out for each other. It is a very special atmosphere only to be found in the Caribbean.

The next day when I was walking around the island, I met the couple from the Irish boat at anchor, the Rival 38. They are from Dingle in Kerry. They had recently retired and sold their house, car and possessions to buy the boat and fulfil their dream of sailing around the world. Later that day I visited the local barber. It reminded me of getting a hair cut in India in a barber with no doors and where no one had a word of English. The Bequia barber was full of locals with reggae and rap tunes blasting away. English wasn't being spoken but a creole language that is widely spoken amongst the locals, known as a 'Vincy'. I explained I would like a trim to my hair and beard. The locals found my red hair very amusing. I went in looking like a woolly sheep and came out with a US Marine style cut and no beard at all! In the mirror I looked like a gang member and you would certainly want to keep your distance. Not a good outcome for my need for social contact. As I walked back to the boat, I noticed many other sailors with the same hairstyle. It seems to be the right of passage after crossing the Atlantic. I have settled into the slower Caribbean way of life and made new friends in my first week. It has been a lovely experience. Now it is now time to move on to the next island.

December 17th, 2018 departure day for the trans-Atlantic sail

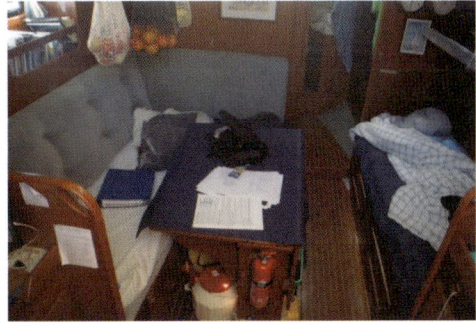

Mending the cruising chute.

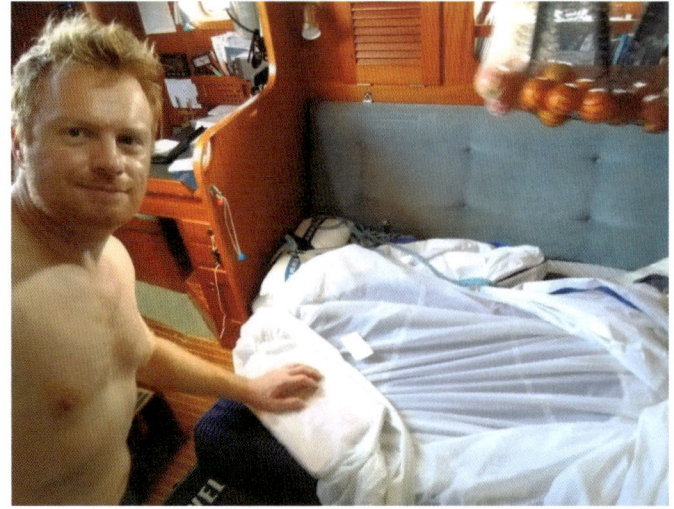

Two poled out jib sails for downwind sailing.

On passage my bed is the starboard bunk in the main cabin where I can see the radar and AIS.

Above: Refuelling from jerry cans. Flying fish start to appear on the deck each day.

Sailing downwind in the trades.

Below: Christmas Day watching 'It's a Wonderful Life'.

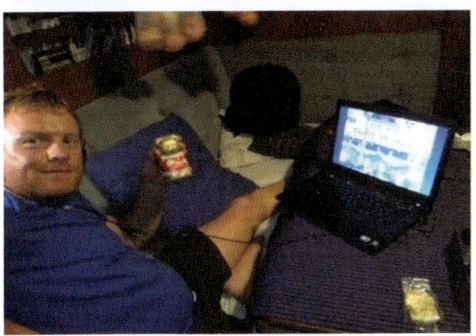

New Year's Eve party on Esperanza. 1,680 miles still to go. I dropped south of 21 degrees North latitude, in search of trade winds.

2nd January 2019, Felicity a French 52-foot yacht appeared behind Esperanza, heading for Barbados. We spoke on the radio over 3 days.

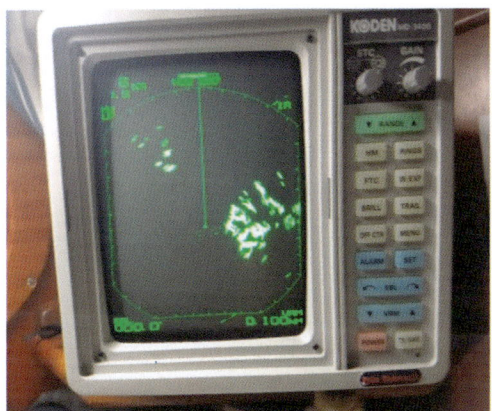

Radar shows Bequia island on the left and island of St. Vincent on the right. It was a night arrival to Admiralty Bay, Bequia.

St. Vincent, Grenadines Courtesy flag is ready to hoist up the mast.

Arrived Bequia, anchored off Princess Margaret beach. Water temperature 26 degrees.

Relaxing on the beach and keeping an eye on Esperanza at anchor.

Haircut in Bequia, before and after.

Princess Margaret Beach, Bequia. Esperanza at anchor Admiralty Bay, Bequia.

CHAPTER 4

Sailing the Caribbean

I left Bequia on the 17th January for the short sail to Blue Lagoon, Saint Vincent where I rendezvoused with my brother who arrived from New York. We sailed up the coast of Saint Vincent to Wallilabou Bay where they filmed Pirates of the Caribbean: Curse of the Black Pearl. An interesting picturesque bay with a mountainous backdrop. Lovely scenery for walks and hikes with a waterfall to visit nearby. The boat boys were a bit more assertive here. Boat boys work in small open fishing boats with fast engines and can approach your yacht when you are on your way to an anchorage. They are private unofficial enterprises offering to guide you into the bay and help you on a mooring for which they charge anything from $10-20. Usually to be avoided as they are not necessary.

Saint Vincente

On the mooring in Wallilabou Bay a local guy with Caribbean dreadlocks rowed up to Esperanza offering to sell us fruit, which looked over ripe and not great. To keep him happy and support the local economy we bought some bananas and coconuts. But then he demanded aggressively we exchange euros coins for local currency and started waving his machete around when we said we did not have spare change. The atmosphere was a little tense. The angry man eventually rowed away. I was left with an unsettling feeling that he may be returning tonight to rob us with the same machete. My guard was up as Saint Vincent has a bad reputation. I debated if we should even stop here at all, most boats choose not to. The reason being that in 2016, a German sailor was shot dead on his boat in a robbery. Two masked armed men boarded the boat at 1am. He was with his wife and children. There was a similar incident here 13 years ago. Maybe this is the time to put up my sign 'Beware of the Electric Fence'.

We went ashore and explored the film set for Pirates of the Caribbean. The village they built for the movie is still here with lots of remaining props. After lunch we noticed the other two boats in the bay had left and Esperanza was now the only boat anchored in the bay. Now I was even more worried as we stood out like a real target. But later that day all was well, four more boats arrived so we had safety in numbers. Myself and my brother went exploring into the mountains. We waved down a local minivan bus and jumped into the overcrowded van not knowing where we were going. It was driven at crazy speeds up and down steep and winding dangerous mountain roads. All you can do is squeeze in and hold on tight. We were dropped off in the mountains but we were not sure where we were. Walking towards us is a guy swinging a machete. It is at first a bit frightening when you see people holding machetes. We see it as a weapon where in reality this is just their multipurpose farming tool. Everyone walks around waving machetes; I must get one myself.

That night back at Wallilabou Bay we got chatting and had drinks with the crew of a German boat also anchored in the bay. Their boat was called Imperosail. There were two German guys and an English woman. The German skipper was retired in his early 60's and seemed to have hooked up with Caroline, the English crew member. We discussed skiing in Ischgl where they have been visiting annually for the last thirty years. It was a very enjoyable evening and our last day in Saint Vincent.

Saint Lucia

Next morning we sailed to Soufriere Bay, Saint Lucia and anchored in a lovely picturesque bay. In the background were the Pitons, two stunning volcanic mountain spires stretching up into the sky. Napoleans' first wife Josephine spent a lot of time at Soufriere Bay. I swam in the same hot springs bath that she is said to have bathed in at Diamond Falls Botanical Gardens and Mineral Baths. My brother left from here to fly home to New York. It was sad to see him go so soon as I really enjoyed his company.

I am back on my own. Being on your own is fine when you are sailing as you are busy going from A to B. It is much more fun to have family or friends with you to explore the islands. Who would not want to visit the Caribbean, a chance in a lifetime to do some tropical weather sailing? I stayed one more day to relax as it was Sunday. So much for relaxing as I got stuck into boat jobs and spent some hours servicing my winches, which were stiff. The sun is setting so that means it is rum and Coke time in the cockpit. I will look for the green flash as the sun dips below the horizon. This is a popular activity here on the beaches at sunset. The green flash sometimes occurs when the sun dips below the horizon, for a second the upper rim of the sun looks green in colour, an optical illusion.

21st January 2019: I motored out of Soufriere Bay at dawn. I am single-handed for Rodney Bay, Saint Lucia. It is just 18 miles, 3 hours to the north. There is no wind at all so I will use the engine all the way. Rodney Bay is where the Atlantic Rally Cruise boats arrive each year after their Atlantic sail from the Canaries. They arrive for Christmas so I am sure most boats will have moved on by now. I left early as I am back to work today after the weekend. I want to arrive early so I can remotely log in to my email and get ready for a day of conference calls.

The sea is nice and flat so it will be a fast motor. Yesterday on the mooring it felt a little isolating. I felt less safe leaving the dinghy unattended here than Bequia. If you try to leave your dinghy at the dock someone usually comes looking for money to mind it, which is annoying. The good old protection racket is alive. I expect if you don't pay then you come back to a damaged dinghy. There was a slight edgy atmosphere in Soufriere Bay so I am keen to move on. I might berth at the marina in Rodney Bay. $30 a night seems good value to experience the comfort of a marina. I have not been on a marina since I arrived and batteries also need a long charge from shore power. I plan to party in Rodney Bay as the local street party, 'Jump Up' is on Friday night. In the Caribbean the big party night is Friday, not Saturday.

I am having my cornflakes as I motor along at 6.6 knots in flat glassy seas. It is one hour after I left Soufriere Bay. Bang, crash, sudden stop… what the hell! There was a loud bang and the boat suddenly stopped dead in the water. What is going on. It feels like I hit something. The boat went from 6.6 knots in flat calm water to 0 knots in seconds, I must have hit a whale, container or something big. I also think there is also something around the propeller. The first thing I do is to go down below into the cabin and look into the engine room and bilge for any water. All looks ok. I see no leaks so we are not sinking just yet. There is definitely something around the propeller so I must swim down under the hull to inspect the damage. I get into my swim togs, put on goggles and dive down with my big diver's knife. At least the water is flat calm. Under the boat I found a green fishing net wrapped around the propeller blades. I was able to pull it off and all seemed ok with the propeller. No damage that I could see. Back onboard I got the engine going again and all seemed well, which is very surprising. I continued on route towards Rodney Bay.

I am trying to understand what happened. The net indicates I did not hit a whale or container. Looking around in the distance I can see a small open fishing boat and it looks like they are pulling in nets. Is this where the net came from? When I heard the bang, I was moving through a field of sargassum seaweed, which may have hidden a net lying just below the surface. The most likely explanation is I sailed into a fishing net. Amazingly nothing seems damaged and no water in the engine room. The force required to stop dead in the water, a

9-tonne boat making 6.6 knots must have been immense.

I arrived at Rodney Bay. I decided to keep it simple and anchor. I had to log on for work anyway so it was quicker than going into the marina. I will soon need the marina to take on more fresh water as only a quarter of a tank remains. This evening I will go on a recce mission to the marina on the dinghy. It is always easier to go into a marina when you know what to expect rather than going in blind. Marinas are stressful when single-handed and often there is no one to help ashore. When you find the right fairway where the berth is located you have to turn down into the fairway, which is usually a cul-de-sac, there is no way out but the way you came in. That means to get back out you need to be able to spin the boat in its own length, 180-degrees while at the same time countering any tide and wind. It is common now for boats to have bow thrusters, a small propeller at the bow to help turn the bow of the boat around, which greatly helps turning in tight situations. My boat does not have a bow thruster. Esperanza has a tighter turning circle when turning to port, so I must think ahead and position the boat for a left-hand tight turn. To make a 180-degree turn I need short blasts of throttle alternating between forward and reverse with the wheel fully turned to port. The key is to hold your nerve, don't change your mind mid turn, even if it looks like you are not going to make it and a collision is inevitable.

I have been using a single-handed trick for years to dock the boat. It involves just one single rope to stop and secure the boat to the marina. One end of the rope is around the winch in the cockpit so I can adjust the length while standing at the wheel steering the boat. The rope passes through a cleat middle of the boat and the other end is a loop held open with a bit of plastic pipe. The procedure is to come slowly into the marina berth. Then I drop the open loop end of the rope over the first cleat on the pontoon and then give a blast of reverse to stop the boat. The throttle is then put into trickle forward gear, a little power allows me to control and hold the boat alongside the marina pontoon. I can fine tune Esperanza's position in the berth by adjusting the length of the rope from the cockpit winch. Now I can step off the boat at my leisure and make the boat fast with bow, stern and spring lines. But with all the best plans in the world anything can happen in reality. The risks of things going wrong are greater when single-handed as you don't have crew to help.

I moved onto the marina a couple of days later. I thought being on the marina would make it easier to socialise. I got a nice berth and had my first hot shower since Lanzarote, 5 weeks ago! It felt so good to have unlimited hot water to stand under. I am sure some of my tan washed off.

I was feeling lonely in the marina so I went to the marina bar hoping to find some sailors to share sailing stories with. To have a good conversation would make all the difference to me at the moment. Two guys arrived at the bar beside me. They looked to be sailors around my age in their 40s. I took the opportunity to ask if I had possibly seen them in Bequia. I hadn't at all but it seemed a good conversation opener and it worked. Dennis is Dutch, 44 years of age and his then partner Thomas is German. They are on an around-the-world voyage in a Hallberg Rassy 49-foot yacht called Mach3. It was great to meet people my age as most sailors I meet are retired. We had a great chat. I was impressed with Dennis's story. When his long-term relationship ended, he dreamt of a lifestyle change, sailing. He put his dream into action and sold his business, home, car and possessions to sail around-the-world. Lucky for him he seems to have made enough money to retire and explore the world. It is a brave decision to sell everything and sail away.

Dennis introduced me to the Gilmores, an Irish family of four who had sailed from Ireland on Pogeen, a Pogo 35-foot racing style yacht. My brave 'hello' at the bar has suddenly resulted in a whole range of new friends. It just shows how wonderful life can be when we reach out to others. I was informed that Instagram is the main sailor communication method. I never used Instagram but I will download the app tonight and connect to the other boats.

A few days later I am on the Irish boat Pogeen, having drinks with the Gilmore family and a Scottish couple Trevor and Eileen, who are sailing the same type of boat as mine, a Hallberg Rassy 352. It was a great group chat with seven of us down below in the cabin drinking rum. This is the social side of Caribbean sailing that is so fantastic and special. In Europe you go into a marina and there is little interaction. In the Caribbean everyone talks to each other. We are all unconsciously bonded together because we share the same adventure. We have all sailed the Atlantic and we are all living on our own boats that we have spent years preparing for the trip. Everyone is sharing their stories of the best places to explore in the Caribbean. People want to help each other; we are one big extended sailing family. I appreciate how lucky and fortunate we all are to be members of the Atlantic and Caribbean sailing club.

The 'Jump Up' street dance party is tonight in the newest town of Saint Lucia called Gros Islet. It is not far from the marina. I am going with Dennis and Thomas and I am looking forward to it as it is meant to be very mad. Today I walked to Pigeon Island national park and climbed the hill to look over the bay. To get there I had to walk through the town Gros Islet. It was a shock to see the poverty, with many families living in shacks. There was an edgy feel to the town. We were told to stick to the main street, but I cut through the side streets, keeping a fast pace. I stuck out as the only white man and clearly a tourist. Saint Lucia is the honeymoon destination with 5-star hotels and private beaches but in the local towns, gangs rule with guns and drugs. A lot of the Caribbean islands look like paradise on the surface but dig deeper and you find a darker side. The wealth difference between locals and tourists must be the cause of a lot of the tension. The locals see the big cruise ships arrive daily. Tourists disembark for just a few hours and then they are gone. The sailors see themselves as separate to the tourists. Sailors are living in the Caribbean for 6 months or more, experiencing the real local people and culture. Though I am unsure how favourably the locals look at the sailors.

That night the 'Jump Up' street party was packed with locals and tourists drinking and dancing at a crossroads in the town. Big bass speaker systems were set up by the locals on street corners. There was no official organisation that I could see, rather local DJ's getting together on the streets. At 10pm it was like a curfew came into force, as all the tourists left and were bused back to their 5-star hotels. Dennis and I were left amongst hundreds of drunk and drugged locals. We watched the local guys stripping their tops off and dancing madly to loud punching dance music. It got wilder as the night went on. We were the only two white people left on the street and it felt maybe we should not be there. Before we went out that night, we were told not to bring a wallet, camera or anything valuable, as it will be stolen. We only had enough cash for beers and a taxi home. We watched the locals dance into the early hours and then slipped away in a taxi back to the marina. A fantastic night and what an experience. This trip is all about new experiences. It was time to leave and sail onwards.

Martinique

The French island of Martinique is a six-hour sail. It is strange to be in the Caribbean and so far from mainland Europe but now I am going to Martinique which is part of France. It will be good to be back using the Euro and I will have free data roaming on my phone. I am looking forward to shopping in Carrefour supermarket to buy French wine and cheese.

26th January 2019: I arrived in Martinique and anchored in a fantastic bay with well over 100 boats looking onto the pretty little village seaside of Sainte Anne. Rain showers are a daily occurrence in the Caribbean so every time I arrive in a new harbour, I put the cockpit tent up. This covers the cockpit completely and keeps it dry. It is like having an extra room on the boat where I sit in the evenings.

Martinique is big, it feels less like an island. Everyone is speaking French, very few people speak good English. Most people here are holiday makers from mainland France. Club Med has a big resort here. Sainte Anne is very clean and tidy compared to Saint Vincent and Saint Lucia where rubbish is common on the streets. Martinique didn't opt for independence and seems to be thriving with no poverty that I can see. The island is supported by the French social welfare system and government jobs. Saint Lucia and Saint Vincent took their independence from Britain and seem to be struggling economically. Was it the right move, I wonder? Martinique has the full weight of the French government behind them for support and development. But in my opinion the smaller islands such as Bequia, Saint Lucia and Saint Vincent offer a more real and authentic Caribbean island experience. Martinique and Guadeloupe feel like extensions of mainland France.

I spent a few days walking the coastline and exploring the beaches. There is much more rain here than the other smaller islands. It is very nice to have my mobile phone working and roaming again at no extra charge as I am in the EU. The bad news is I am back to European prices with €5 for a beer where I have been used to half that price on the other islands. An Irish boat, a Lagoon 45 catamaran from Dublin, dropped anchor beside me in Sainte Anne bay. The boat name Realta Bheag, is Irish for 'small star'. George and Mary own the boat and are recently retired. They bought the boat new in Dublin and are sailing to Australia where they will sell the boat. They are making this a 2-year adventure. It was an interesting idea to sell the boat in Australia as they don't then have the long, sail home from Australia. Since they bought the boat new, it is under warranty for their entire trip. They were making use of the warranty in Martinique as some jobs needed to be done and it was going to be at no cost to them. George told me that boat resale prices for catamarans in particular are higher in Australia than Europe so in theory this trip may cost them very little. Smart idea, they are in effect on a multi-year delivery trip with near free use of a new boat.

Today marks the end of the first leg of the trip as I move to the marina at the port of Marin, Martinique. I will spend a week on the marina doing engine and boat maintenance before I fly home for a 3-week break to see my family. The engine has done 117 hours since I left the Canaries so it needs an oil and filter change. Some of the winches need to be serviced. In the Caribbean evenings I am still having fun listening to the Amateur/Ham radio guys chatting on the radio. I heard the US military in Guantanamo Bay calling as they were running a radio group. It is very hot at night in the boat and I keep waking up during the night with the heat. I don't think I have had a full night's sleep since I arrived. My body is still conditioned to being awake regularly during the night from the Atlantic sail. It might take some weeks to get back to normal sleep patterns.

29th January 2019: I motored over to marina Marin in Martinique. I was not expecting the marina to operate Mediterranean style moorings, which means there are no finger pontoons beside the boat to tie onto. I motored into a space between two boats on the marina. I gave the bow line rope to the marina guy on the pontoon and he made it fast. He then gave me a rope, which I walked back to the stern and pulled on, it was attached to a bigger rope, which I pulled up from the seabed. I used this rope to secure the stern. The boat was now docked Mediterranean style. The only option to get off the boat is at the bow. But the bow is high in the air, 5 feet above the pontoon. The solution is to clip onto the bow pulpit a small ladder that came with the boat. But where is the ladder? After searching the boat I realised it is at home in my shed! I remember being told that I would never need the ladder and leave it in the shed. Now I need it. A German man on the boat beside me gave me a wooden box to use as a step onto the pontoon. It is awkward and not a very gentlemanly way to get on and off the boat. Ideally, I should have reversed the boat to the pontoon as then I could just step off from the bathing platform. But I was not going to attempt this on my own as Esperanza never goes backwards the way you want her too. Reversing is a journey into the unknown so you need crew with fenders at the ready in case you get too close to other boats.

It is nice to be on a marina as I can go often for walks around the town, which is full of sailors. In the last week I have been hiking with Dennis and Thomas from the Dutch boat Mach3. They also arrived at Marin the same time as me. We had great fun exploring the island and socialising at night. We all hiked up the Mount Pelée volcano, which has been dormant since the last eruption in 1932. In 1902 it erupted and destroyed the town of Saint Pierre, killing a shocking 29,000 people in minutes. This was the worst volcanic disaster of the 20th century. There were only two survivors, one a prisoner whose dungeon-like prison cell protected him and a young girl who hid in a cave. It was a beautiful but strenuous hike to the 4,500-foot summit where we walked around the rim of the crater, which is heavily overgrown with green vegetation. We have a clear view down to Saint Pierre, the town that was destroyed in the eruption.

After a week in Marin on the marina, I am leaving today to spend a few days at anchor in the bays of Anse Mintan, Anse Dufour and Anse Noire. I have heard from other sailors that these small bays are worth exploring. Anse Noire is where you can swim with turtles; this is something I don't want to miss. When does anyone get a chance to swim with turtles? I am working normal Irish hours during the week so when arriving in each of these anchorages I have to do the 'anchorage signal dance'. This involves motoring around the anchorage looking for the best 3G internet signal, with the other boats watching and wondering what I am up to. So far so good, as work is under control. It is great that my salary keeps coming through each month to fund this trip as well as the family back home. I am pushing this remote working to the limit but I am making it work. It would make a great case study for the company to show how technology has changed where we can work from. I have to force myself to focus on work during the mornings, which is not easy in the Caribbean heat, especially when my work attire is a pair of swim shorts. In the afternoons I go for a swim off the back of the boat to cool down, then ashore to explore.

7th February 2019: I am anchored in little bay Anse Noire and after work I go for my swim with the turtles. There 5 metres below me is a big old turtle swimming around on the seafloor. The water is crystal clear and the turtle is chasing a crisp packet around the seabed. It makes me realise the importance of keeping plastics out of the water as this fellow looks like he is trying to eat the old crisp packet for dinner. When swimming I always look around the boat hull and propeller to check it is clean of weed. While I was swimming, I noticed something looking out of place with the bolts that hold the propeller shaft housing on. I swam down again under the boat to take a closer look. My God, two bolts were loose and sticking out of their holes! Am I going mad and seeing things? This is impossible, this can't be happening. It is bad, really bad. I start to panic thinking of the consequences, which could be epic - the boat may already be taking on water and sinking right now as the damage is where the propeller enters the hull of the boat. There is a rubber seal inside the boat where the propeller shaft enters the engine bay. If this has broken, Esperanza will sink. I rush back on board to check for water.

In the engine room I do not see any water and the bilge is dry, thank God for that. For the moment we are not sinking. It feels like I am in a dream and this can't be happening. I need to sort this out. Maybe I can re-tighten the bolts but deep down I know this is unlikely. I get some tools and go back in the water, which is at least warm. I have to dive down under the dark hull to get to the propeller. It is awkward to do this and I have only seconds under the boat before I need to come up for air. It takes some getting used to diving under the boat as the dark hull is looming above your head. Your brain is screaming warnings that being under the boat is not a good place to be. The risk is I get stuck under the boat for a few seconds longer than normal and run out of air and panic.

As I expected the bolts won't tighten, they just keep turning; it looks like the threads in the propeller housing have ripped. On closer examination the bolts are bent and may have sheared or broken in two inside the housing. Only a truly massive force could do this as these are solid 10mm marine grade stainless steel bolts. I know the bolts were perfect as they were only changed a year ago. The propeller bearing housing is cracked and as the bolts have sheared it is coming away from the hull. This is structural and not a job you can do a quick or temporary fix on. I realise now this may be the end of the Atlantic adventure as the boat has to come out of the water and I need to find a boatyard to do extensive repairs. This is a non-standard repair and could take weeks or months, assuming I can find someone to take on the job in the first place.

What to do now. I am two hours from the nearest marina and I am afraid we may sink on the way back. But I have no option as there are no facilities here. All I can do is try to get back to marina Marin. Maybe I can use the engine as little as possible and sail back. The vibration on the propeller shaft when the engine is running is going to be bad and the shaft could separate from the engine. The propeller and shaft would then fall to the seabed leaving a large 50mm diameter hole into the engine bay. Water would flood in at high-pressure as this is the lowest point of the boat. There would be little chance to stop the flow of water so the end result is that the boat sinks in 15-20 minutes.

I sailed some of the way back but then I had to turn the engine on as the boat was pointing into the wind. I took it very slow but as we turned into the channel for Marin the wind picked up to 22 knots right on the nose and the sea turned white with big waves. A rough sea is the last thing I need to add to this already dangerous mix. I am checking regularly for water in the engine room. I can feel the vibration from the propeller shaft. I am very worried about what may happen. Will I make it or will I lose the boat? Esperanza is only making 4 knots over the ground as we crawl towards the marina into increasing waves. I am ready to deploy the life raft as a last resort. My head is full of all the things to consider such as being ready to send a Mayday over the radio for help and to remember I must grab the ditch bag with the emergency beacon and flares to bring into the life raft. This is where a non-believer suddenly decides to pray again.

After another hour, thank God, I am back on the marina. This was the closest yet I have been to losing the boat. What an ending this would be for my Atlantic adventure, sunk in the Caribbean. How would I explain this back home in the yacht club? At these moments you wonder what the hell you are doing here. I made a call to the local boat yard in Marin. It was Thursday so it was late in the week but by luck they had a spare slot to lift the boat out tomorrow at 1.15pm. I am flying home Sunday so I must find an engineer who I can leave the job with. As you can expect my stress levels are at maximum.

The next day the boat is lifted out of the water and the damage can be seen. The cause must be from when the boat suddenly stopped when I hit that fishing net off Saint Lucia. It is odd that no damage was visible at the time. There is huge difficulty in trying to find an engineer and no one speaks any English. It is total confusion in the boat yard. The long French two-hour lunch breaks do not help. I am stressed out as we are running out of time to get this repair organized, my flight home is in 2 days. Eventually I located an engineer who thinks he can carry out the mechanical work but he could not carry out fibreglass repairs so I had to then find someone else for that work. This meant dealing with two separate people who have not worked together before and do not speak English. Lots of head scratching and arm waving as they considered the job. The conclusion is that they are also unsure how to make the repair until they take off the propeller and housing and that won't be until next week. I just want the peace of mind that this can be fixed while I am back home in Ireland. The uncertainty is unsettling.

10th February 2019: I am sitting on an Airbus A330 to Paris. I have left the boat in the hands of the French, there is no more I can do. Vive la France! I told the engineers the repair has to be a perfect job as I am sailing the boat across the Atlantic. I can't have a half job done and then end up sinking mid-Atlantic. If I am sinking anywhere, it would be much better to sink in the 25-degree Caribbean waters than the icy cold Atlantic, but I prefer not to sink at all. I am going home to see the family. I will be home for three weeks before flying back to Martinique. I am glad to have a break. The last few days after finding the damage have been mentally and physically exhausting. It is so much more difficult to deal with a complex situation like this when you do not have the language. As I fly home, I think about all the amazing times I have had. The weather has surprised me, as I thought the Caribbean was all sunshine when in reality there is also a fair share of cloud and rain.

While I was back home in Dublin there were many emails and phone calls with Jean Michael, the French engineer who speaks not a word of English. It was a real struggle to understand their proposed solution. I was very grateful to Cecile who works with me, for acting as my translator. She gained a crash course in boat engineering. A few days before I was due to fly back to the boat the job was completed.

Below is the work carried out:
- Removal of propeller, cutlass bearing and housing
- Removal of filler and preparation around bearing housing
- Epoxy two metal 35mm diameter bushings into GRP for bearing housing bolts
- Refurbishment of the stern tube thread
- Inspection of propeller shaft
- Reassembly of bearing housing and propeller
- Finish with epoxy filler and shape following the line of the boat
- Applied epoxy primer and four layers of Coppercoat
- Total cost to repair damage: €2,666

I won't know the quality of the repair until I see the boat and inspect the workmanship but from the emails and phone calls back and forth, I was confident they did a thorough job. I am looking forward to getting back to the boat. I want to do more sailing and explore the islands north of Martinique.

7th March 2019: I am back in Martinique and back in the sunshine. It's great to be back on the boat. Esperanza has been repaired to a high standard. I am glad to leave Martinique and get moving again. Next stop are the islands of Les Saintes, which are just off the coast of Guadeloupe. The sail time will be 18 hours, covering 92 miles. It will be my first night sail in a long time. I will be passing the island of Dominica, keeping at least 7 miles offshore to avoid any fishing nets. Unfortunately, I do not have time to stop at Dominica. It was recommended by other sailors as an unspoiled island for hiking.

Guadeloupe

I arrived at the island of Terre de Haut, the larger of the Les Saintes islands. I had to move my anchor spot three times to find the best 3G data signal as I am remotely working this week. I need a good signal as I have a busy week at work planned. This is just a brief stop at Les Saintes as I will be back on this island later this month with my friend Bernadette who is coming out for a couple of weeks' sailing. Terre de Haut is a nice little island with a rustic holiday atmosphere.

My next stop is Malendure, a small seaside holiday village northwest of Guadeloupe. Three scuba diving schools are based here, including Jacques Cousteau Underwater Reserve. Jacques Cousteau was the French oceanographer who explored more of the Earth's oceans than any other explorer. He filmed an underwater documentary at Melendure and divers can find the French explorer's statue resting on the seabed. The waters are teeming with turtles, tropical fish and coral. The sail from Les Saintes to Malendure was fast and wild sailing with 25 knots of wind between the islands. The boat speed was up to 7.8 knots. Once in the shadow of Guadeloupe on the west coast the wind dropped as expected to 13 knots. A few hours later I was pulling into the bay at Melendure. I anchored in 11 metres with 50 metres of chain.

Ashore at Melendure, there is a nice little beach full of sun bathers and a few beach bars. At night they play traditional island music in the bars. There are lots of divers and young people around. I like the vibrant hippie atmosphere here. This is just an overnight stop. The next day, it is a short two-hour motor sail north to the small town of Deshaies. There are lots of boats anchored in this sheltered bay. It is a lovely town with the magnificent Grande-Anse beach nearby. I spent two nights here. I topped up the boat fuel tank by filling two jerry cans from the local petrol station in the town. Carrying the heavy jerry cans back to the dinghy was hard work. The dinghy is working out great for hauling my supplies. It is a large dinghy for four people so plenty of room.

The reason I am here at the northwest point of Guadeloupe is that I have arranged to meet my brother again on the island of Montserrat for the Saint Patrick's festival. Montserrat is a British Overseas Territory and has a long-standing Irish heritage. It is the only island in the Caribbean that celebrates St Patrick's Day. It sounds intriguing. I am looking forward to seeing my brother again and it will be good to have company on the boat. It is my last evening in Guadeloupe and I am on the white sand Grande-Anse beach. This is one of my favourite beaches to date. I had a lovely swim and sat on the beach watching another sunset. Pity to be on my own but I am content with the beautiful surroundings. On the horizon, 42 miles away I can see Montserrat's active volcano with clouds overhead marking its position. This is where I am off too in the morning.

13th March 2019: 6.45am is the earliest I can leave Guadeloupe as I must wait for daylight. The anchorage is too packed to try to leave in the dark. The anchor is up and I am off. I point the boat at Montserrat. There is a two-mile exclusion zone around the south of the island due to the huge volcanic eruption in 1997. The capital of the island, Plymouth, had to be evacuated and 19 people died. Two thirds of the island's population emigrated to the likes of the UK, Antigua or America. A new port was built at Little Bay on the northwest coast of the island and this is where I am headed. On the chart I see three volcanoes, one is called Galway Soufriere, named after Galway city in Ireland, I assume. Soufriere is the name for a volcano across all of the Caribbean. The last eruption was 2005 and the volcano is actively monitored. As I sail up the east side of the island, I can see the result of the volcanic flow from Soufrière Hills volcano, which ran down the side of the volcano and into the sea. The area looks like the moon. The eruption reclaimed new land and made the island bigger but this is in the exclusion zone where no one lives. Through the binoculars I can see bubbling green gases with steam coming out of the rocks on the side of the volcano. This volcano is very much alive. The two-mile exclusion zone out to sea is because lava flowed into the sea and changed the seabed levels and it continues to change so who knows what the real depths are and if new obstructions have popped up.

Montserrat

I arrived in Little Bay anchorage, Montserrat and dropped anchor. I had to reposition the anchor three times as it was windy and the anchor was not catching in the seabed. I am a bit far out now for the dinghy but it will do for today. Ashore and in customs here is another island still using carbon paper to make copies of their paperwork. A very old-fashioned system versus the simple French system where you clear yourself into the islands using a computer in less than 5 minutes. They are setting up tents here at Little Bay for St Patrick's week and there are a few bars and restaurants also here. Live music and steel bands are performing every night so good fun ahead. The main town is two miles away but Little Bay is developing as a small settlement based around the port. The officials did not seem impressed that Esperanza was an Irish boat that had sailed all the way from Ireland to be here for St Patrick's Day. I thought I would be the talk of the town especially that I am also the only Irish boat here, not to mention the red hair.

Montserrat is nicknamed "The Emerald Isle of the Caribbean" because of the Irish ancestry of its inhabitants. Many of the surnames and even the street names are Irish names like 'Sweenys'. The locals who are all black trace their Irish heritage back to the 1700/1800's. Catholics were 'tolerated' in Montserrat where on the other Caribbean islands they were persecuted. Many of the Irish originated from the crew of slave ships or were those managing tea and sugar plantations. You would wonder how well the Irish treated the local native people of the island but that is a long time back in history. My brother arrived on a small Islander 12 seat propeller plane from Antigua. We took a guided tour of the exclusion zone, including the ghost town of Plymouth, which is submerged in ash from the volcanic eruption in 1997. The pyroclastic flow spread into the town and covered buildings in ash, raising ground level. You can still see the upper level windows of the taller buildings but the lower floors are below the new surface of ash and mud. Just like what happened in Pompeii.

My brother and I had a great week exploring the island. One night we went to the main town on the island for the biggest concert of the year. DJ Nappy, a top DJ from Antigua, was playing. We had no idea who this guy was but everyone was super excited to see Mr Nappy. Everything starts so late here. It was 3.30am in the morning and DJ Nappy had still not come on stage, only the support act had played. We could not keep awake any longer so we left without even seeing the main act. We were just too tired. The locals sleep all day and party all night, and I mean all night to dawn. This week there are many expats back from America and the UK for the Saint Patrick's week festival. They still have family on the island so they all tend to come back this one week in the year to visit and party. There is lots of heavy drinking so they have inherited that trait from the Irish.

We met Quinten, an interesting character who is 70 and English. In the 1980's he was sent to the nearby island of Nevis by the UK government to establish and teach Bee Keeping to the islanders. He liked the island so much that he never went back to England. He had come over to Montserrat on the ferry for the weekend. We had a great chat with Quinten. I asked where he was staying on the island, he said he was sleeping on the beach. I was very surprised to hear this at his age, but it turns out this is the old traditional way to travel in the Caribbean, you just curl up on the beach at night. It is warm enough to sleep outside but I am sure there are lots of bugs to nibble at you as you sleep.

While out enjoying the St Patrick's festivities I was wearing the only green thing I had on the boat, a running t-shirt with the name of my hometown 'Dun Laoghaire' written on it. A guy stopped me when he saw my t-shirt and said he was Irish and from a few miles from my hometown. We had a great chat with him and his buddy. It turned out they were both pilots flying the small propeller Islander aeroplanes from Antigua to Montserrat. He had actually flown my brother to Montserrat. During the week a naked Italian sailor arrived in the anchorage. He was single-handed and we watched him running around the deck while anchoring. So I am not the only mad single-handed sailor out here but at least I wear a pair of shorts when arriving in a new port. It was a very enjoyable week, completely different from what I expected, which made the week even more interesting. It is unlikely we will both be back here again; it was a once in a lifetime opportunity.

18th March 2019: It is time for both myself and my brother to leave Montserrat. I dropped Paul at the dinghy pontoon and he got a taxi to the airport where he flew to Antigua and then onto New York. I went the opposite direction, my next stop is the French island of Saint-Barthelemy, known as St. Barts. An island for the rich and famous. I am not sure I want to go there as I am not rich and famous but I will stop at St. Barts for a rest on my way to Saint Martin. I have organised to meet Dennis again from the Dutch boat Mach3 in Saint Martin, so there should be some going out and partying. It is nice now that I have friends on other boats that I can organise to meet along the way. I noticed today when stowing the anchor that the bow roller is cracked. It is made out of a very tough plastic so I will bring it home with me on my next trip to get it fixed.

Today will be a 12 hours of sailing, arriving into the anchorage in the dark. The marina in St Barts is not an option as it is only for big money boats so I will creep into the anchorage and drop the hook. I like anchoring, not only because it is free but it gives a real sense of freedom and independence. On the sail today I passed the islands of Nevis, St Kitts and Saba, the Dutch island, is ahead to the northwest. I will leave these islands for the next trip to the Caribbean as I have no time to stop. I am certainly coming back to the Caribbean so I am not too bothered about skipping these islands. My time is limited as with work commitments I can only really sail to the next island on the weekends. I then spend the working week on anchor, working in the morning and exploring the island in the afternoon and evenings. I am getting all my work done per normal and no one is any the wiser that my office is in the Caribbean. It was pitch dark at 7pm when I made it to Gustavia Bay anchorage, St. Barts and dropped the anchor in 10 metres of water.

St. Barts (Saint-Barthelemy)

I spent 2-days enjoying St. Barts. I loved the island and it is not as crazy expensive as I had expected. The marina is full of super yachts and it is great fun to watch the professional crews coming and going. In the anchorage behind Esperanza there are two mega super yachts. Eclipse is the second largest yacht in the world owned by Russian billionaire Roman Abramovich, who also owns Chelsea football club. She cost $500 Million to build. Onboard are two swimming pools, two helicopter pads and a crew of 54. I watched as a hanger door opened on the side of the ship and a pontoon extended outward to form its own mini marina for the smaller boats stored inside the mega-yacht. Another Russian billionaire's superyacht called Black Pearl is also anchored in the bay, which looks more like a spaceship than a yacht.

The St. Barts Bucket Regatta is next weekend, which is an annual boat race for big yachts over 30.5 metres. Esperanza is excluded being just 10 metres. The prize is the St. Barts bucket, whatever that looks like. There are 26 very beautiful classic yachts docked in the marina getting ready for the race. I am going to Saint Martin next but I hope to come back to St Bart next weekend to see the race, it is only a three-hour sail.

The big reason I wanted to do Saint Martin was to visit the airport where you can stand on the beach at the end of the runway and feel the jet wash from the airliners landing and taking off. This has been on my bucket list since I was a kid. A few weeks ago I was going to skip Saint Martin completely, as it was a long sail to the north, especially since I had decided to leave the boat in Guadeloupe for a few weeks in April and fly home. But I said if I don't make the effort now to visit Saint Martin, I will regret it, as I am so close. Grab the opportunity while I can. It just means I have to sail 180 miles back down south again to Guadeloupe.

Saint Martin and back to St. Barts

Saint Martin has an unusual arrangement. The island is split 60/40 with France occupying one side and the Dutch running the other side. I anchored in Simpson Bay Lagoon, which is a huge inland water area that separates the two sides. The French side of the island is an 'Overseas Collectivity' of France with semi-autonomous status. Guadeloupe and Martinique are Overseas Departments of France and fully governed by France. French Saint Martin has a population of 32,000 and seems poorer to me than the Dutch side. The Dutch side forms part of the Kingdom of the Netherlands and has a population of 41,000. To get in or out of the lagoon the road bridge lifts at designated times during the day. The lagoon is sheltered with calm shallow waters of 1-3 metres. It is known as a hurricane hole where boats anchor for protection if a hurricane is forecast. In October 2017, category 5 Hurricane Irma devastated Saint Martin. The hurricane caused billions of dollars in damage. In the lagoon hundreds of boats were at anchor seeking safety but Hurricane Irma scored a direct hit and boats broke anchor and crashed into each other. Boats were adrift and sinking all over the lagoon. The Dutch side has carried out a big clean-up of wrecked boats while the French side still has many sunken boats emerging out of the water.

I took the dinghy on a long 5km trip across the lagoon from the Dutch side, where Esperanza was anchored, to the French side to explore. This was the longest I have travelled in the dinghy, 10km return. I had to take extra fuel and refuel halfway across. A bigger engine with separate fuel tank and more speed would have made this trip easier. A good seagoing fast dinghy allows you to explore around the islands where a yacht can't go, such as shallow snorkelling spots, up rivers, into caves or nearby bays. I had many opportunities for such exploration but I did not have a capable dinghy. On the French side of the lagoon, I tied up the dinghy and walked into the town of Marigot to explore. I continued 10km around the coast to the small French airport Grand-Case, the main international airport is Princess Juliana Airport on the Dutch side. I saw the destruction from the 2017 hurricane everywhere with roofless houses and damaged buildings dotted along the coast road. Reconstruction looked very slow on the French side but they did take the full brunt of the hurricane force winds.

I enjoyed my time on Saint Martin, the island has lovely beaches, nice walks, bars and nightclubs. I had fun nights out with Dennis. Since we met last in Saint Lucia, he had broken up with his partner Thomas. Thomas had gone home to Germany leaving Dennis alone on the boat. Lots of drama. I went to experience the landing airliners touching down on Princess Juliana airport runway at Maho beach. There is even a bar there to service the spectators. They publish the daily flight times on a blackboard to tell you when you need to be ready in position on the beach for the next landing or take-off. It was so much fun that I went there twice. Even in the water you get an amazing view, as a Boeing 777 on final approach swoops low over the water for landing. I am delighted I made the effort to visit and experience Saint Martin.

I returned to St. Barts for the weekend. The Bucket Regatta is underway with 100-foot yachts racing around the island. There will be a great atmosphere on the island. I doubt these super yachts are any more fun to sail than my own 35-foot boat. On my smaller boat I am in full control and without the need for crew to sail the boat. On a big yacht you need many crew just to move off the marina.

While walking the coastline of St Barts I stumbled across a 'white party' at the celebrity famous Nikki Beach. Everyone was dressed in white except of course me. I was unprepared, wearing a red t-shirt and blue shorts but I tried to blend in as I gate-crashed the party. I stayed in the background by the bar taking the role of the anthropologist watching the rich and famous in their playground. Two waiters appeared, carrying over their shoulders on a pole, six bottles of Dom Perignon Champagne lit up by sparklers. What did that cost I wondered? I made do with my small beer - live-aboard sailors have to watch the pennies. After a really lovely weekend I sailed back to Saint Martin.

I am heading back south again unlike my boat friends who will continue north to visit the BVI's (British Virgin Islands). I would have loved to visit the BVI's but I am out of time. I have a reservation for five weeks in the main marina in Guadeloupe so I can fly home. I wanted to leave the boat in Saint Martin and fly home from there but it was cheaper to leave her on the French islands so I decided on Guadeloupe. Another reason for Guadeloupe is there are low cost flights to Dublin via Paris. The first thing to consider when deciding where to leave your boat for an extended period, is to find the airport that works best for your route and then work from the airport to the nearest marina. Bye bye Dennis and all my sailor friends, unfortunately our paths are unlikely to cross again.

27th March 2019: I am sailing single-handed to Antigua. On the direct route it is an overnight sail, 90 miles. I am feeling slightly nervous about sailing alone through the night since the damage that occurred to the boat off Saint Lucia. I need to be cautious and safe. Added to this is the wind is anything but ideal, it could not be from a worse direction as it is blowing straight from Antigua. The forecast is for strong 20-25 knots winds. I can't sail directly into the wind and motoring with the rough seas would be very slow going. My plan is to first head to St Kitts, which is slightly off the track for Antigua, but I hope this direction will allow me to sail. I can also anchor at St Kitts to rest for a few hours during the night. St Kitts is 55 miles away. Then it is another 53 miles east to St John's, the capital of Antigua. I have heard many great things about Antigua and it's English influence so I'm looking forward to it.

I was anxious to get going and away from Saint Martin into deeper water so I would be clear of lobster pots and fishing nets before it got dark. I left at 5pm from Simpson Bay. That night I was off the island of St Eustatius, another island I will not get to see and must add to my list for next time. I sailed down the gap between St Eustatius and St Kitts. I noticed a small rip in the jib sail so I have decided to anchor for a few hours and fix it. 2.30am: I dropped the anchor in the Bay of Basseterre at St Kitts. I tried to sleep but the swell was awful and I did not get much rest. 7am: I am up to look at the rip in the sail. I decided it was best to change to the heavier jib sail. This heavier jib sail while smaller, is better at punching into the wind which is what I need for the rest of the trip.

Anchor up and I am off again sailing on a tight beat west of Nevis island, which looks like a very nice place. The wind has risen to 25 knots, a Force 6 and there are rain showers around. The sea is getting a bit wild. It is a bit mad to be trying to sail to your destination, which has a Force 6 wind blowing from it. The sensible sailor or a sailor with time on his hands, would have stayed in Saint Martin waiting for the wind direction to change, before attempting the trip. But my time constraints do not allow this as I have organized to meet Bernadette Fox, who is flying from Dublin to Antigua. She will crew with me for 2 weeks. I already messaged her that I will be late due to the weather and it is best she finds a hotel for the first night in St. John's. Normally for crew changes I plan to arrive a few days beforehand to allow for weather delays and to have some flexibility but I was committed to staying in Saint Martin. Sailing involves lots of logistics: planning where to pick up and drop off crew, where the nearest airport is, how the crew get from the airport to the boat, and where best to leave the boat for an extended period.

The sailing guide says watch yourself in St John's as there is an edgy feel to the place and a history of crime. Although, to be honest, the book says this about a lot of places that I have been to and I have not seen any trouble. Dublin city is far more dangerous in my view. My priority on arrival is to find a laundrette as I have two weeks of laundry stacked up and no more clean clothes to wear. I also need fresh water and fuel is down to the red line and critical. I used a lot of fuel on this trip from Saint Martin, 17 hours was motor sailing using 51 litres. I estimate I have just 24 litres left in the main tank or 6 hours on the engine. It is time to resupply the boat. With two people onboard we need lots of water.

Antigua

I arrived in St John's harbour at 9pm; it really is a big port. My initial opinion is that this looks like an awful place, an industrial port, big and smelly. Up to now I have been in picturesque anchorages and harbours. I will stay one night here and pick up Bernadette in the morning and get moving. I will get the laundry done here as well. I dropped anchor by a busy road near the harbour. There was no wind at all but the anchor did not bite. On the second attempt the anchor catches. I decided not to try to reverse the boat to pull it into the muddy seabed and just let it sit there and slowly dig itself in. On other occasions I found the anchor skips out when I try to dig it in with the engine in reverse. It is a bit unnerving to try to sleep wondering if the anchor is going to hold or not. But so far, the new French Spade anchor has been the best purchase I made. I can trust it, which allows me to sleep.

30 March 2019: Bernadette Fox has joined the boat. I signed her on as crew with port officials, more paperwork and more money exchanged. We left St John's harbour, the main working town on the island. It is not too pretty but the people were friendly. I felt safer here than Saint Lucia. We sailed around the corner just 2 hours to Jolly Harbour as we were nearly out of fuel. We went onto the fuel berth, had lunch and fuelled up. Jolly Harbour was actually a jolly place. The sailing guide described it as an artificial golf resort, which put me off but it has lovely sandy beaches and would have made a more picturesque stop than St John's. We were not staying as we wanted to get to English Harbour before dark. English Harbour is one of the main yachting centres in the Caribbean. It was an uneventful sail arriving at 6pm in Freemans Bay.

As anchorages go this one was small and tight, it was also full of boats. It is useful to remember to try to arrive into a new harbour or marina before lunch, as by then boats have already left and free slots will be available. Arriving in the evening can mean all the anchor spots are already taken. We dropped anchor but ended up too close to a Catamaran and had to move. Other boats were watching us carefully hoping we would not drop anchor near them. An old English sea dog on his yacht started hailing us. He said this anchorage is odd as the boats lie in all different directions due to the swirling tides and the gusts of wind that flow down from the hills. In most anchorages the boats will be facing the same direction and you all swing together with tide and wind. If boats are swinging all different directions there is more chance of boats colliding. I was now unsure what to do and it was getting dark, the stress was building.

We decided to go deeper into English Harbour, further up the estuary, passing the marina and into Ordnance Bay. The anchorage here was also full and it was shallow. We spotted an old looking mooring buoy and decided to grab it. There was no wind at all and it was a private mooring so we had no idea who owned it. Was this even a mooring? It might be just a lobster pot marker. It would have to do for tonight. Taking an unknown mooring is dodgy as you have no idea when it was last maintained and what it is connected to on the seabed. Maybe it was designed for a light rowing boat and not a 9-tonne yacht - so it breaks when you are sleeping and you and your boat end up on the rocks. This happened last summer to a visiting family in Skerries Harbour, Dublin when the mooring broke and their yacht washed up on the beach.

In the end we stayed on this mooring for two nights. We went to the famous Shirley Heights Sunset Party, which looks out over English Harbour. There was a fantastic view of all the boats at anchor with Esperanza amongst them. The spectacular sunset provided a perfect backdrop. A truly Caribbean view. The next day we motored around to Falmouth Harbour, which is the next bay right beside English Harbour. Both harbours are separated by a just small spit of land. Antigua Yacht Club is based here and holds the world-famous regatta: Antigua Sailing Week. Falmouth Harbour is huge and a great anchorage with lots of room and nice sandy beach to look at. I spent the next couple of days working and when ashore walking and exploring. Antigua was more expensive than Saint Martin but very enjoyable. I did not have enough time to do the island justice, it would be nice to come back here for a week.

Les Saintes French Islands & Guadeloupe

2nd April 2019: We are sailing back to the town of Deshaies in Guadeloupe. This is the town with the spectacular beach nearby, Grande Anse beach. I really enjoyed my time here and I am looking forward to going back. Work has got very busy so I am trying to clear the email backlog. The good news about having crew is that I can work on the day job while they do the sailing. Bernadette and I have sailed together for many years so I know I can trust her in charge of the boat. At times it is a bit of a nuisance and stressful to work from the Caribbean. I feel I am on holiday, and it looks like I am to all around me, but to the working world it is as if I am still in Dublin. That evening we are between three islands: Antigua behind, Guadeloupe ahead and Montserrat ahead to starboard. It is nice to see Montserrat again; I have fond memories of my time there with my brother.

Bernadette has been asleep for 3-hours, I will soon be waking her up with the air horn. I never thought I would say it but I am now looking forward to getting back to France (Guadeloupe). One benefit is the 3G data phone signal is much better than the other islands and there are no roaming charges as I am back in the EU. I am spending in the region of $150 dollars a month on internet coverage on the smaller non-EU islands. Esperanza is sailing very nicely, making 7 knots. It is a tad rough but I am well used to that; poor Bernadette is fighting seasickness. Flying fish just popped out of the water, I haven't seen them in a long time. Approaching Guadeloupe waves start to reduce and we motor into the nice sheltered anchorage of Deshaies as the sun sets. It is useful to see on the iPad charts the track from the last time I was here so I can find the same anchor spot. This location had a good 3G internet signal. That was a 46-mile sail in just under seven hours, a fast sail.

We spent 2-days here but the 3G signal kept dropping and causing all sorts of problems on my Skype conference calls. I was running out of excuses for my poor data connection. We decided to motor two hours south and back to the diving bay of Melendure, where the 3G signal was better. It is funny how my anchorage decisions are now driven by searching for the best internet data spots. We anchored in 12 metres of water with 50 metres of chain out. We stayed just one night in Malandure and then we are off again to Les Saintes island, 13km south of Guadeloupe.

5th April 2019: Once we sailed past the south tip of Guadeloupe the sea got rough. Away from the wind shadow of the island, the wind cranked up to 29 knots, and we are back to white water sailing across the exposed gap between Guadeloupe and Les Saintes. The wind continued to rise to a steady 32 knots, a Force 7. This was becoming a south easterly gale. We are reduced to sailing solely on a heavily reefed mainsail, the jib sail is completely furled away as there is too much wind. We are banging into the waves but still making 6.4 knots. Once again, we seem to be the only boat out here. We aimed for the main island Terre-de-Haut where I had been briefly before on my way to Guadeloupe.

When we get into the bay at the small town of Le Marigot, all the moorings are occupied. It seems no boats have decided to sail today with the strong winds. I was hoping to take a mooring, which you pay a daily rate for as it means you are closer to the dinghy pontoon. It is a big bay and we end up anchoring at Anse Galet, which is a 1km dinghy ride to the pontoon. That does not seem far but when the sea is choppy and it is windy it can mean a wet and slow dinghy trip ashore. It is not much fun going out for the night when, before you even get to the bar you are soaked. It is Friday, so I have the weekend off and no work, yippie. It is time to explore the island properly. Last time I was here it was a quick stopover.

My first tourist activity was to walk up the steep and winding hill to Fort Napoleon. No surprise that this was built by the French for protection of the islands from the British, who were nearby on Antigua. The story is that the fort is haunted by the spirit of a French girl who fell in love with a British officer. Her lover went to sea and promised to return for her when his duty was completed but after waiting several years the young woman lost hope. She thought the British officer had found another woman so she threw herself off the cliffs into the sea. The young officer did eventually return for his love. After finding out she had ended her life, and believing he had betrayed her, he too threw himself from the cliff to his death. I am not sure what the moral of the story is meant to be but keeping away from cliffs is certainly one and the virtue of having patience and hope seems to be another.

On Saturday night Bernadette and I planned to go ashore as we heard the party was going to be good in Coconuts cocktail bar. The problem was it was still windy and the sea in the bay was choppy. We got into our party attire. Bernadette offered to helm the dinghy but as skipper I thought it best I did. We jumped in and she took her seat in front of the dinghy with me behind steering. Off we went and as luck would have it, it just happened I was blocked from the splashy waves by Bernadette. Within a minutes Bernadette was soaked by a number of incoming splashing waves and progress towards the shore was slow. Understandably, Bernadette was not too happy as she had just dressed up for the night out and washed her hair. We decided to abort and returned to the boat for the night. It would have to be rum in the cockpit for me while Bernadette washed her hair for the second time. Here again is another example where a more seagoing dinghy with a more powerful engine to power through the waves would have got us to the bar on time.

7th April 2019: It is time to leave Les Saintes as I have a reservation in the marina at Pointe a Pitre, the capital of Guadeloupe. I am leaving the boat here for five weeks and flying home to remind the family I still exist. It is actually nice to go home and take a break. When I return to the Caribbean, I really appreciate the climate as you are escaping the cold Irish winter. You feel refreshed and ready for the next sailing leg. Before I go home, I have a week of boat maintenance scheduled in the marina with a long to do list. This will be my only preparation time for the return Atlantic trip back to Europe. When I arrive back in Guadeloupe in May, I need the boat to be ready to sail immediately with all jobs complete. It can't be lackadaisical this week, as everyone keeps telling me the return Atlantic trip can be expected to be more difficult.

Our short 4-hour passage of 24 miles to Pointe a Pitre was again rough. We passed a Sperm whale going the other way. He/she gave us a blow and then dived down to the depths.

Pointe a Pitre, Guadeloupe

We arrived on the fuel dock at Marina Bas-du-Fort, in Pointe a Pitre the capital of Guadeloupe. We filled the fuel tanks to the very top as well as the jerry cans, in preparation for the transatlantic. The marina boat man came over to us in a rib to bring us to our berth. This was another Mediterranean style marina with no fingers or pontoons between the boats. We were directed down a narrow fairway where there was no room to turn and get out! With no bow thruster I was snookered. The berth itself was tiny, it looked more for a 20-foot boat than my 35-footer. I was trying to explain there was no way I will ever get into that little berth, but it looked like he did not speak English. He was giving me all sorts of instructions in French and waving his arms wildly. At this stage I had already passed by the berth. The only option was to reverse in but my boat is a pig in reverse. It looked like I was going into this berth whether I liked it or not. I said in an authoritative voice if he could use his boat as a tugboat and push my bow around. I shouted 'pousser, pousser', push me. He understood. With the marina boat pushing the bow, I reversed in between the two smaller boats and pushed them out of the way, to enlarge the space for Esperanza. The French man was annoyingly right, we did fit after all by pushing the other boats out of the way. It was the most stressful arrival yet of the trip. Time for a beer and to allow the blood pressure to return to normal.

Pointe a Pitre is not a pretty place, it is an industrial working port. The marina is reasonably priced and a safe place to leave a boat unattended. A big plus is that it is only 10 minutes from the airport. It is a modern marina complex with fancy bars and restaurants. At the marina there is everything you need including a Carrefour supermarket which also sells gas bottle refills, two chandleries for boat parts and a sailmaker. It makes it an ideal place to resupply a boat. I had 4-days of non-stop jobs to do on the boat. I serviced the engine, changed the oil and filter, replaced the fuel filters and all looks well. The sailmaker fixed the tear in the jib sail and strengthened the mainsail, which he felt was weak for an Atlantic passage. I am glad he did this as I don't want the mainsail to blow out. The big question I need to think about, over the next few weeks while I am home, is how much fuel to bring. How much is enough, there is no way to tell. I can work out all sorts of scenarios but who knows what the winds will be. I elected to buy four more jerry cans in Guadeloupe. That is another 80 litres or 40 hours of fuel for motor sailing at low revs. I will secure these on deck mid-ships, two cans either side, ratchet strapped to the stanchions.

I became friendly with a French guy on the boat beside me who skippers catamarans. He gave up his life in Paris to try a new lifestyle in the Caribbean. It is a common story that I hear in the Caribbean of people leaving behind their 9-5 jobs at home and changing direction by sailing away. They sell everything to buy a boat as their new home. It sounds great but I wonder after a year or two would it be a bit tedious living solely on the boat. It is nice to know you have a home to go back to and have a break from the boat. It is the time away from the boat that makes you appreciate how much you love the sailing lifestyle.

So that's a wrap, my Caribbean cruising is completed. I have sailed 738 miles (1,336 km) in the Caribbean. The distance sailed since leaving the Canaries including the Atlantic passage is 3,795 miles (7,028 km). The total distance since leaving Dun Laoghaire June 2nd, 2018 is 5,522 miles (10,226 km). Bye Esperanza, I will see you on the 17th May. I am going home for Easter so it is time to switch back to my other life with my family for the next five weeks.

Boat boys offering their services to find an anchor spot.

Wallilabou Bay, St. Vincent where Pirates of the Caribbean was filmed.

My brother Paul McMahon arrives.

The Pitons, two volcanic spires rising to 798 metres, St. Lucia.

Soufriere Bay, St. Lucia with Pitons volcanic mountains in the background.

Below: The fruit boat called by each day to boats at anchor.

Working from the Caribbean.

Rodney Bay, St Lucia

'Jump Up' street party Rodney Bay, St Lucia with Dennis and Thomas from the Dutch yacht Mach 3.

Esperanza's dinghy, which became my car in the Caribbean, for bringing supplies back to the boat.

Relaxing in Dennis's Hallberg Rassy 49 yacht, Mach 3.

Climbed Mount Pelee, an extinct volcano, which was cause of the worst volcanic disaster of the 20th century. 30,000 people died in 1902.

Above: Guadeloupe: Grande-Anse beach, Deshaies, one of my favourites.
Below: Les Saintes islands, Guadeloupe.

Guadeloupe. Above: diving resort of Malendure. Below: Deshaies.

13th March 2019, celebrating St Patrick's Day on the Ireland of Montserrat with my brother Paul. An island of Irish descendants.

Active steaming volcano Soufriere Hills, Montserrat.

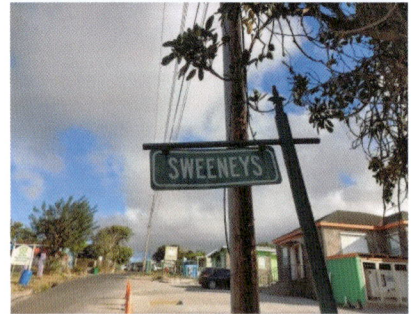

Anchored beside me in Bequia was 107 metre super yacht Ulysses with its own helicopter, owned by billionaire Mark Zuckerberg of Facebook. Below: superyacht with its own 40 foot yacht onboard for day sailing.

Bernadette Fox joins as crew in Antigua.

Route planning using the PredictWind app. Weather forecast models are downloaded from Iridium satellite. The solid yellow line is the direct route but the Azores High pressure system, shown in blue is on-route. Blue indicates slack or no winds, red shows strong winds. The best suggested routing from the four different forecast models is to go north, around the Azores High.

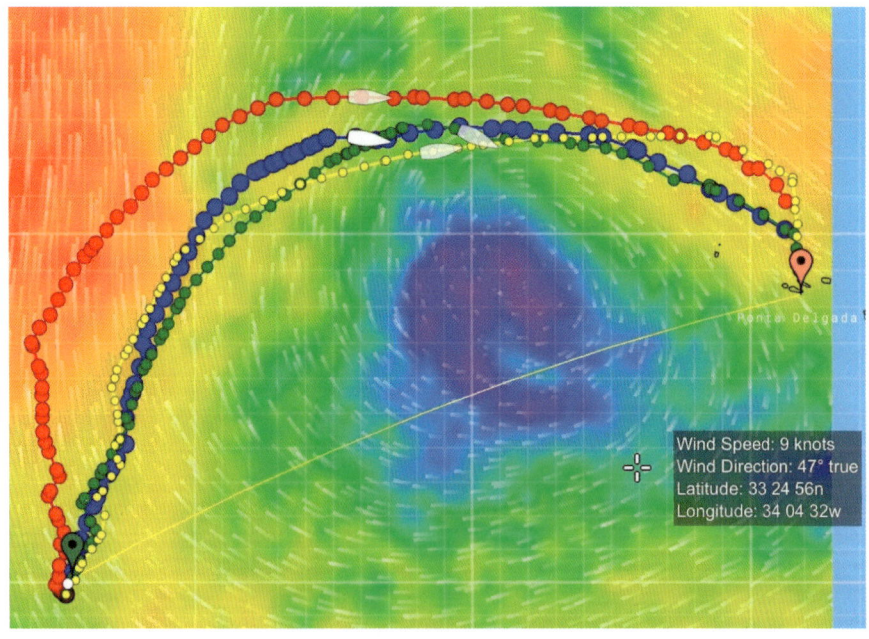

CHAPTER 5

Back to Europe

My route across the Atlantic will follow the traditional old sailing ships to first sail to the Azores and then onto mainland Europe. The Atlantic low-pressure systems and storms move out from the east coast of the USA and race across the Atlantic towards Europe. I do not want to be in their path so the objective is to avoid these. Boats sailing to Europe wait until the spring, as then the low-pressure systems move north, giving an opportunity to sail from the Caribbean to the Azores. To fit in with work and family my departure is set for the 22nd May 2019. This could be considered a little late to leave the Caribbean since hurricane season starts June 1st. I will be in the middle of the Atlantic during the start of hurricane season. I am leaving Guadeloupe, which is at the latitude of 16N and the Azores is at latitude of 38 north. In distance terms this is 2,200 miles or 4,074 km on the direct route. A duration of approximately 23-days. I will explore the Azores islands before continuing to Portugal.

The next decision is what route to take. The Atlantic Cruising Guide says for comfortable sailing stay south and take the direct route to the Azores through the high-pressure area of slack winds. The direct route strategy is to keep as close to the Great circle route as possible, which is the shortest course between two points on the surface of the earth. When the wind dies and the speed drops to less than 4 knots, turn the engine on. The risk is going too slow on the Atlantic crossing as then you are adding days to the trip and exposing yourself to a longer time at sea and more of a chance of hitting a storm or hurricane. The recommendation I was told by a sailor in Guadeloupe is to carry enough fuel to motor at least 800 miles. That means lots of jerry cans of fuel on deck.

The other option where there is more certainty of wind is to sail towards Bermuda. This will mean 300-400 miles of fast and furious sailing, beating into the wind. Either stop over at Bermuda or continue north until the latitude of

38N where there is the best chance of favourable winds. Sail the westerly winds around the top of the Azores high-pressure and pick up prevailing south-westerly winds to the Azores. June is considered a good month to cross the Atlantic on the route with 1% chance of winds of greater than Force 7. The advice is to watch the weather forecast daily, in order to position the boat to avoid the bad weather from low-pressure systems to the north and the slack winds from Azores High to south. The best sailing conditions are between the two systems. Expect lots of squalls, which are described as looking like the gateway to the Bermuda triangle. This is the traditional sailing route and longer than the direct route at approximately 2,900 miles (5,370km).

18th of May 2019: I am back on the boat in Guadeloupe getting used to the four-hour time difference. The boat is ready to go on the big long trip to Azores. My plan is to do a shakedown passage or a test sail to the northwest coast of Guadeloupe and back to my favourite little bay Malendure. I always carry out a shakedown sail to make sure that the boat is ready. I also need to check I am ready as I have not sailed in five weeks. I will have to use the engine for a number of hours on the shakedown cruise to get out of the long inlet where Pointe a Pitre is located. This will be using up my Atlantic fuel supplies but I know there is a petrol station in Melendure where I can get my jerry cans refuelled. It is crucial to leave with every last drop of fuel - looking at the weather forecast I might need it. End of this week I will be officially on three weeks of holidays from work. Every single vacation day is allocated and accounted for to make this Atlantic voyage possible.

I have been studying the Atlantic forecast charts daily over the last week. Guess what, Murphy's Law has struck again. In the Atlantic 700 miles south west of Bermuda, there is a 40% probability of a cyclone or low-pressure system developing. The forecast says it could develop into a more severe tropical cyclone late Monday or Tuesday, moving north or northeast. This could become a Hurricane and needs to be watched closely. A US Hurricane Hunter reconnaissance aircraft is scheduled to investigate. I received an alert for all vessels in the Bermuda area or heading to Bermuda to monitor the progress of this system. My plan had been to go north towards Bermuda where I have the best chance of finding westerly winds to take me all the way to the Azores. Now this possible cyclone is changing my plans.

I have two options: 1) wait a few more days and see how the cyclone develops and then go north behind it or 2) take the direct route through the Azores high-pressure. I can't wait unfortunately as I do not have the vacation time to allow this. I need to be back to working remotely from the Azores by June 24th. My family have also booked flights to meet me in the Azores June 17th so I have hard deadlines to meet. It is not a good idea to have deadlines when sailing as it means you can push yourself into dangerous situations but this is the reality of making this trip possible.

The day before leaving the marina it is back and forth to the French Carrefour supermarket to load up on bottles of water and food. I must have made 10 trips filling my big blue Ikea bags. I have 510 litres of fuel onboard so at low revs and motor sailing that is 8-days of motoring, allowing for fuel to charge the batteries each day. I have 450 litres of water onboard with 300 litres in the main tank and 75 two litre bottles. This time I had to stock the boat on my own and it felt rushed and disorganized. The Carrefour supermarket was one of the smaller local branches so it had a limited selection. I have enough cheese for sure. Anything I missed, including fresh fruit and veg I can get in the supermarket in Malandure.

Shakedown Cruise

19th May 2019, 10.30am: I motored out of Marina Bas du Fort, Pointe a Pitre, Guadeloupe. I managed to get out of the tight marina berth no problem and got the mainsail up in the bay. I am glad to get out of Pointe a Pitre and on the move again. The marina staff in the office were not very friendly or helpful. The locals seem a bit curt and miserable, maybe it is all the rain they get. Of course that is a general statement and I met the exceptions who were very friendly. For example the Dutch boatman from the marina was very friendly and brought me to and from the fuel dock to fill a couple more jerry cans of fuel. I have 8 jerry cans of fuel tied down on deck and 3 in the cockpit locker. It is a lovely sunny day but it is hot and the day has the look of heavy showers for the afternoon, surprise surprise.

While underway I noticed the speed was reading zero so the little wheel on the transducer sensor under the hull must be stuck with weed. Simple job to pull the transducer out and clean it and I can do this at anchor in Melendure. It is 11 miles to just get out of the big inlet from Pointe a Pitre and around the corner of the headland. This is actually more than just an inlet as it splits Guadeloupe into two islands. Basse Terre is the western island while the eastern island is Grande Terre. The two islands are separated by the Salee River, up to a couple of years ago, before the last Hurricane hit, a yacht could sail up the 5km river to the north side of Guadeloupe. There was a lifting bridge allowing you to quickly pass through. The bridge was damaged in the Hurricane and the route is closed. Instead I have to sail 42 miles to get to the northwest point of Guadeloupe. I much preferred Basse Terre, the western island of Guadeloupe as it was more rustic. The people living there or visiting were more alternative with lots of divers and young people.

The batteries are reading 86% charge. I need to use the engine to get them up to 100% full charge. The boat was not on shore power in Guadeloupe while

I was back in Dublin. I thought the batteries would be up at 100% from the charging by the solar cells. This is puzzling so I must check it out before I sail for the Atlantic as I need the solar power working. I add this job to the shakedown cruise list. There are many lobster pots around and I just motor sailed right over one without seeing it, all ok as it did not catch the propeller. I need to keep a better watch out while I am still near the coast.

The next problem is I cannot connect the iPad to the Iridium satellite system so I can't download the weather. Without daily weather forecasts I ask myself whether I should be going offshore into the Atlantic. After two hours of puzzlement and by trial and error, I found it was the boat alarm control box that was the problem. It is located in the locker behind the Iridium Go satellite device and seems to have been interfering with the WiFi connection to the iPad. The alarm has an aerial and a SIM card so it can text me it's position. I had put the alarm back on when I left the boat to go home to Dublin. I pulled the fuse on the alarm as it is not needed when sailing and I don't want it using power anyway. Everything is working ok now. I can connect to the Iridium satellite and I am downloading weather. Pure luck that I found the problem as I would never have thought of it.

2pm: I am at the southern corner of Guadeloupe abeam Vieux Fort where I will turn north and sail up the west coast. Lunch is cheese, ham, tomato in a yummy fresh French baguette from the boulangerie earlier today. I notice the French baguettes are baked to be eaten that same day where at home Baguettes from the supermarket bakery can last a couple of days so they must be putting in long life additives. I have another problem and it is not the baguette. The revs or RPM will only go to 2200 RPM on full power when it should reach 3000 RPM. This indicates something fouling the propeller. I hope the hull is clean and not covered in weed after the six weeks it has been sitting in the marina.

I was thinking of getting the boat lifted out of the water and power washed at the marina and the price was reasonable. In the end I did not bother as it was becoming complicated. For some reason that could only occur on a French island, the boatyard who lifts out the boats did not have a power washer. You had to go yourself and see if you could find some other company to rent you a power washer and no one knew who to ask. Very mad to offer a boat lifting service without the option of washing the hull of the boat since every boat that is lifted out of the water is full of weed and needs to be washed. I must inform the boatyard of this business opportunity, which they must not yet have realised... Every other boat yard that I have encountered around-the-world charge around €70 for a 60-minute power wash. It is easy money for them. On the French islands it was little things like this that seemed completely illogical.

My plan is to stay a few nights in Malendure. I can't leave before 5pm Irish time on the 22nd May as my holidays from work don't start until then. I have

Back to Europe

lots of work emails to do before then. It is a lovely sunny evening with very few clouds as I motor sail up the coast. I am in the wind shadow of Guadeloupe with a light 10 knots of wind. I am sitting in the cockpit feeling a little nervous of the upcoming Atlantic sail. Especially with everyone back home in the sailing club telling me it was going to be much harder to get the boat back to Europe than my passage out from the Canaries. The weather for the next week is showing light winds, 8-10 knots and many no wind areas ahead, which does not suit my 9-tonne boat. Esperanza likes 15-20 knots of wind to get her moving fast. It could be a slow sail. The routing software models are all advising me to head direct for Azores for the first 5-days and not to go north towards Bermuda. The reason being that the cyclone or low-pressure, which had a 40% probability of becoming a storm, has developed into one. Even worse it is now a fully-fledged named storm, Tropical Storm Andrea. Anything named on the weather chart is bad and the advice is to keep well away. Storm Andrea could easily develop into a Hurricane so everyone is watching closely to see what she does. I need to keep well clear of angry Andrea.

Storm Andrea has decided the route for me, she has blocked my preferred option to go north towards Bermuda so I must go direct towards the Azores. I am conscious that Atlantic hurricane season starts in just two weeks so I need to get moving. Most boats have already left the Caribbean. To get out of the hurricane zone, boats leaving the Caribbean either go north to the US mainland or back across the Atlantic to Europe. The boats that want to stay in the Caribbean head south to Grenada or the ABC islands, which are just outside the hurricane belt. All going to plan by June 1st I should be moving out of the hurricane zone myself on my way to the Azores. Hurricanes usually form south of where I will be sailing around the Cape Verde islands and then head towards Caribbean. But there is a precedent for hurricanes to spin north instead of west. This happened when I was in the Canaries last year when Hurricane Ophelia emerged near the Cape Verde islands and tracked directly north towards the Azores. It then wiggled around the middle of the Atlantic for a few days before it decided to plough into Lisbon.

6pm: I arrived in Melendure bay and dropped anchor in 8 metres of water. This time I am the only visiting boat. Last time the bay was full of boats. The tourist season in the Caribbean ended mid-April, so there are very few tourists around. The beach village feels quiet, the vibrancy is gone but it is still a nice place. It feels a little worrying that all the boats have already left. It looks like Esperanza will be the last boat to the bar in the Azores. It is a little lonely here on the anchorage with no other fellow cruising boats. I pull out the little Honda generator and get her running to supply power to the boat. It would be nice to figure out the RPM problem before I go to sleep tonight as it is bugging me and

I won't sleep. There is only one option; dive down and inspect the propeller and the hull. I will get in quickly before it gets dark. The water is cooler here as it is deep. As I swim down and under the hull, I do not see anything wrapped around the propeller, there is a little weed on the blades that is all but nothing to cause the large RPM reduction. The hull of the boat though is another matter, it is covered in barnacles, hundreds of them! I can't cross the Atlantic like this as the barnacles will slow my speed right down. A 23-day trip could become 30-days or more. I am kicking myself for not getting the boat lifted and washed in the marina. Now, what do I do?

Back onboard I think of my options: 1) try to clean the 35 foot long hull myself with a paint scraper, it will take some time but isn't it good exercise; 2) see if I can find a diver to do the job as where I am now in Malandure which has three dive schools; 3) I will be passing right by Antigua on my way to the Azores so I could stop there and get the boat lifted out of the water and cleaned, but how long will all that take and I am already on a tight schedule; 4) sail back south to Pointe de Pitre marina and get the boat lifted and washed there but I hate to go backwards and the thought of going back to the unfriendly marina does not appeal to me. Why do these problems always appear at the last moment when I am ready to set sail? At these difficult points in time you just want to sell the boat and take up stamp collecting. I am kicking myself for not planning the boat lift and wash, which is what I did in Lanzarote.

I am now wondering if I am really prepared for this trip, what else have I missed in the preparation. This is going to be a serious passage with all sorts of possible bad weather. It is funny how careful we are when we do something for the first time, but the second time we are more blasé and it is then you are more likely to make mistakes. To add to the barnacle problem I am still unsure why the propeller RPM is not making 3000 RPM at full power as it used to do. Is this an indication of an engine issue? What I am trying to figure out is the RPM lower because of the dirty hull full of barnacles. The unclean hull would certainly cause more drag just like when the wing of an aeroplane is covered in ice. Increased drag means a slower boat speed so to make the same boat speed as a clean hull you need more engine power or a higher RPM. But at full power I would have expected the RPM to still reach the same 3000 RPM and just that the boat speed would be slower. It is a puzzle, if my Dad the engineer was here, he would have helped figure this out.

Reading a blog it says an unclean boat hull covered in weed is like putting an 8 x 4-foot sheet of plywood on the front of a car and going full acceleration. The additional drag created by the wooden sheet will mean the car speed will be slower and the wheels of the car like the propeller on a boat will also turn slower. So maybe this is the answer, all I need to do is clean the hull to solve the RPM and slower boat speed problems at the same time. All this fluid dynamics has made me thirsty so I give up and have a beer. I will sleep on the problem and let my unconscious mind turn it over. As I drift off to sleep, I am thinking that I started the day ready for the Atlantic but by bedtime I wasn't ready to go anywhere. Today does show the value of a good shakedown test sail, where would I be if I only discovered this deep in the Atlantic.

20th May 2019: It was Sunday, the day of rest. I woke up with the conclusion that if I was a real sailor, I should be able to clean my own bottom, by that I mean the bottom of the boat. Before I left Europe, I heard many stories of sailors in the Caribbean swimming around their boats each day to clean their hulls, making it part of their daily exercise routine. Though I never actually met anyone that did this. How difficult could it be to scrape off the barnacles. I rig a rope from one winch on the starboard side under the boat to the other port winch. This allows me to pull myself down under the boat and work using a wallpaper scraper to knock the barnacle suckers off. Unfortunately the wallpaper scraper is just 2 inches wide so this is going to take some time. I put on my snorkel mask, attach my divers knife to my belt and jump in. The barnacles fall off easily so it is going well. I spend an hour or so getting the propeller nice and clean. Then back on board for a Coca-Cola break.

Even though this is the Caribbean and the water is warm you get cold after a while so I put on a wetsuit. The barnacles are sharp and I have already cut myself. I do not have proper diver gloves, which would be useful. All I have is a pair of garden gloves, which fill with water but they sort of work to protect my hands. Mental note to buy a pair of diver's gloves for the boat, an essential item that I have not seen mentioned by anyone else before. I work away for most of the day until I am absolutely exhausted. I have covered maybe one third of the boat. I am a little disappointed with the lack of progress. The chief reason that progress is so slow is that I can't stay under the water for very long. I have just a few seconds of air before I need to go to the surface to take a breadth. I can't hold my breath for long. This is hard work and at this rate it will take three more full days of scraping to get the job done. I don't have the time as I have a very busy work week lined up. I will also be covered in scrapes and cuts from the sharp barnacles. As Sunday ends, I am feeling a bit low, there has to be an easier way than this. I realise that I was not born to be a free diver.

21st May 2019, a Monday and I am back at work. My new plan is to see if I can get a diver and pay them to finish the job but how do I even find one. There are three dive shops ashore and I don't have the time to be knocking on doors trying to find a diver. I decide I need help and fast. I phone my French work colleague and she offers to make some calls to the dive schools. Within minutes like magic she has it all arranged. I am to meet two divers outside a pink coloured dive shop after dive school at 5pm. It will cost €100 but they will only have 45mins to do the job before it gets dark. They don't have dinghy so I must pick them up. This sounds great and I just hope they do a proper job. I prepared the boat with a few additional ropes running under that they can hang onto as there is a current flowing under the boat.

5pm: I am ashore looking for the pink dive shop. The divers are expecting me, a guy and a girl in their late twenties. They don't seem to think the request to clean the hull is unusual. I explain I am crossing the Atlantic alone and they are noticeably impressed. I try to make it clear that the success of my trip depends on the thoroughness of their work, no pressure then. My little 2.3 horsepower engine struggles to get us across the bay to where Esperanza is anchored. The poor dingy has never been so overloaded with me, the two divers and all their equipment. Their oxygen bottles are unbelievably heavy, I could barely lift them. With all the weight I was having visions of the dinghy sinking in the bay but my little dinghy did not give up. Divers are used to dropping into the water backwards from the side of the dinghy but I was afraid this would capsize us, so I suggested they get into the water first and I would lift the air bottles down to them. Down they went and with a few bubbles they were gone. I went back onboard and let them work away while I did some email. As I worked in the cabin, I could hear them scraping away on the hull. 45 minutes later they were done, I was amazed it was so quick. I brought them back ashore, paid them and said goodbye. Hopefully this solves my engine and speed problems but I won't know until I sail tomorrow.

While I am ashore, I need some final supplies in the supermarket. I will refill two jerry cans with the diesel to replace the diesel I used on the sail from Pointe a Pitre to Melendure. The next problem is the petrol station is 1.5km down the road and lugging two very heavy full jerry cans 1.5km back to the dinghy won't be fun. It is a job that just has to be done as I see no taxis here. Off I go walking down the road to the petrol station with my two bright yellow empty jerry cans. A car stopped in front of me and a French girl jumped out and asked did I want a lift. She said she saw the jerry cans and knew immediately I was a sailor. It turns out she is also a sailor and her boat is in the next bay. She and her partner sailed here from France. She was so nice to offer to drive me to the petrol station and even better drive me back to the boat. We had a great chat as we drove along about sailing. At the petrol station two girls appeared and asked if they could also get a lift. So in addition to 40 litres of diesel in the boot we have two German girls in the back. The problem of carrying the heavy jerry cans back to the dinghy was solved. It just shows, don't overthink things, get on with it and things work out themselves in the end. I am not back onboard for the last time with my fuel and supermarket shop. Tomorrow is departure day.

CHAPTER 6

Caribbean to the Azores

Day 1: 22nd May 2019 - *Bye bye Caribbean*
N16° 17' W61° 78'

Bye bye Caribbean, I loved my time with you but I won't miss the daily showers. I am sad to leave but I am equally excited about the Atlantic passage and exploring the Azores. Tropical Storm Andrea is making her presence felt, the sky to the north is dark and threatening. This is why I am not going north and I am taking the direct route to the Azores. It is 2,250 miles to the Azores on the direct route taking a northeast heading of 67 degrees magnetic. That works out at 19-days if the speed can be kept at an average 5 knots or 120 miles per day, which is my target. The latest weather shows a 10-15 knot easterly wind for the next 3-5 days. Then lighter winds as the Azores high-pressure moves south into the lower Atlantic where I am heading. It looks like light wind sailing ahead.

1pm: It is 5pm back home in Ireland and work has finished, I am on holiday for the next three weeks. I motor out of Melendure bay heading north. I need to motor sail 12 miles to get clear of Guadeloupe, then I can sail towards Antigua and out into the deep Atlantic. The good news is the hull cleaning has really worked. It has solved the low RPM engine issue. That proves that a hull with weed or barnacles will not only slow the boat down but it also reduces propeller revolutions per minute and therefore engine RPM. I have learnt something new again, that's sailing for you. It is a reason I like sailing so much as a hobby, you are always constantly learning new things.

It is a dull, showery and humid day. I am in my usual Caribbean attire, just swim shorts. This will soon be changing as I head north into cooler air. Three hours later I clear Guadeloupe and have a lovely sail making 6 knots. 2,216 miles to the Azores sounds a long way, but it is better than when I left Lanzarote when the distance to go was 2,788 miles. I notice a 2 millibar drop in pressure in the last 4 hours as we head more towards Storm Andrea. There on the horizon to port is Montserrat, a familiar site to me by now. Antigua lies dead ahead. I am getting pushed into Antigua so I tacked away from the island to allow more room. Night-time checks: nav lights on, AIS on and transmitting, VHF radio listening on channel 16. This time on my route back across the Atlantic I will leave all the equipment switched on to highlight my position to other vessels. On my voyage from the Canaries to the Caribbean I ended sailing past the Atlantic Rowing team so you never know what vessels are in the Atlantic.

Day 2: 23rd May 2019 - *Dinner: Pizza and Carib beer*
N18° 10' W60° 67'

It is Friday and breakfast time, which is a bowl of cereal, mug of coffee, pot of yogurt and to finish a small chocolate bar. I feel happy to be at sea again. Funny how quickly I have slotted back into being at sea, it took just a couple of days. The days at anchor helped me adjust to the motion. Today is a lovely sunny morning compared to the dull day of yesterday. I managed to sleep a few hours through the night. The good news is the engine has not been needed since yesterday evening. The latest weather download shows the high-pressure will push down on top of me Saturday and then I can expect little or no wind. It will then be motoring for the next while to get across the centre of the high-pressure system. Of course, things are unlikely to be that simple. Out here there is nothing to see at all. No sea life, no seaweed. I am alone in this vast ocean. For Atlantic entertainment I started a new William Boyd novel.

Dinner was four cheese pizza and a bottle of Carib, a popular Caribbean beer. The boat while sailing was well healed over on its side so it was tricky to use the oven. I was feeling down after my super positive day. I am wondering what the hell am I doing out here! It is on day 2 you have the realisation of the magnitude of the journey ahead, another 20 or more days at sea. It is the same feeling I had after leaving Lanzarote. Maybe this always happens when you start a long voyage. Did Columbus feel the same I wonder? I am back sleeping in the starboard bunk in the main cabin. It is too hot in the aft cabin.

Day 3: 24th May 2019 - *Do I go to Bermuda?*
N19° 54' W60° 21'

I slept well even though I was up twice because of the wind shift alarm. This alarm is warning that the wind direction has shifted and the autopilot may disconnect so I had to get up and check. Today is a day of indecision about the route. Do I keep going on the direct route or change course and go north up to the westerly winds? Let's see if the weather offers any clues. The high-pressure at 36N 39W is moving south east towards me at a speed of 30 knots! This is very fast for a high-pressure; yesterday it was travelling at 15 knots. There is another high-pressure system at 32N 77W moving south at the more usual 5 knots. The 48-hour forecast shows a third high-pressure developing north of Bermuda so this may be the answer to my question. There is no point in burning all my fuel to run north if I end up in yet another no wind high-pressure region.

I did some fuel calculations. I estimate I have 800 miles of motoring fuel. Bermuda is 860 miles from where I am now. The only realistic option if I go north is to stop and refuel in Bermuda and then continue the 1,700 miles to the Azores. This would be adding 600 additional miles to my trip versus direct route and it would likely mean I would be late for meeting my family. It is not advisable to have people meeting you at your destination unless you allow plenty of leeway as it is additional pressure you don't need. I am also concerned that I could get stuck in Bermuda for some reason. With the hurricane season starting, I do not want to be on this side of the Atlantic after June 1st.

Well it is hot today, 32 degrees in the cabin. I spent a nice hour before sunset on the wheel to give George the autopilot a rest. For entertainment I have started listening to 'Waiting for Sunrise', an audiobook by William Boyd. The narrator Robert Ian MacKenzie will become my virtual travelling companion. Netflix is driving me mad. I had downloaded a series on the iPad to watch before I left Guadeloupe. When I press play it says 'error can't connect to Netflix'. Luckily, I have the same series 'Better Call Saul' downloaded on my phone but I have to watch it on the small screen. To save diesel fuel I started using the Honda petrol generator at night to charge the boat batteries. The plan was for the generator to sit in the locker on standby in case the engine failed but I see no reason not to use it. I have 20 litres of petrol so I might as well use it.

Day 4: 25th May 2019 - *Norwegian yacht Alize*
N21° 53' W58° 57'

7.40am: I have been up and down all night as the wind shift alarm keeps sounding. I will have to see if I can set a wider angle for the wind alarm so I can sleep. By 9am it is raining. A soft day as we would say in Ireland. I am very tired so I spent most of the morning in bed dozing, listening to the audiobook. In the cockpit while on lookout I noticed the mainsail furling rope that runs from the cockpit to the winch at the mast has come off its track. The rope is now twisted so I need to go on deck and figure this out. I am not great at untangling twists. It always amazes me how a rope can work its way into the most complicated tangle. The rain has stopped and the sun is out so it is a good time to fix this. A nice sense of achievement from a small job that could have turned into a big one - for once it didn't. It is going to be hot today as the breeze is dropping. Coffee time and book reading is my next trick. I am taking it easy today. The forecast is for a bit more wind, so I am feeling more positive.

6.30pm: the wind has shifted easterly and dropped to just 6 knots. The boat speed is down to 3.9 knots so the forecast was wrong. I am nursing the boat along in a flat calm, deep blue sea under a cloudless sky. In the light winds there is complete silence and stillness out here. It is so peaceful. I am reading up on sail trimming in order to get the maximum performance. I won't turn the engine on unless the speed drops below 3 knots, my rule was 4 knots but to save fuel I am compromising further. Today's Atlantic weather chart shows a gale to the northwest of me with 35 knot winds and 21-foot seas, not nice so I will keep away from that. The two high-pressure systems continue to move south into my position so it could be slow going. I am actually wondering if I have enough water in case, I am out here 30-days or more. I have been drinking lots of water each day as it is so hot. Do I need to be rationing water? I did a water audit and found 120 litres in bottles and about 260 litres in the main tank. At 10 litres of fresh water per day I can survive for 40 days, I hope to have arrived in the Azores well before then! To be safe I won't use any fresh water for washing the dishes, I will only use sea water. I will drink from the water from the boat's tank first and keep the bottled water as standby.

Dusk is falling with dark squall clouds building ahead and closing around Esperanza. Tonight, I am cooking a Thai veggie rice dish, which is a concoction of whatever I can find that is to hand and thrown into the frying pan. I have many fresh carrots to eat so a couple will go into tonight's dinner. A bird flew by the boat as I was preparing dinner. This is the only life I have seen since I left Guadeloupe. 9pm and the engine is back on. It feels like today is the big decision day where I decide if I should keep the engine on permanently for the next few days to keep the speed up and make some distance. Under sail my speed is slow at 3 knots which is no fun. I hope to pick up wind in a few days' time so it might be best to keep the engine on until I find wind. But with every decision there is self-doubt and many 'what ifs'. In these situations, having a crew to discuss options would be helpful.

What's this, a ship is passing my bow with big deck cranes. It is called Watkins going to the US. It is all happening tonight: a yacht called Alize pops up on AIS, 4 miles to port. She is a 37-foot Beneteau yacht from Norway, her speed is 5.9 knots so she must also be on engine. I called Alize on the radio and had a great chat. They are also going to Horta on the island of Faial in the Azores. Their original plan was to go to Bermuda but they had to also take the direct route to avoid Storm Andrea. They only brought 6-days of fuel and are worried about running out but they are confident wind will come. Their plan was simple, keep motoring until fuel runs out. It was reassuring to know another yacht is on the same route as myself. We have the same plan, unless we are both wrong and then will both run out of fuel together. Later that night I can see the lights of yacht Alize as we sail in company towards the Azores. I am not alone.

Day 5: 26th May 2019 - *Engine on then off, burning more fuel*
N23° 04' W57° 26'

I am motoring at 5 knots with the sails completely furled away as there is not a puff of wind. This morning I feel uneasy again with the decision to keep motoring until the fuel runs out. It is difficult to relax and enjoy the trip with this feeling. Once the fuel is all gone the only option is to drift and wait for wind, which could be days as I will be trapped in the centre of Azores high-pressure also known as the Horse latitudes. The Horse latitudes were named by the crews of sailing ships, who sometimes threw their horses overboard to conserve water, when their ships were becalmed in the high-pressure area 30 degrees north and south of the equator. I have no horses or crew to jettison. A ship positioned mid-Atlantic offering the services of a fuel station would be a great business, yachts could rendezvous at the ship for a fuel pit stop, chat, food and beer. It would make a great party in international waters. It is not unheard of for cargo ships to drop off fuel drums for yachts out of fuel but I am not sure how you would get a heavy 55-gallon drum onboard a yacht. More likely the ship would drop the fuel drum on top of Esperanza like a depth charge and sink her.

From this morning's weather chart, a cold front is moving south over me tonight, which should mean wind. As I study the weather, I eat my breakfast cereal with UHT long-life milk. I am used to UHT milk as it is the norm in the Caribbean. I just heard the yacht Alize, talking to another Norwegian boat on the radio so there are now three of us out here. It is getting busy. Looking at the AIS on the iPad, I see this new boat is called Borea, a 39-foot yacht. I notice they are taking a more northerly track; hmm I wonder what they know that we don't. I called yacht Alize on the radio for a chat. Jim is the skipper and Norwegian, he has three crew onboard: a Portuguese woman, a Polish girl and her boyfriend from America. A true international crew and a young bunch in their thirties and forties. We agree to meet for drinks in Peter's Cafe bar in Horta when we finally arrive.

After breakfast I got the cruising chute up and tried to sail but the speed was only 2 knots. At this rate I will be out here for weeks! There is no option but to put the engine back on and roll the sails way. In the back of my head is the nagging feeling that I should quit the direct route and instead turn north to find the prevailing westerly winds. But I feel comfortable sailing in company with Alize. By 2pm I feel a light breeze so back up goes the cruising chute. With a little engine revs Esperanza is making 6.1 knots, not bad at all. The flat seas are helping keep the speed up, as there are no waves to slow the boat. The engine is getting very hot with the slack winds as very little fresh air is getting into the engine bay. My solution is to open the engine bay side doors in the cabin to let more air circulate though I am aware by doing this I am letting carbon monoxide into the cabin. I need to be careful or tonight when I go to sleep, I may never wake up. Now it is time to relax and read my book in the cockpit, it is too hot to do anything else. I leave the transfer of fuel from the jerry cans into the main tank until this evening, when it will be cooler.

In the afternoon I am able to turn the engine off and sail. It is great to give the engine a rest. I can see the clouds of the front ahead, which get darker as the hours go by. It feels like thunderstorms are building, the air is heavy. As darkness falls, I am flying along under sails alone, at 7 knots. A lovely fast sail in a totally flat sea. I am having a tin of Spaghetti Bolognese heated on the stove for dinner with a tin of corn and mushrooms added in. I turned on the HF radio and had a chat with Radio Amateur G6MC, Neil from York in the UK. I heard another boat on the radio that was sailing to the island of Montserrat in the Caribbean where I was with my brother for St Patrick's Day. Great memories! 8pm is movie time on Esperanza. I am going below into the cabin to watch the French series 'Marseille' with a cold beer. As I go down below, I can see the lights of the two Norwegian yachts following me. It is nice to feel I am not alone in this featureless ocean. 10pm: guess what, the wind has died and boat speed falls to 4 knots. I put the engine on for a while. This is the pattern of the night, engine on then off, sails in then out. I am up and down all night with little sleep. This is the reality of the so glamorous life of a sailor.

Day 6: 27th May 2019 - *Biggest decision of the trip*
N24° 58' W55° 06'

Once again, I am obsessing over the weather or lack of it. The engine is on far too often for my liking, the fuel is going fast. In my head I am exploring two options. One is to go more south for the best wind angle, sail around the bottom of the high-pressure and then face headwinds to the Azores. It would be a slow slog beating into 20-25 knots of wind and possibly big waves. This option looks less favourable. The second option is to go back to the plan of motoring 400 miles north for a few days onto the traditional sailing route between Bermuda and the Azores. Here, westerly winds are the prevailing winds. This is similar to my original plan, but this time I would not stop in Bermuda. What concerns me is that if I keep going as I am now; I will run out of fuel in 4-5-days. I would then be trapped. All I could do is pace the deck waiting pensively for the high-pressure to move away and for wind to arrive. High-pressure systems can stick around for weeks in summer months. I might go mad out here. I think going north has higher odds of finding the winds to blow me east.

I can't decide what is the best option. I feel lonely and a bit unsure that I know what I am doing. Motoring every day also feels like I am failing as a sailor. I should be using the sails and not the engine. Esperanza is not a motorboat. The latest weather shows favourable winds at 31N to bring me to the Azores. I called Jim the skipper of Alize on the radio to discuss the situation and my thoughts to go north. They were also unsure what to do and were concerned, as they have less fuel than I do, but they are on a lighter boat that will sail better than Esperanza in the light winds. I am becoming conscious of groupthink and that it feels comfortable to stick with sailing with them but it also feels that maybe I am the blind following the blind. It would be difficult to break away from Alize and say goodbye. I would be sailing away from another boat and help if I needed it. I don't want to end up following the crowd and then kick myself for not going with my gut feeling. I want to be able to say 'I did it my way'.

Later that night after dinner I eventually made the big decision. Procrastination was getting me nowhere. It has been one of the bigger decisions that I have to make in my life. I decided to leave Alize and motor direct north to a latitude of 31N where there is wind. I can't handle the uncertainty on the direct route. It would be easier if I had no time constraints but I have family to meet in the Azores and do not want to miss them. So let's go north into the weather and onto the storm route above the high-pressure and see what happens. It feels great to have made the decision and to be taking control. I called Jim on the radio and told him of my decision. He said they will continue on the direct route for another couple of days and see what happens. Their worry about going north is the possibility of being hit by a storm. I alter the boats heading from 67 degrees northeast to 12 degrees north.

Isn't it strange how the boat's progress becomes linked to your mood? When you are going slow and not making much progress with little hope of improvement you feel anxious, low and powerless. When there is a steady wind and you are speeding towards your destination, you feel alive and master of your destiny. I want some fast and furious sailing. I am excited and ready for the challenge.

Day 7: 28th May 2019 - *Course change, sailing North to 35N*
N26° 35' W55° 12'

I feel great today. I had a long deep sleep, which must have been brought on by my final decision to change course and go north. I thought last night I was coming down with a bug and felt weak. I can't let myself get sick when sailing alone. Today though I feel refreshed. My stress levels have dropped and the weather forecast continues to support my decision to go north. Once I get to 35N, I am expecting westerly 15-20 knot winds all the way to the Azores. I am motor sailing today making a comfortable 6.5 knots. Another cold front is ahead, which I may hit tonight. A mental note to myself that I have been lazy at recording my daily runs, I need to get back into the routine first thing each morning. In the last 24 hours I sailed 148 miles. It is the slack winds of the last few days that have made me lazy. Calculating my new time of arrival, it is looking like the 14th of June but it is too early to be accurate. As I was eating my breakfast in the cockpit, I had a private air display of seabirds showing off their flying skills. They circled the boat looking for some breakfast. I told them I have no fish for them as this is a fish-free boat. They left.

It is another hot day and I am doing my steering duties. I am wrapped up like an Arab Sheik in a Sarong. I bought this Sarong in Martinique and it has been the most useful item yet when ashore or at sea. I decided to have rum and orange juice. It needed ice, which of course I do not have as I don't have a freezer onboard. I have many bottles of Mount Gay rum onboard, which is sold across the Caribbean at very cheap prices. It makes me think of my favourite Caribbean drink, Ti Punch, which means small punch. It is a very popular drink in the French Caribbean islands. To make a Ti Punch is simple: rum, fresh lime and cane syrup as the sweetener, no ice required. I have a bottle of cane sugar onboard; I am well prepared. Tradition says for a Ti Punch you are supposed to knock it back in one go in the morning but I prefer to sip it in the evenings.

It is time to move the clock forward. I write down my plan in the logbook to move the clock one hour forward every 15 degrees at longitudes: 53W, 43W, 33W, 25W. The clock on the wall in the cabin is on local time. This dictates mealtimes. The clock on the GPS and the iPad for navigation are kept in UTC / GMT time. My logbook is always written in the same UTC time zone. It was 7pm but after my clock change it is now 8pm and it is getting dark. Dinner tonight was Ravioli, one of the French meals in a tin from Carrefour, not bad actually. As I am eating, I am listening to the Amateur Radio guys chatting about the Tornados today in the US. Later that night a ship pops up on AIS on my iPad. It is close, just 6 miles away. Keros as she is called is a Greek crude oil tanker, 748 feet long. She is heading to Antwerp, Belgium. I have gone under 1,500 miles to Horta, yippie! Night all.

Day 8: 29th May 2019 - *39 degrees in the cockpit, it's really hot*
N28° 41' W54° 54'

The forecast today shows the wind shifting from the northeast to the east, which will give a better wind angle and more speed. But the reality is the wind dies off completely so I am back to motoring with no sails up. I am a motorboat. Just 129 miles travelled in the last 24 hours. A visitor arrived today; a flying fish who crash landed on the deck. In the afternoon I raised the cruising chute to see if I can get an extra bit of speed. The cruising chute is still filling as I motor sail so I will leave it up. 39 degrees today in the cockpit that is crazy hot. God knows what temperature it is in the engine room. I am afraid to think of that. I have the engine doors off again today to let air circulate as I do not want the engine giving up on me from the heat. This morning's job was to figure out why the battery charge monitor was frozen and not working. I traced the wiring back to the battery and pulled the fuse to reset it and it looks back to normal. After working in the hot cabin, the sea looks very inviting for a swim but instead it is buckets of cold sea water over my head. The seaweed floating by looks very nice and I am sure one could eat it.

It is not best practice to run a diesel engine at low power for an extended period like I am doing now. So every few hours I move the throttle to full power for a few minutes to burn off any carbon deposits on the engine injectors. Today when I did this, I noticed the RPM on full throttle was only 2,400 RPM when it should be near 3,000 RPM. Here we go again, the same problem I had in Guadeloupe, which I thought was solved by cleaning barnacles off the hull. I hope it is a simple fix and just a clump of seaweed around the propeller. This is likely, as lots of seaweed has been floating past the boat. I remembered the old reverse trick I used on the Atlantic outward voyage. I bring the throttle back to neutral and put the engine into reverse and give it a blast. It should spin off anything wrapped around the propeller. It worked - the RPM is back up to the normal 2,900 RPM. The speed also shot up from 5.4 knots to 6.2 knots so I was probably towing a big clump of seaweed and slowing the boat unnecessarily. Not to mention wasting valuable fuel! That explains why I was so slow last night, only 129 miles sailed in the last 24 hours. I need to check this more often.

It is a lovely clear night and I am star gazing as they twinkle back at me. In the cities and towns where most of us live we rarely notice the stars. We take the universe above us for granted. Only in the ocean, where the stars are so bright do you realise how many billions of stars must be out there and our tiny planet relies on just one of these for life. The wonder and size of space is impossible to fathom. After my philosophical star gazing it was time to come back down to earth and experience the pleasure of Netflix. I finished the series 'Marseille', I truly enjoy my hour of escapism from the ocean.

Tonight's weather shows an Occluded front ahead. It will pass over me tonight. An Occluded front is where a cold front overtakes a warm front and they join to give a wide variety of weather, thunderstorms and squalls are possible. The Jetstream today is very far north at 45 north and meanders over Ireland. The Jetstream is dividing the Atlantic in two: bad weather to the north of it, and to the south, balmy sunny weather with calm winds dominated by the Azores high-pressure, which is stretching across most of the southern Atlantic. It looks like it is sunbathing weather in the Azores.

Dinner tonight was fried noodles with tinned veg with lashings of soya sauce. Very tasty, you can't beat soya sauce for giving vegetables a kick. Tonight, I dropped the cruising chute and went to the effort to get the pole up in the darkness to keep the jib sail from collapsing and flapping. Again I praised the bright LED deck light, which nicely illuminated the deck while I worked. This sail configuration with the pole gives me an extra half a knot. The boat speed rises to 6.1 knots. While doing this I saw an airliner passing high overhead. This is the first aircraft I have seen in 8-days so I must be coming onto the flight path from Europe to South America.

Day 9: 30th May 2019 - *No wind again! Fuel is becoming critical*
N30° 57' W54° 26'

I woke up to no wind again! This is getting crazy. The sea is flat and glassy except for the odd ripple now and again. I have sailed 1,000 miles so far. The miles are now coming down more slowly as I am no longer heading direct to the Azores but instead going north. Pressure is rising, it is now 1019 millibar. I hope I am not heading into another high-pressure slack wind system. I will download the latest weather over breakfast. Doing my calculations the engine has been running for 93 hours since I left Guadeloupe, 190 litres of fuel has been used. Out of the 9-days at sea I have only had 3 good sailing days where the engine was not on. Six of the jerry cans of fuel have been used with 4 full cans remaining on the deck and three in the locker as emergency fuel. Fuel is becoming critical. From tomorrow, I can't motor anymore as I would be eating into the fuel allocated for running the engine to charge the batteries. I also need to keep fuel to allow for motoring as I approach the Azores. I am not a religious man but I am praying for wind by tomorrow. Now I understand why some of the yachts had rows of jerry cans tied the full length of either side of their decks. They probably had enough fuel to motor at least half the way across. I just did not have the room to take on more fuel.

Today I tried everything to get some speed from the little puffs of wind. I had the cruising chute up but it does not work well when going directly downwind. I really need the spinnaker sail but that is also in my shed back at home. I did not bring it as I have no experience flying the spinnaker single-handed. There is a high risk when flying it alone that it would wrap around the forestay or mast. I thought it was best to play it safe and use the easier to manage cruising chute. I am only making 3.3 knots and in even worse it is in the wrong direction towards New York. The wind speed is 6 knots and swinging around all over the place. It feels like the wind is on the change so hopefully it is a sign of more steady wind to come. Tonight's dinner plans are very dull to follow my mood: two eggs, beans on toast and a mug of tea. I have developed a fondness for tea at sea.

Man Overboard! One of my yellow empty jerry cans fell overboard. At least it is not me overboard and just a jerry can. As I watch it drifting away from the boat, I am wondering should I bother to try and rescue it. It's only worth €20. The risk is that in trying to pick it up I cause a bigger problem like falling in myself. But it is the excitement of the day so I decide it must be rescued. Time to launch Esperanza's Man Overboard Drill. I turn the boat towards the yellow casualty, which is floating away behind me. My man overboard skills are a little rusty but after three attempts, the casualty is safely back onboard using the boat hook for the pickup. Good training, I say to myself. The boat is now completely stopped and it is very hot. All the looking at the deep blue ocean when rescuing the jerry can has given me the urge to have a swim. The flat calm ocean is serenading me.

There can't be too many people that have swam mid-Atlantic where the water is four kilometres deep. Hmmmm, why not have a quick dip in the cool water. The wind is reading zero as is the boat speed. Searching the horizon I am alone, there are no boats around. I don't see any sharks so why not have a swim. I decide to go for it and have a quick plunge in the inky blue ocean. I head for the boarding platform at the stern. I will stay right by the stern of the boat by the boarding ladder. I know you should tie a rope around yourself if you go for a swim off the boat, but I don't think I need a rope this time as we are stopped and I will be in the water for just enough time to jump in and then get back out. Let's go, the shorts are off. Boarding ladder down and snorkel mask on. Here I go, I launch myself into the 4,000-metre deep Atlantic. With my big jump I submerged under the water deeper than I expected. It is dark under the water and cooler than I expected. Now I am shooting back up to the surface. When my head breaks the water and I open my eyes the boat has moved 20 metres away from me. Oh my God, the boat is drifting away without me!

I have one thought that the boat will sail away and I will be left stranded here alone. I get the fright of my life; any puff of wind and the boat will be gone. There must be an ocean current running. What the hell am I doing. I panic and swim like a madman to the boarding platform and grab the ladder. I keep a firm grip of the ladder as I can feel the pull of the boat moving. I am truly frightened of what could have happened if I stayed longer underwater. I clamber back onboard in shock. A stiff coffee sorts me out as I kick myself for being so stupid. Of course now I realise that the boat will drift at a different speed to me as it weighs 9 tons and I weigh slightly less. Even when you think the boat has stopped there is always some ocean current at play even with no wind. But attempting a swim when alone is adding unnecessary risk. What if I hit my head or got stuck in the water a little longer? The boat would be gone. I would be left there floating in the ocean watching the boat sail away. I would not last very long as there is no one nearby to rescue me and no way for me to raise help. That's enough excitement for one day. Two beers tonight, I decide.

The near-death swim earlier has shaken me more than I realised and lowered my mood. It is so important to be aware of your moods when alone and try to stabilize yourself. There is no point in being a single-handed depressed sailor. Music helps lift my mood. I put on my Spotify dance mix and turn the volume up loud and blast the tunes inside and outside the boat. I recognize I am over-tired. I am just not getting enough sleep. I am not good at napping and being single-handed means I am always in alert mode; I never fully switch off even when asleep. People who can put their head on a pillow and immediately fall asleep are so lucky. Tonight I am writing my feelings into the logbook and remind myself it is the journey that matters and to enjoy it. It is not all just about the destination and getting there.

Sailors in the old sailing ships would also suffer from periods of low mood. Crews would go mad when becalmed in the Atlantic for weeks on end with no wind and no engine. I write in my log that tomorrow I will force myself to take a 1-hour nap during the day no matter what. I also make the decision from tomorrow to go back sailing and not use the engine no matter how slow I go. When you are sailing you feel in control and good about yourself as you are using the free resource of the wind to move the boat. For me nothing beats this feeling, it makes me feel alive, in flow and content with the world. Sailing can be a spiritual experience as it is just you and nature doing battle. I feel a new lease of life and a sense of energy as I make the plan to sail the remainder of the way without the engine. I will sit back and read more books and enjoy the journey. It will be a test of my sailing skills to nurse the boat along in the light winds.

Day 10: 31st May 2019 - *Strange alien creature: Portuguese Man-of-War*
N32° 41' W54° 12'

I am sailing! Yippie, my prayers have been answered. I awoke to 10 knots of lovely steady breeze, which has filled in from the south west. I am on a beam reach where the wind is blowing 90 degrees to the boat - this is the best sailing angle for speed. I am at latitude 32N and on the traditional sailing route from the Caribbean to Azores, which is where I was expecting to find wind. I slept very well so I feel like a new man today. By lunchtime I have both jibs poled out. The wind speed has risen to 14 knots. Boat speed is 5 knots and the motion is comfortable. I am enjoying the sail and reading in the cockpit, while keeping a lookout.

Whale! A big whale passed to starboard, not much to see it dived straight away. There was more sea life today, as hundreds of strange jellyfish-like creatures floated by. They look like a plastic air-filled bag with a big black slug inside and long tentacles hanging down in the water. I tweeted out the description and waited for friends to reply. They were identified as Portuguese Man-of-War and I would like to meet one in the water. They paralyze fish or plankton with their long venomous tentacles before reeling their prey inwards to be eaten. The sting is very sore and can be serious. I was going to scoop one into a bucket and do a closer examination but I decided it was best to leave them alone. Despite their appearance, they are not jellyfish which are single organisms. Portuguese Man-of-War are zooids, made up of four different organisms that can't live without each other. There is the gas filled bag which allows it to float;

the tentacles for defence and capturing prey; the digestive organism; and the final part is for reproduction. The floating gas filled bag acts like a sail to catch the wind and they drift along in ocean currents. It was named Portuguese Man-of-War for its resemblance to the old Portuguese sailing ships. Turtles for some reason love to eat them.

After lunch it is poles down and cruising chute up as wind drops back to 10 knots. I am getting good exercise with all these sail changes. ETA is coming back to 16th June as we have a little more speed. Tonight I decided to leave the cruising chute up for the first time as the boat was going nicely at 4.5 knots in a 7-knot wind. It is frustrating not to have more wind at 32N, but all I can do is keep going further north to get out of the grip of the high-pressure. It is Murphy's Law again as the high-pressure has now decided to move north with me. I can see on the weather chart there is nice wind just a little north of my position so I need to get up there. Tuning around on the HF radio I can again pick up the BBC World Service. It is comforting to hear the English voices again. It feels like I am returning to civilization.

The air is damp, which I am not used to. It reminds me of sailing in Scotland. Bedtime, to help me relax and drift off to sleep, I am listening to an audiobook. I am not feeling as tired tonight as the forced nap during the day worked. In the bunk I am thinking of home. There is a family wedding this weekend and I feel a little lonely knowing everyone is together having a great time. I am halfway now with 11-days or so to go. It will be great to see the family again and I feel excited to think of us all together in the Azores. I am missing home such as going to my son's favourite cafe for the 'Big Big Breakfast'. Normal life always returns, so I will enjoy the isolation while I can.

Day 11: 1st June 2019 - *Slowing down: only 93 miles in the last 24 hours*
N34° 20' W53° 43'

It is Saturday June 1st, the bank holiday weekend in Ireland, but there are no days off in the Atlantic. The latest weather shows a nasty gale only 120 miles away with 30-foot seas. This will bring more wind from Monday. I only sailed 93 miles in the last 24 hours, I am slowing down and below my target of 120 miles per day. Today was a day of trying all the sail combinations to squeeze some more speed. I feel the need for speed, but I am stuck at 3.5-4 knots all morning. A slow morning, with not much to report other than the carrots, oranges and yogurts are all gone. Today's jobs include re-running ropes to stop then chafing.

I am feeling the effects of being further north, as it is noticeably cooler in the mornings and at night. The damp air at night is getting into my bones, I must be getting old. I have to decide if I will fly the two jibs poled out, which means I would be heading directly north when I now want to head northeast towards the Azores. The other option I ponder is bringing in the poles and flying the cruising chute on a broad reach allowing me to aim for a more direct route to Azores. I prefer to be always heading towards the destination and knocking off the miles even if it is slower. I tried the cruising chute on its own without the mainsail, as on a broad reach the mainsail was blanketing the cruising chute. This worked as I am getting an additional 1 knot boat speed and even better, I am now on a direct heading to Azores. By lunchtime I am having a beautiful sail, flying along at 6 knots. The cloudy sky from earlier this morning has lifted to become a lovely sunny day. Time for my afternoon nap. I am enjoying my new routine of daily naps listening to an audiobook to help me relax and mentally switch off from sailing.

A word to the wise: be aware of the cruising chute. It needs to be watched if the wind is not steady. At one stage the wind dropped and the cruising chute collapsed, wrapping around the mast and radar. I was able to get it untangled and luckily there was no damage to the lightweight nylon sail. It would be a dodgy situation if the cruising chute got stuck and would not come down. I would have to put on the self-climbing gear and climb the mast. This is not something I want to do in a hurry as at sea it is exhausting and dangerous work. I have a nightmare of being at the top of the mast and the climbing gear jams and I am trapped hanging out of the mast with no one below to help! It doesn't bear thinking about.

Day 12: 2nd June 2019 - *Bloody hell, I nearly went overboard*
N35° 43' W53° 27'

I am at longitude 53W, so I am moving the clock forward another hour. Time goes fast at sea. The days seem to fly by. Maybe it is because I am alone and there is always a list of boat jobs to keep things ship shape. If I was with a crew I might be bored as there would be much less to do. I am at 35N and the Azores is 38N so I am nearly on the same latitude. I will keep going a little more north to 38N, which on the chart shows stronger and more reliable winds for a passage to the Azores. I am still on the edge of the high-pressure system and do not want to drift back into its grip. I did not sleep well as the boat was rolling side to side with the two jibs poled out for downwind sailing. I will definitely need an afternoon nap today. I switched the sails to the traditional mainsail and jib configuration. I am hoping I can keep the sails like this for the next few days, as the boat is going nicely with no rolling. It is a relaxing motion today compared to last night. I didn't feel 100% last night; I felt a chill and shivery. I hope I am not coming down with something from the damp night air.

Today's job is to patch a small tear in the cruising chute before I need to put it up again. I carry out the repair in the cabin by applying strong self-adhesive sail repair tape as a patch to both sides. Then it is time to settle down to reading my book with a cup of instant coffee and a Madeleine French fairy cake. The boat has a lovely motion, it is peaceful and quiet at sea. Speed is back up at 6 knots, yippie! On AIS I see a Spanish yacht called Champagne - they are also heading to the Azores. I must remember these yacht names when I arrive in Horta so I can say hello. Horta is the port where traditionally all the yachts heading across the Atlantic to Europe make their first landfall. The days have got much longer at this higher latitude compared to the Caribbean. This was the one thing I missed in the Caribbean, the long bright evenings. The nights are long when it starts to get dark at 6.30pm. The downside of being this far north is I now need to wear a fleece at night. The bucket of sea water for my shower is also noticeably colder. I let out a little scream every time I pour it over my head.

Tonight, grey clouds are forming all around me. It might be the first bit of rain of the trip. I am debating whether to take down the cruising chute for night-time. I am making good speed with the cruising chute, and it would be a shame to lose this speed by changing the sails. Though I don't want the added risk of a squall scoring a direct hit on Esperanza with the lightweight cruising chute flying. I decide to leave it up as everything looks stable, 9 knots of wind and no squall clouds on the horizon. I checked the weather forecast and it looks ok. The good news is the high-pressure that I am on the edge of is slowly moving away and dissipating. That has to mean more wind to come over the next few days. I could be arriving as early as 12th June, which would mean 5-days alone to relax, sleep and recover, not to mention plenty of time for hanging out with the other yachties. I think I might sleep for days when I arrive. It is 9.30pm and I am off to bed for an early night.

I am woken at 1am by the wind howling. The wind has increased a lot from when I went to bed. In the cockpit I see the wind gauge is showing 15 knots. The boat speed is over 7 knots, which is too much pressure on the cruising chute and I fear it may blow out. What do I do? Leave it up and wait until daylight to take it down or get it down now in the dark? I am hesitating as I know going on deck in the dark and trying to lower the cruising chute alone is a risky business and could lead me into even worse problems. I am kicking myself for not taking it down before night-time. The one time on the trip I leave the cruising chute up for the night, the wind picks up. I have a bad feeling about this but I need the cruising chute intact, so I am going to take it down. I must make sure not to let the sail fall into the water. As if it did it could be sucked under the boat and wrap around the rudder and propeller, disabling the engine and steering. That would be a real mess. The other risk is the cruising chute wraps around the jib forestay or the mast and gets stuck. Lots can go wrong here. Flashing through my mind is the story of a couple crossing the Atlantic last year: as the wife slept below, the husband tried to lower the spinnaker at night and he was pulled into the ocean with the sail, never to be seen again.

I put on gloves and a safety harness to clip myself to the boat while on deck.

I let out the boom and mainsail to blanket the cruising chute and depower it somewhat. Ok let's get on with it, so I can get back to that comfortable bunk. Sitting on the deck midships on the port side, I am looking out into pitch darkness. The sea is up, the boat is bouncing along and, even though it is dark, I can see the white wave crests breaking. The cruising chute looks very much alive; it is full of power and close to bursting with the wind. I start by trying to pull down the 'suffer' or bucket-like device at the top of the mast to collapse the sail but it won't budge. There is just too much wind pressure. I try to half stand-up to get leverage and I am getting some movement but the wind is too strong to collapse the sail. I need to try to depower the sail so with one hand I keep pulling on the rope to pull down the bucket to collapse the sail, while my other hand is controlling the halyard rope to lower the sail. If I can lower the sail slightly maybe it will depower and allow me to collapse and control it. But instead the sail billows outward and gains more power! The bucket shoots back up to the top of the mast ripping my gloves off and overboard. Ahh, the rope has cut into my gloveless hand. Then the deck rolls and I am thrown off balance. Bloody hell I was close to going overboard there! Sit down I tell myself and wait for a lull in the wind to try again. I take an opportunity and pull like hell hoping the thin rope won't snap. I succeed through brute force to get the cruising chute beast tamed and down.

I quickly stuff the sail back in its bag as I want to be back in the safety of the cockpit as fast as possible. I must get the boat sailing again. I power up the mainsail and roll out the jib. Damn, I have hurt my hand lowering the sail. Down in the cabin I wash my hand in disinfectant, it looks ok and just a rope burn. I am in shock and shaking from the experience. I very nearly met my maker tonight; it is the closest I have been to going overboard. I can't even remember if I was clipped on properly, it is all a blur. Even if I was, I could have been dragged through the water with no way to climb back onboard the boat. A glass of Oban Scottish whisky does the job to calm me down. I tell myself to slow down, be safer, be overly cautious for the next 10-days until I arrive, please! This is a valuable lesson of the fragility of life: one moment we are here and then next we can be gone.

There isn't much more I can do tonight or want to do. I am shattered so I go back to bed with the boat steaming along at 7 knots in a rough sea. I am very glad the cruising chute is down but I have a dissatisfied feeling that I could have done things better. How do I depower the cruising chute when single-handed if I hit a squall again?

Day 13: 3rd June 2019 - *Luna Verde, a Dutch 50-foot sailing yacht 6 miles to port* N37° 34' W51° 36'

I slept until 10am, a much-needed sleep after last night's antics. I look outside and the sea is still rough. It was the right decision to take the cruising chute down as there is no way it would have survived. It was not a temporary squall that I sailed into last night but it looks like I have moved into the prevailing westerly winds and out of the calming influence of the high-pressure. The daily run in the last 24 hours is improving, at 129 miles. I am now on the Middle route to the Azores, which is where I want to stay, so no further north. I will keep going east directly to Horta. The real bad weather is just north of me with constant low-pressure systems accelerating out of the Hudson Bay area of New York on a storm track east across the Atlantic. This is where the 30-foot seas are, another reason not to go further north. I have forgotten what a bouncy rough sea feels like as over the last 10-days it has been so flat and calm. During the night I heard a ship calling the Norwegian yacht Alize. I hope Jim and crew are ok. Looking around, there are no vessels on the horizon, I am alone again in my Ocean, which suits me just fine.

Today's job is no surprise: to bring the cruising chute into the cabin, unpack and untangle it. Then check for any tears and repack it like a parachute so there are no twists when I launch it again. I had a new idea this morning on how to get the cruising chute sail down quickly and safely in high winds – sleeping on the problem has worked. I can depower the cruising chute by releasing the Tack end, which is the end attached to the deck at the bow of the boat. Then it should immediately depower and flap harmlessly like a flag. Shouldn't it? Well, I think it should. I study my sail trim book on flying spinnakers but it does not mention this as a solution, so this is going to be an experiment. It sounds logical to me but what other issues could it cause?

The big question is how do I release the sail at the bow and be at the mast at the same time to lower the sail. I would need very long arms, in the region of 5 metres. These are the challenges of single-handed sailing. My idea is to put a quick release shackle on the tack, the corner of the sail that connects to the bow. The quick release shackle has a pin, which when pulled, releases the sail. To solve the issue of being in two places at the same time, I came up with the simple solution of tying a length of rope to the release pin. The rope is then led back from the bow to the mast where I will be in position sitting down. Standing is too dangerous when both my hands are occupied holding ropes, I could easily lose my balance and go overboard. It sounds like a good plan and I am excited to try it out, but also a little anxious. I prepared the quick release system and packed everything in the sail bag ready for when the conditions are right for a trial. It was fun improvising at sea which is central to be a successful ocean sailor. Stuff breaks all the time and out here there is no one to help you; you just get on with it and improvise and find solutions. It looks like a job well done so I deserve an afternoon nap.

5pm: Luna Verde, a Dutch 50-foot Contest sailing yacht, is 6 miles to port also heading to the Azores. I called her on the VHF radio and we had a chat. They said to look out for them in Peter's Bar in Horta. This makes three boats that I have promised to meet in Horta, I am going to be busy on arrival. They left 5-days ago from Bermuda with 3 onboard. They said Bermuda was very expensive so maybe it was good I did not stop there. After the Azores they will continue to the Canaries where they will leave the boat for the winter. They want winter sunshine so the Canaries are right for them. I feel energised after chatting so I must be missing social contact after my 13-days at sea.

It is getting dark and I need to charge the batteries so I pull the start rope on the little Honda generator. I will leave her running for a couple of hours while I retire into the world of Netflix. The batteries are at 73% charge so they need a little juice. Esperanza is still flying along at 7 knots consistently. It is strange down below in the cabin as the motion is so smooth that it feels we are not moving at all. We are on a beam reach, the wind is at 90 degrees, which is the fastest point of sailing, Esperanza is slicing through the waves effortlessly with very little healing. I put a small reef in the mainsail to balance the boat and we are actually going faster with the slightly smaller main sail. The expression is that boat is 'in the groove', so I won't change anything.

11.45pm: boat speed continues to rise; it is now 8 knots. Esperanza is not a slow boat after all. She is heavy and a bit fat in the midships but when there is a decent wind to push her along, she gets into her stride. I reefed the sails some more to bring the speed back down to 7 knots, which is more comfortable. I turn the Honda generator off as it has charged the battery from 71% to 75%. It's satisfying not to have to turn the engine on to charge the batteries. On the HF radio tonight, I listened to a US Amateur radio group called the 'Hole in the Wall Gang Net', which gets together each night on 7.188MHz. It was interesting to hear the group chatting about US politics and everyday life. It was difficult to pull myself away to go to bed.

3am: I am up again as the wind dropped a little so I removed the reefs in the sail. I have just gone under the 1,000 miles to Horta. I feel a sense of achievement as I am getting nearer. I just hope I do not get hit by a storm with all the depressions I see rolling out of the US into the Atlantic.

Day 14: 4th June 2019 - *Icebergs just 120 miles ahead bring freezing fog*
N39° 04' W49° 14'

10am: I don't want to get out of bed but I must have a look outside to see what sort of day it is. Looking around the horizon from the cockpit it is cloudy and gusty. It looks to me like it might rain. I am now heading east on a heading of 80 degrees, directly to the Azores. This morning I am wondering what time zone I should be in. Azores is one hour behind UTC but then it also has summertime so it's local time must be the same as UTC, which is one hour behind Irish time. I have two more one-hour forward clock movements to get into the Azores time zone. The next one will be at 43W, in 360 miles or 3-days. This morning I ran the Honda generator again for two hours and the battery charge percentage rose from 69% to 74%. This covers the power use during the Night-time from navigation lights, VHF radio, AIS and iPad. I run the generator each night for 3 hours, which burns 1 litre of petrol. I have 20 litres of petrol onboard so I have 20-days of charge time available from the generator. Even at this latitude, during the day I am getting enough energy from the sun to keep up with my energy needs, Esperanza is energy neutral during daylight hours. Though today is an exception as there is no sun, just clouds. When you are used to blue sky and fluffy white clouds it is a bit of a shock to encounter a cloudy overcast day.

I am listening to Air Traffic Control for the Atlantic on the HF radio. I can hear airliners checking in with Santa Maria radio, which is based on Santa Maria island, in the Azores. I also came across BBC News: Trump is in the UK meeting the Queen, I would love to know what the Queen says to Prince Philip afterwards. By night-time the wind has swung a little and I am moving more onto a beat. The pressure is falling, maybe a sign of more wind to come. Tonight in the cabin, my feet are cold so I have to resort for the first time since leaving the Canaries to put on socks! What a come down and soon I may have to pull out my slippers. I am also wearing a hoodie fleece at night. I am still in shorts but on the edge of moving to long pants. The miles are rolling down, we have just gone under 900 miles to go. Esperanza's boat speed is 6.6 knots tonight under mainsail and jib, lovely steady sail, no real heeling and once again I hardly feel we are moving. Dinner tonight is two boiled eggs, warm baguette bread and hot soup. The cooler weather is making the soup in the cupboard look inviting. In the hot weather I was wondering if I would ever want to drink soup again.

3.30am: I am woken in my bunk and it is freezing cold inside the boat, which is very odd. Just an hour ago it was not cold at all in the cabin, there has been a sudden drop in temperature, and now it is freezing. I got up to have a look and I am in the thickest fog I have ever experienced. I can just see the bow of the boat but no further, visibility is down to 10-15 metres. I immediately turn the radar on as I have no idea what I am sailing into. The radar and AIS both look clear of any vessels. Not only is it foggy but it is freezing fog and even smells like dry ice. Is it odd to have fog in the middle of the Atlantic? I opened the Atlantic sailing guide and it says icebergs have been reported up until July on the Bermuda to Azores route. I am at 39N 47W and it turns out I am in the iceberg zone! The guide warns that when you encounter freezing fog like I have now, beware as a big iceberg is not far away. I never considered icebergs would be an issue on this route. If an iceberg sank the Titanic, I am sure it could sink Esperanza. I switch on the iPad and download the latest weather. Amongst the weather charts from

Boston there is an ice chart, which I have never bothered to look at before. Yes, there on the chart two icebergs are shown just 120 miles from my position. To be marked as icebergs on the chart they must be huge things.

The fog is caused by the iceberg cooling the air in its vicinity and the light winds are carrying this as fog south into my area. Hopefully there are no 'growlers' or broken-off chunks of ice in my path as they can drift further south than the main iceberg. I see nothing on the radar. Icebergs have smooth wetted surfaces that produce low radar reflections, which means they are stealthy and difficult for the radar to pick up. All I can do is keep sailing through the fog tonight and hope for the best. To keep warm I put on a woolly hat, slippers and my body warmer. I will sleep wrapped up in my warm sleeping bag tonight.

Day 15: 5th June 2019 - *Ship on lookout for a yacht in distress*
N40° 15' W46° 22'

I woke up late today at 11.30am. I am not feeling great as I may have gotten a chill from the cold fog last night. I feel weak and more tired than normal. I also have a sore left leg for some reason but don't remember banging it off anything. I will struggle on but I am hoping for an easy day. The wind has dropped to 8 knots so expect I will need to raise the cruising chute. I will wait as I have no energy for sail change at the moment. My daily 24-hour run was good at 152 miles. I got a call on the VHF radio from a ship called Polaris 4, a big chemical tanker who is crossing my bow heading for London Thamesport in England. They asked if I am ok, which sounded odd. I said I was fine, in no danger and the boat is ok. I asked why they were asking and they said a navigation warning was issued for a missing yacht that had sent out a distress signal in this area. They were checking if I was this yacht in distress. I hope it is not any of the yachts I have spoken too. Nice to know the ship is looking out for us yachties and checking in on me. It is cloudy and raining today, the first day of proper rain, yuck. I miss the heat and sunshine. On the sail across to the Caribbean, everyday got a little warmer as I went further south, now on the return trip every day gets a little cooler and wetter. All good things come to an end.

I am now at the latitude of 40N, which is as far north as I want to go. Horta is slightly south of my position at 38N. The winds brought me a little further north than planned, but this is not a problem, as I will come back down south when the wind direction allows. The plan now is to head direct for Horta, 795 miles to go. An airliner flies overhead heading in the direction of Europe. I am thinking of the passengers comfortably sitting in their seats watching movies, that was me six weeks ago on my way home to Dublin, now look where I am.

During the day I leave the second iPad running at the navigation table, connected to the HF radio to download synoptic weather and wind charts. It is reassuring to know that if the satellites stop working, we still have weather forecasts transmitting over good old-fashioned radio waves for anyone to receive. The latest weather chart shows that I am now bang in the middle of three high-pressure systems so I am lucky to still have wind. The slack winds from the high-pressure systems are moving out of my way, allowing wind to fill in from the west behind me, it should allow me to sail all the way to the Azores. I do think coming up this far north where there is a higher probability of steady winds was the right thing to do. I am enjoying the sailing versus last week when I was on the southern route with little or no wind and the constant work to nurse the boat along. That's no way to sail.

My reworked ETA is on the 12th June. Updating the fuel log, I have plenty of fuel left but I have run out of pages in my logbook. I use a regular A4 hardback copybook instead. I rule it myself for the columns of data I want to record. I have filled 192 pages in my A4 logbook since I left the Canaries on the 17th December 2018. The right-hand page in the logbook is the boring nautical position information, which all vessels are required to keep by law. On the left-hand side I record my thoughts, fears and emotions. It is therapeutic to offload your thoughts each day and, when I look back in future years, it might make interesting reading.

Day 16: 6th June 2019 - *Luckily, I spotted a broken pin in the crucial shackle that connects the boom*
N40° 34' W44° 26'

Last night was very rough from midnight onwards. Lots of white surf in the waves. The waves were coming at odd angles and breaking on the side of the boat, slowing me down. When a wave hits the boat, the whole boat shakes and vibrates like crazy for a few moments, speed falls, then George the autopilot recovers and Esperanza speeds up again. The current wind at 13 knots is not enough to be generating these big seas, which are more in line with a Force 6 or 7 wind. The big waves must be coming from a storm to the north of me.

I am still puzzled as to why my GPS speed over the ground is slow and not moving over 4.5 knots; it indicates there is an unfavourable ocean current slowing my progress. It feels like the waves are grabbing the stern of the boat and sucking me backwards, the opposite of surfing down a wave where you get a speed boost. I am getting a speed drop with every wave it just does not feel right. To check I was not towing anything under the water, I furled the sails away and turned on the engine. I tried a few 360-degree turns and reverse manoeuvres to see if I can shake off anything that might be hanging onto the rudder, keel or propeller. Afterwards I go back on track but unfortunately there is no difference to the speed. All I can do is just keep going and hope things sort themselves out. Daily run over the last 24 hours was 141 miles.

This morning I was lucky to spot a broken pin on the key shackle that connects the end of the boom and mainsheet rope to the boat. The forces on this shackle are huge. I was surprised to see that an 8mm solid stainless-steel pin had completely snapped in two. It must be metal fatigue as the break was very clean and just before the threads on the pin. Just by luck everything was still attached but at any moment it could give way. The unsecured boom would then swing dangerously back and forth. Real damage could be done to the boom but also to me as I would have to manhandle it back onboard. Imagine that happening at night-time. I have plenty of spare shackles onboard so I was able to change the shackle no problem. I just spotted this by accident so I need to do more checks – what else is about to break? On deck I will check all the shackles, pins and connections. It is a lesson to use certified shackles and not the cheaper unbranded Chinese look-alikes.

I am staying in the cabin this morning to avoid the miserable weather. It looks like it will rain all day. I am curled up on the sofa with a good book, coffee and a blanket, as it is now officially cold. I gave in and had to move from shorts to long pants combats. The cooler weather is not agreeing with me as I have mouth ulcers, a sign I am run down. I loaded up on Vitamin C. I am just not made for cold climates. I had the engine on for an hour at lunchtime but I was still only able to get the speed up to 4.6 knots. The cruising chute is now out and I am making 4 knots in the light winds. I am seeing lots of ships on the horizon heading towards America. A giant aircraft carrier size container ship passed across my bows. It is nice to see such a huge ship alter its course because of Esperanza. On the weather chart I see a cold front ahead, which must be where all this cloud and rain is coming from. I can expect squalls, gusts and wind shifts so I need to be prepared and not have the cruising chute up. I don't want to get caught out again with the chute up in ever increasing winds at night-time.

I got a chance today to test the new quick release system to lower the cruising chute and it worked very well, woohoo! It was a textbook operation, if I say so myself. I sat down midships by the mast with the quick release line in one hand and my other hand holding the rope to pull down the bucket to collapse the sail into its sock bag. One pull of the quick release line and the shackle at the bow sprung open, the cruising chute immediately depowered and flew from the bow like a flag. There was no risk of it wrapping around anything as it flew away from the boat. Now that there was no energy in the sail, it was super easy to pull the bucket down all the way to the deck and the sail was scooped into the sock bag. All that was left was to lower the sail in its bag to the deck in a controlled fashion. I am pleased with my little invention.

7pm: I may have fixed the slow speed issue. I ran the engine for a while on full power to get the boat crashing through the waves. On full power the bow of the boat seemed to be in a higher nose attitude than normal with the stern more dug in, which is odd. After some minutes crashing into the waves the speed over the ground on the GPS jumped back up to normal, so it looked like I was towing a big clump of seaweed after all. While the engine was on full power, I noticed the engine oil pressure is a little low, 58psi at 2100RPM. Hmm, let's hope I am not moving into engine problems. I am back sailing tonight and making 4.1 knots with just 9 knots of wind from the south west, the usual speed I would expect.

It is that time again, the clock moving ceremony, which is an enjoyable routine as you feel you are making real progress across the Atlantic. The new local time on Esperanza is 9.40pm. The weather today went from rain in the morning to sunshine in the afternoon. Tonight it is back again to thick fog with very little wind. Looking at the latest weather it has all changed again. The weather ahead is looking dodgier from Monday as a new low-pressure depression is powering its way towards me from the west at 30 knots. It is on a direct course to hit me Monday. That will mean waves as big as houses, I assume. It looks like I will not escape this one. I might keep ahead of the high winds but I am sandwiched between the oncoming low-pressure behind me and the high-pressure in ahead. There is nowhere to run or hide, I will just have to deal with it. Didn't I say I wanted to experience some fast and furious sailing? Here it comes.

My ETA is shifting around due to the changing winds. It could be anywhere from Wednesday 12th to Friday 14th June. I have fuel so I can motor sail the last couple of days if I need to keep the speed up, but what's the rush? I am fine as long as I get to Horta before my family arrives. I am more relaxed these days and I am enjoying the journey rather than fixating on arriving and the destination. I am feeling very happy tonight. The boat is sailing nicely at 5.9 knots with a lovely steady motion.

2am: I am awake, the jib sail is flapping with the changing wind, causing the jib sheet/rope to flick around on the deck, which sounds like the cracking of a whip below in the cabin. This is keeping me awake, very irritating. The wind is flaky so to ensure some sleep I roll in the jib and continue on just the mainsail downwind. I should have put up the two poled jibs before night-time. I will do this in the morning. I am still making 5 knots on the mainsail alone.

4.45am: I am up again in the cockpit to check things, all well, but the motion is a bit rolly with just the mainsail out. 657 miles to Horta, 5-days to go. For breakfast I would love an Irish fry with baked beans, a mug of tea and toast. That would hit the spot on this damp morning.

Day 17: 7th June 2019 - *Storm preparation as low pressure storms towards me at 30 knots*
N40° 32' W42° 03'

It is storm preparation day. I got the storm jib out and attached it to the inner forestay wire, ready to hoist if required. The storm jib is a small bright orange sail that is very strong. Its purpose is helping the boat to keep some forward momentum into the waves in storm conditions. It is important to take the breaking waves at the bow of the boat which is the strongest point and not to allow breaking waves to hit the side or beam of the boat, which could roll the boat upside down. It would be bad luck to get wiped out a few days before I am due to arrive in Azores. I am feeling a little anxious, as I have not had any bad weather yet on this trip, and this morning's weather shows that even higher winds are on the way than forecast last night. I can see the bad weather on the horizon behind me, as a dark black skyline. I am trying to keep the speed up to see if I can run ahead of the depression.

I have the parachute anchor also rigged, which I can drop into the sea from the cockpit, to hold the bow to wind if I feel conditions are getting too much for me or the boat. I can then ride out the storm below in the cabin. I have never launched or tested this system. The big decision is at what point does one decide to launch it. If I launch too late in the height of the storm, it may be far too dangerous to go up to the bow to make adjustments. You would more likely be washed overboard as 20 foot plus waves crash over the boat. It is unlikely I will need to use the parachute anchor but it feels good to have it in my storm arsenal.

As I am preparing the boat for the bad weather a pod of dolphins drops by. There are small baby dolphins with their parents swimming, jumping and frolicking around the bow of the boat. Later that morning the wind decreased to 6 knots, the calm before the storm. I have slowed down in the last 24 hours, covering just 125 miles. By lunchtime the wind has picked up again and the speed is back up to 5 knots. By dinner time it is back to no wind at all and I have to turn on the engine. It looks to be a motor sail through the night when I thought I was back to pure sailing for the rest of the trip. Tonight my stomach feels a bit iffy; being over tired can't help. A good idea would be for me to keep a sleep log to monitor how much sleep I am actually getting. I am aware from my flying training of the danger of exhaustion – it has been the cause of many accidents, mistakes and bad decisions. I am napping during the day but it is more dozing and I am not falling asleep. I will cut down on my coffee intake and move to decaf to see if this helps.

Reading up on Horta, it looks like a nice small port town. I am looking forward to exploring and pottering around. I can see myself sitting in a coffee shop having a custard donut or a Portuguese Pasteis de Nata custard tart. Now that I am thinking of food, a burger and chips would be lovely for dinner, washed down with a pint of ale. I do need to eat lots of salad when I arrive as my diet is low on greens.

3am: I was woken in my bunk as I felt the speed increasing and the boat accelerating, which means wind. Up I get, engine off and sails out. I am back to sailing and back to bed. I feel at one with the boat and know instantly when she needs me to do something for her.

Day 18: 8th June 2019 - *Near disaster as I could not find the spare oil filter*
N40° 35' W39° 56'

I slept well last night which was just what I needed. There are a number of ships now showing on AIS as I get nearer the Azores. I have set the AIS alarm to 3 miles, so any vessel that comes within that radius will sound the alarm, which is loud enough to wake me from the deepest sleep. I got the cruising chute up before breakfast. Breakfast this morning was cereal, tinned fruit, coffee, an odd tasting French yogurt and, to round it off, a mini size chocolate bar. There is no point in starving myself. It is cooler again this morning and I need to wear a fleece and woolly hat. The daily run was 122 miles. By lunchtime I am flying along directly to Horta. I couldn't be happier when sailing fast in the right direction, especially when the sun is shining. On deck this morning I found a small squid looking at me with his big black eyes. I flung him back to sea as I found he had no ticket for the voyage.

I was wondering about the lower than usual oil pressure so I decided to do some engine maintenance and checks today. First, I removed and cleaned the air filter. I checked the oil level and it was low at just half full. Is this the cause of the low oil pressure reading? I added engine oil to bring the level to full. I will change both the fuel filters in case they are clogged with dirt, reducing the fuel flow and engine power. I am not sure this would lead to a lower than usual oil pressure reading, I doubt it, but I might as well try it. I am not an expert on engines but I can service my own engine, which is an essential for a sailor.

As I was changing the fuel filter there was a near disaster. After figuring out which way to unscrew the filter, I eventually got it off but, in the process, destroyed it. I went to get the spare filter but I could not find one! Oh my God, don't tell me I have run out of spares. If I do not have a new filter, I can't start the engine for the rest of the trip. This is really bad and once again I am kicking myself. Normally I would first gather the spare parts that I require before starting the job to make sure I have the spares. I am panicking, pulling out and opening all the boxes of spares. There are three different types of fuel filters on this boat and I have plenty of the other two types. My heart is pounding with dread that maybe there is no spare fuel filter onboard. I thought I checked this in Guadeloupe months ago but must have missed this. Silly of me to be sailing the Atlantic without spare filters! I should have spare filters onboard as it is common for dirt in the fuel tank to clog filters in rough seas. An hour later and with every spares box opened I found the very last filter. I am saved. I fitted the filter successfully and all is well.

I needed a break after that stressful morning and near disaster, so I had a refreshing cold glass of Coke in the cockpit. This afternoon's job is to wash the pillowcases and sheets as they are ingrained with salt; at times it feels like I am lying on pieces of broken glass, a horrible prickly feeling. I put up a makeshift clothesline from the canopy to the backstay and I peg out the washing where it dries in the breeze and sunshine. Although you never really get all the salt out, as the air itself is salty. While I am at it, I treat myself to a hot shower as I have plenty of water reserves. Lovely to feel the hot water again and wash away the salty sea dog feeling.

All day I am seeing fantastic speeds of 7-8 knots from the cruising chute. It will soon be dark and the cruising chute has to come down even though it is performing so well. I do not want another night of having to drop the sail in a panic in the dark. The winds are also increasing in line with the forecast. I can expect to see 30 knots of wind soon. The low-pressure depression, which is trundling towards me like a steam train has been upgraded to a full gale. The eye of the storm is clearly shown on the satellite image, it is a big system with gale Force 9 winds near the centre. The good news is that its track has changed slightly as it is being forced more to the northeast because of the blocking high-pressure ahead of me. Extending from the Low is a front, which is also chasing me with 35 knots winds. The Jetstream is going to take it eventually towards Ireland. I need to keep moving or this thing will catch me.

Dinner time and I am making a Thai green veg curry with an assortment of tinned vegetables. I am serving this with boiled rice. Yum, a spicy curry hits the spot in the cooler evenings. I must say rice is very nice on an ocean passage and not something I would have considered before. After dinner it is time for a mug of tea and a biscuit or two or three. I will read in the cockpit this evening and listen to BBC World Service. Movie time tonight is The Bodyguard, an English drama series, with a Ti Punch rum drink. Today can be summed up as lovely speed, lovely evening and lovely smooth motion. I am very happy and lucky to be here. By midnight it has all changed! The sea has whipped itself up into a frenzy, it is rough sailing from here on in. The stronger winds are catching me, the cold front will be over Esperanza tomorrow. It feels as if I am moving into a new chapter in the journey, the time for fast and furious sailing. Back to bed in the rough seas.

Day 19: 9th June 2019 - *In the groove: carving through the waves at 7 knots*
N40° 31' W36° 32'

6am: I am already up and out of the bunk. The daily 24-hour run is improving, 148 miles. The plan is to keep going as fast as possible so this gale does not catch me. The centre of the gale is now located 300 miles to the north of my position at 45N 38W. The Azores High is centred right over the Azores, which is protecting me as I sail the edge of the high-pressure. This is going to develop into a full-blown storm.

Caribbean to the Azores

6pm: I have had to put another reef in the mainsail as the winds have increased. That is three reefs in now. I am listening again to Santa Maria Air Traffic Control talking to overflying transatlantic aircraft. Like the aircraft, I am flying along, with my speed showing a steady 7 knots. It is a bouncy ride and the boat is well healed over on its port side from the moderate wind. I am very impressed with the boat speed. Dinner is simple tonight, garlic bread with leftover curry from yesterday. I am taking a more southerly course as I curve down around the top of the high-pressures to the Azores.

10pm: the Honda generator is running nicely, pumping 40 amps an hour into the batteries. I spoke on the HF radio to a Radio Amateur called Sergey in St Petersburg, Russia, call-sign RW1F. Even with today's abundance of modern technologies I still find it fascinating that I can talk around the world using just radio waves. The only equipment you need is a transceiver and a set length of any old bit wire for the aerial. The radio enthusiasts get their real buzz from experimenting with new equipment and aerials. For many it is all about 'DXing', making contacts with far away stations and getting a radio report as to signal strength and readability.

3am: the wind has woken me as it has risen to 25 knots. Esperanza is in her element, carving through the waves at 7 knots. The sea is angry, I can hear waves breaking on the hull. An hour later the wind is 30 knots. It feels like I am in a washing machine. I am beating into the wind and waves. I got up once again to reef the sails some more. It is wild out there, even in the darkness you can see the white boiling water all around the boat. Best not to look and get down below back to bed. George the autopilot is handling the boat very well. Slam bang, slam bang, slam bang is the pattern as the boat crashes into a wave, slows down a little and then accelerates away until the next wave. When a wave crashes on the bow, the boat shudders and mast vibrates. The poor boat is taking such a pounding. Will she hold up to this punishment, I wonder? I remind myself that Esperanza is a Hallberg Rassy, built for the ocean. She is as strong and sturdy as you can get.

Day 20: 10th June 2019 - *Speed record for Esperanza: 164 miles in 24 hours, average speed of 6.8 knots*
N39° 27' W33° 26'

11am: no real sleep last night as it was so rough. I think it was the roughest that I have experienced in my sailing career, that is all I can say! The wind continues to rise, now Force 8 gusting 9. I am still flying along at 7 knots with the sails heavily reefed. I am bashing into big breaking white crested waves, which look bigger in daytime than night-time. The motion is very uncomfortable, the boat is like a bronco horse, up and down, side to side, bang, slam, bang. This is the joys of sailing, I tell myself, as I jam myself into a corner and use all my muscles to stay there. Though I don't feel seasick at all. How long is this going to last, I wonder? I need to see what is going on with the weather. The Global Maritime Distress and Safety System (GMDSS) forecast shows southeast winds Force 4 or 5 and rough seas. These are average wind speeds; the actual wind speed can be 40% higher and the maximum actual wave size can be twice the forecast height. That is not very reassuring... The rule of thumb is to add half the wind speed onto forecast winds to get a more accurate picture of what to expect in the Atlantic.

I was considering raising the storm jib as it is perfect conditions for this strong sail but there is no way now that I can go safely on deck, as the waves are crashing over the bow and flooding tonnes of seawater down onto the deck. If I went up there, I would most likely be washed away. The bow of the boat is a very scary place to be in rough seas. Why do I bother having a storm sail when I can't get up to the bow to hoist it? The sail needs to be put up before the strong winds kick in, but Force 8 winds were not forecast, so how was I to know. Safety items on the boat make a lot of sense from the comfort of an armchair back at home but out in the raging Atlantic the practicalities are a very different story. In these conditions I have the jib sail reefed to the size of a handkerchief and the mainsail reefed to the size of a pillowcase.

This morning I am sitting in the cockpit huddled under the canopy looking through the glass windscreen in total protection from the waves. I am in awe at the wildness of the sea, the sure ferocity of the waves, which seem to never tire in their attacks. One of the best design features of a Hallberg Rassy yacht is this solid glass windscreen offering excellent protection from the elements and super clear visibility.

Last night from my bunk I heard dolphins swimming underwater with the boat. At first, I thought I was imagining it, but I could hear high-pitched whistles, which were dolphins swimming alongside the hull. I never thought I would hear them from inside the boat, but it makes sense as when I am in the bunk, I am just a couple of inches from the ocean outside. Amazing to be so close to my friends, the dolphins who visit me regularly on these ocean passages. The dolphin singing lasted about 5 minutes and then they were off. The longer I am out here the more the sea becomes part of me and me of the sea.

4pm: I have jammed myself at the navigation table with my feet up on the side of the engine bay door to stop myself being flung onto the floor as it is so rough. My daily distance sailed is the best ever in my sailing career, 164 miles in 24 hours. This is an impressive average speed of 6.8 knots, which is very fast for my boat. It is a new record for Esperanza. I spend some time on the wheel steering through the white-water waves but it gets tiring after an hour so I put George the autopilot back on. George has so much stamina, I wonder where he gets it from. I cannot believe it is only 201 miles to go to, I am nearly there. Very

Caribbean to the Azores

soon yachts should be popping up all around the horizon as we are all converging on Horta. It is too rough for any kind of cooking so dinner is cancelled. It is so rough I can't even boil the kettle. This is the first time on a boat I have not been able to make a cup of coffee due to sea conditions. The ability to boil the kettle or not has become my new metaphor to describe how rough the sea is.

5pm: the wind is reducing as the low-pressure system moves off to the northeast. Thank God for that, as I had enough. The wind has dropped back to a more manageable 25 knots but the sea is still rough. I would not like to be on route to Ireland as in 48 hours this storm will hit Ireland with 50 knot winds and 24-foot seas forecast. These are averages, you could get 40-foot waves – the height of three double decker buses – bearing down on you. I am sitting in the cockpit keeping more of a lookout than usual as I near the Azores. Suddenly I see a big black thing in the water not too far away to starboard. I grab the binoculars and have a look. It is a floating pontoon, made up of plastic cubes that you attach together. What the hell is this doing out here? It must have broken away from a marina in the Azores. It was big enough that I could have gone alongside and tied up to the pontoon, stepped off and claimed it as salvage. I am not sure what I would do with a floating pontoon. It would be funny to tow it behind me into Horta harbour and anchor my own pontoon in the bay with Esperanza.

I am keeping an eye out for whales. From April whales pass by the Azores on their migratory paths. Sperm whales are residents of the Azores all year around. Then, whale! There is a whale on the bow, very close. I can see its black back and blow spray, magnificent. On the HF radio today I am picking up Gander Air Traffic Control from Newfoundland who control the air traffic over the western Atlantic. They are talking to a US military aircraft called Reach 504, which turns out to be a big four-engine C-17 Globemaster transport aircraft from 437th Airlift Wing, South Carolina. I wonder where they are going Europe, Iraq, maybe Afghanistan. I started a new book today, the autobiography of the most famous test pilot in the world, Captain Eric Brown. He has flown more aircraft types than anyone else in history, 487 in total. An amazing career and a surprising long life to 97, considering all the risks involved in test flying. Like the first Atlantic voyage, audiobooks continue to be my best friend at sea, they are the key to keeping loneliness at bay. I have been listening for 19-days to William Boyd's novel Waiting for Sunrise, an excellent story. The narrator Robert Ian MacKenzie has become my traveling companion on the crossing.

I have the Azores pilot book out and I am studying the approach to Horta. The first sign you are near the Azores is that you will see the volcanic island of Pico, the tallest point around this part of the Atlantic at 7,713 feet or 2,351 metres. Pico is the youngest of the Azores' nine volcanic islands and twice the height of any other peaks in the Azores. It can be seen 50 miles away sticking up on the horizon guiding the way. Columbus mentions Pico in his logbook. I am looking forward to seeing land again, after 21 days. It is a special feeling that only long-distance sailors will understand. I will keep a watch on the horizon for Pico.

Horta on the island of Faial is one of the four busiest harbours in the world for yacht transits. 1,300 boats a year pass through Horta, most on their way across the Atlantic. I hope the bar will be busy and full of sailors with great stories to share. Nothing beats sailing stories and beer. The more beer, the better the stories! Shay from my hometown Dun Laoghaire has left today from Lisbon for the Azores in his Rival 36 yacht. We plan to meet Monday in Horta, which will be great fun. I haven't seen another yacht in days so I'm looking forward to seeing some on the horizon tonight or tomorrow. There must be many boats out here heading for the Azores, I just can't see them yet.

Tomorrow will be my last full day at sea! I can't believe it is coming to an end. I hope I can get into the marina and it is not full. Ideally, I don't want to have to raft up to other boats, which means 3-4 boats all tied together and the inner one tied to the marina. To get off you have to cross over the decks of the other boats, which on a positive note means there are lots of opportunities for conversation and to make new friends. But rafting gets messy when the inner boat wants to leave as all the outer boats have to untie their lines to get out of the way and then come back to reform the raft. Not easy to do when you are on your single-handed. I am getting a little anxious about coming into a new marina, as I have no idea what to expect. The pilot book has basic information on Horta, but until I see the harbour with my own eyes I am sailing into the unknown. I called home and Sonya, who speaks Portuguese, called the marina to see if I can book a berth. They laughed and said the marina is completely full. Boats are rafted four abreast, it has been a record year for visiting boats. There is no room at the inn for Esperanza. Anchoring inside the harbour will be the only option, c'est la vie. That will mean pumping up the dinghy again, which is a bit of a pain, as I thought those days were over and it would be marinas all the way to Portugal.

The beer supplies are holding up, so I can have two small bottles of beer with the film. On the HF radio I have found a French station teaching English, funny to listen to. Midnight and the latest weather forecast is that the wind is expected to reduce overnight to 13 knots and then further drop to 10 knots tomorrow. 154 miles to go. ETA is Wednesday 12th June at midday, which is perfect as it will be daylight. The speed is good, between 5 and 6 knots. I have purposely slowed the boat down, which I hope will allow me to sleep through the night. I need to build sleep reserves, as I won't be able to sleep at all once I get closer to the Azores. Hopefully I will not need to get up to reduce sail during the night.

Caribbean to the Azores

Day 21: 11th June 2019 - *Last full day at sea, I arrive tomorrow in the Azores*
N38° 40' W30° 45'

6.45am: today is my last full day at sea. It feels a bit like a dream to be arriving so soon. I am now abeam the island of Flores but I can't see it, as it is 40 miles away. I slept well but had mad dreams that I was flying through the sky and using the sails to control my height and direction. It must be from all the flying that I am reading about in the test pilot book. Just 99 miles to go on a cloudy day with thunderstorms forecast. I fish out the Portuguese courtesy flag from my big box of ever multiplying flags. I need to have it ready to fly from the starboard side of the mast before I get to Horta. The rule is you fly the flag of the country you are visiting as a token of respect, a tradition that goes back hundreds of years. Every boat does this, from the smallest yacht to the huge super tankers. I also get out the yellow Q flag, which I must display until I have cleared customs in the Azores. While it was relatively calm, I went to the bow to get the anchor out of the locker and attach it to the bow roller so it is ready to drop in the anchorage.

10.30am: the wind had dropped back down to 12 knots and boat speed had reduced to 5.4 knots. My ETA has come forward to 8am tomorrow. I will be arriving in time for breakfast. Here we go, yachts are starting to pop up on AIS. I see a UK yacht with the memorable name Bloodshot on the horizon to port. A bird arrived overhead and started screaming at me, I could hear it shouting at me in the cabin. I went up to see what the fuss was about and watched it circling the boat squawking. It then made a nice precision landing on the solar cell. A chatty bird, I am happy to take it on as a passenger. It is the first bird I have seen in I don't know how long. I have no idea what the name of the bird is but it is small and black in colour. Then its friend arrived and also made a landing on the solar cell. Sorry guys, I have no bread to give you, it was all gone days ago. There is still no weather text on the Navtex screen, which is blank. I wonder if it is working properly. It is not essential as I have the satellite weather but it would be nice to see the local forecast broadcast from the Azores.

I am thinking how I will get on in Horta when I arrive; it will be my first time walking in 22 days. I had no problem walking after my first Atlantic crossing to Caribbean. First thing I desperately need when I arrive is a long hot shower to wash all the salt off. Then all the bed linen and my clothes need washing – that will be one big laundry day. Oh, the thought of soft sheets and pillows washed with fabric softener is heaven! I never considered the benefits of fabric softener before, now it has a special place in my heart. I see this crossing as a real achievement. It has been difficult, not from the storms I was expecting but from the lack of wind and the stress of deciding on the best routing. My view is anyone can cross the Atlantic once, which I did on the way out to the Caribbean but to do it again on the way back means it is more than just luck. A French sailor in Guadeloupe was correct when he said the return trip to the Azores requires real sailing skills. You do have to sail the boat much more on the return trip, adjusting and tweaking the sails in the lighter winds. I now feel I am a real sailor after my double Atlantic.

5pm: the VHF marine radio is alive and busy with boats and ships calling. I am picking up AIS signals from the many yachts at anchor in Horta harbour. It looks busy, I hope there is room for Esperanza in the anchorage. With 50 miles to go, there is no sign of the 2,351-metre-high volcano island of Pico, which is lost in the low cloud. This is disappointing as I really wanted to see it on the horizon. The wind has increased to 17 knots from the south east. It is a gusty unstable wind so I am trying to keep my heading towards Horta and not get blown into the rocky shoreline. I can see squall clouds ahead so I reefed the mainsail in preparation. There are now five other yachts sailing with me converging on Horta. It is exciting to see all these yachts sailing to the same destination on the same adventure. It feels like a race and maybe it is not a bad idea to get into the harbour first in case there is little room left in the anchorage. Closest to me are the following yachts: Bloodshot from the UK and same size as Esperanza at 36 feet; Kairos from the Netherland at just 32 feet; and Aura a 39-footer from Martinique.

Day 22: 12th June 2019 - *Arrival Horta on Faial, Azores*
N38° 32' W28° 37'

1am: in just 28 miles I turn north around the bottom corner of the island of Faial for Horta harbour, which is one hour further up the coast. Bloodshot the UK yacht has been converging from the south and is now just 2 miles to starboard. I can clearly see her port light. I have to watch that we do not collide. There won't be any sleep tonight. I was going to call on the radio but it is too late at night and I do not want to disturb him or her.

4am: I am one mile off the coast of Faial island. I can see the lights on the island and at the airport. I switched the deck light on and let out some more sail for a little extra speed. I am making a comfortable 5 knots. Bloodshot is close to port and I see he has also switched on his deck light. It looks like he is copying me and letting out more sail as well to increase his speed. Is he racing me, I wonder? He may have the same idea, to get to Horta first to win the prize of the best anchorage spot. The race is on, so let's see who will get there first. We are neck and neck and less than a half a quarter of a mile separation between us.

6am: I have rounded the headland south east of Faial. There is less than an hour to go and I decide to bring the sails in and prepare the boat for arrival. I will engine the last hour to recharge the batteries before I arrive on anchor. Bloodshot has fallen close behind my stern and is following. I slow down to allow dawn to break as I do not want to be dropping anchor in the dark in a congested harbour.

6.40am: I am passing the lighthouse at the end of the pier at Horta harbour. Into the harbour we go towards the marina. Dawn is breaking and there are boats anchored everywhere in the harbour. I have never seen so many boats in such a confined area. A guy is waving at me from the marina. I have my radio on and he calls Esperanza to say the marina is full and I am to anchor across from a white building. The pilot book says the holding can be questionable and watch out for old chains on the seabed that were used to anchor seaplanes in 1930/40's. The PanAm Clipper flying boat used to stop at Horta on its route between America and Europe. I find a free spot in the anchorage close to the marina. There is no wind in the harbour, the water is lovely and still. Not a sound to be heard as everyone is still in bed. I walk to the bow and drop the anchor in 6 metres of water. I have arrived in the Azores! The boats at the marina are only 100 metres from me and rafted four abreast. There must be a hundred boats at anchor in the harbour. Sitting in the cockpit and not feeling the motion of the boat moving is very strange.

12th June 2018 is the conclusion to a 22-day transatlantic crossing covering 2,655 miles, 4,917Km. My route ended up 405 miles longer than the original direct route from Guadeloupe and Horta, Azores. This is the extra distance from my decision to go north to find wind and having to take the curved route around the top of the high-pressure to the Azores. I burnt in total 300 litres of fuel and have 210 litres remaining on arrival. In comparison, the crossing from Lanzarote to Bequia took 23-days, covering more distance, 3,057 miles. A successful trip but a difficult voyage. What I need now is rest and recuperation. Here comes Bloodshot, now I can get a good look at the skipper; it is a guy who looks single-handed like myself. We wave to each other as he passes by and he anchors just in front of me. We are the only two people awake in the harbour. I am off to bed feeling at peace with the world, having arrived safe and sound and achieved my goal. I have done it and I look forward to getting ashore to explore.

Horta — *the island of Faial, Azores*

After a few hours of rest, I am itching to go ashore and I can't sleep. It is time to get the dinghy out, inflate it and put the engine on. Bloodshot has been busy, here he comes in his dinghy back to his boat from being ashore to clear-in to the Azores. It looks like he has already been ashore. He comes over and I invite him onboard for a cup of tea. Phil, the skipper is English and at 45 the same age as me. He has sailed from Bermuda. We had a great chat about our trip. We laughed as we discussed our arrival last night. I was right, he was trying to race me, as he saw that I had put my deck light on to let out more sail, so he did the same. I knew immediately I would get on with Phil, the Atlantic had bonded two strangers together. We both have a lot to celebrate and plan that evening to visit

Peter's Cafe Sport, the bar that all the sailors go to when they arrive. Single-handed solo sailors are a rarity, so it was good to talk with someone who understood what it is all about.

Horta is a magical place. Everyone in the small town is there to support the visiting yachts and sailors that pass through each year. Even tourists are brought down to the harbour to be shown the boats in the marina and all the boat names painted on the harbour walls. The tradition is that when you successfully complete an Atlantic crossing, you have earned the right to leave your mark in Horta and add your boat name. Every inch of the harbour walls are covered with painted names from all the boats that have passed through Horta over the years. It is fascinating to walk around and look at this art from simple boat names to elaborative murals and illustrations, from every nationality. I painted the name Esperanza on the pier wall on the island of Porto Santo, Madeira to mark the start of the Atlantic. Now I will paint Esperanza's name again and the Irish flag in Hora to mark the successful completion of my Atlantic voyage.

Peter's Cafe Sport pub is probably the most famous bar in the world for sailors. It was established in 1918 to cater for sailing boats crossing the Atlantic. I had read about Peter's pub many times in all the different sailing books so it was the one place I wanted to always visit but only after I had successfully completed my Atlantic. It felt special to be now here, eating a steak and drinking cold beer. I had earned the privilege. The walls of Peter's pub are covered in flags of all the nationalities of boats that have passed through Horta. I left my mark, adding an Irish flag hanging on the wall with Esperanza 2019 written on it. In return they gave me a Peter's Cafe flag. I was delighted.

For our first night ashore Phil and I planned to go out early so we could be back on our boats early as we were both exhausted. It was a good intention but we did not get back to the boats until 3am. We met up with other sailors and the night rolled on and on. It was a superb night with many wild and bizarre sailing stories shared at the bar. We met a Dutch drug running sailor, an Irish shipwrecked sailor and many interesting lost souls propping up the bar. I found out that Phil also had Netflix onboard and spent his evenings down below in the cabin watching movie after movie. You would wonder how many other boats are doing this with no one maintaining a look out…

Squall time and more Flying Fish on deck.

Becalmed in the Atlantic, time for a swim in 4km deep water.

The Nav table is the centre of operations while at sea. I am writing the logbook, plotting my position and checking the weather.
Below: Cruising chute flying in light Atlantic winds.

Another lovely sunset, a daily occurrence at sea.

Portuguese Man of War, hundreds floated by the boat.

Honda generator charging the batteries each day to save fuel.

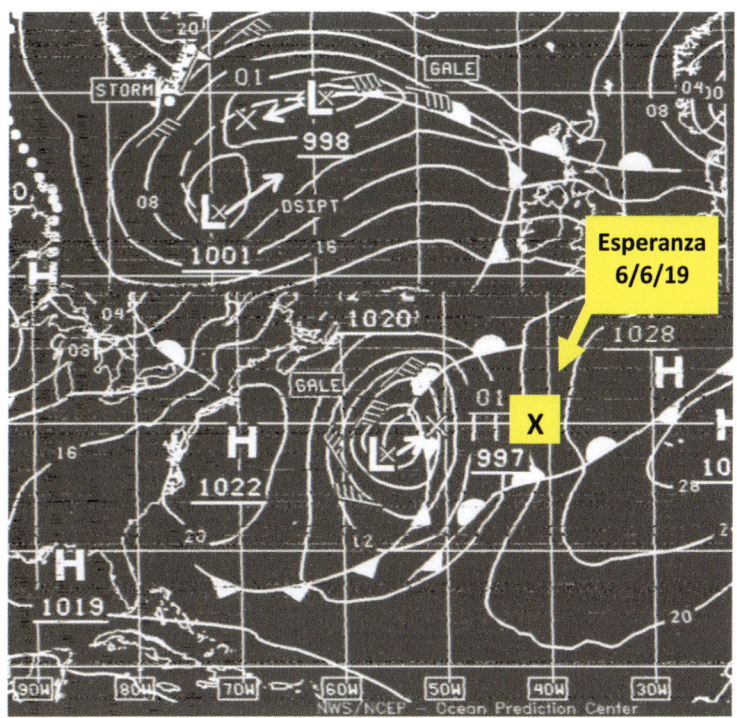

Above: 6th June, weather chart downloaded from the HF radio, showing the 987mb low-pressure system chasing Esperanza. Below: wind chart downloaded from Iridium satellite to PredictWind app. Strong winds are shown in dark red and heading for Azores. I am going fast to keep ahead of the storm.

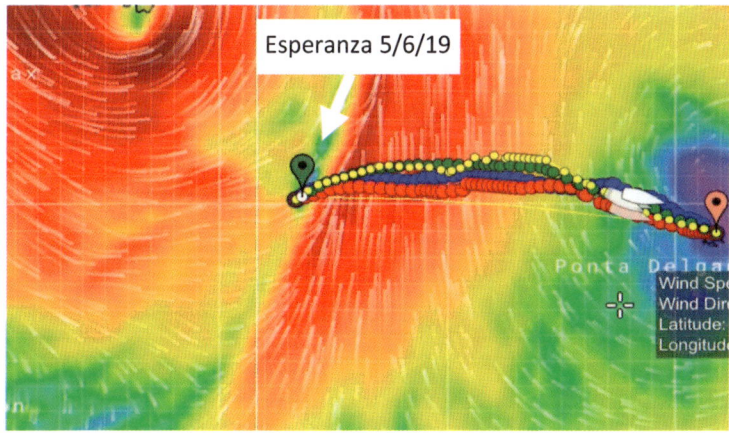

Above: Reading a book about Solitude in solitude...
Across: Some type of Whale

Large floating pontoon from a marina passed close to Esperanza near the Azores. A real collision risk.

Day 22: 12th June 2019 arrived on anchor at Horta, on the island of Faial, Azores. 2,655 miles sailed.

Irish flag added to the flag collection in Peter Café Sport, Horta.

Esperanza's name painted on the harbour wall in Horta.

Phil from UK yacht Bloodshot who I met in the Azores.

Island of Sao Jorge.

Above: Azores island of San Miguel.
Across: swimming pools on Santa Maria.
Below right: Camping on the island of Santa Maria.

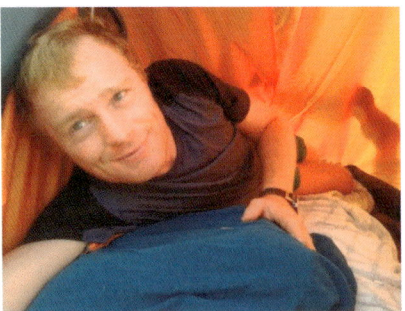

The arch window frame of the chapel Columbus visited in Santa Maria, after his first Atlantic voyage to the Caribbean, when he was on his way home to Europe.

CHAPTER 7

Azores to Portugal mainland

My first few days in the Azores were lazy. I enjoyed walking around the town, exploring the beach and the headland. My treat after 22-days at sea, was to visit a cafe for a Portuguese Bica coffee and a number of custard tarts. Phil and I had many late nights in the two bars in Horta chatting with other sailors and locals. I heard a big storm was coming to hit the Azores. Boats were leaving Horta to get to the other islands or trying to get onto the overcrowded marina for added protection. I decided to stay in the same spot at anchor. I let out more chain to increase the holding strength. Shay, who is sailing his boat Adrigole from Lisbon to Azores, was due to arrive in Horta on Sunday but he called me on the phone when passing the island of Sao Miguel for weather advice. The sensible option was to pull into the marina at Ponta Delgada on Sao Miguel and let the storm go through. When the storm hit, I could not get off the boat until lunchtime as it was too rough inside the harbour for the dinghy.

My family arrived from Dublin and we spent two nights in a nice hotel, which for me was pure luxury. I found it initially difficult to sleep in such a soft bed. From the hotel room I could see Esperanza anchored in the harbour. It felt odd to be sleeping in a hotel leaving Esperanza all alone in the harbour. I was already missing my sea home. After exploring the island of Faial, we sailed to the next island, Sao Jorge and spent a day exploring. This island had lovely sea swimming pools built into the rocky shoreline. We then had a longer eleven-hour sail to Praia Vitoria on the island of Terceira. This is a great location for aeroplane spotters as we are anchored under the approach to the Lajes Field US Air Force base. During World War II it was a very active military airfield being a key stopover refuelling base for transatlantic aircraft. The base still has the same function today. I saw C-17 Globemasters, Hercules Transport aircraft, as well as Hercules Gunships and fighter jets all coming and going as they made Terceira their fuel stop before crossing the Atlantic.

My family flew home from Terceira and I sailed onto Angra do Heroismo, the capital of Terceira, a beautiful small city. It was festival week and I watched a traditional bull fight in the streets. Then it was an overnight 90-mile sail to the biggest island in the Azores, Sao Miguel, where Shay was with his boat Adrigole. I spent 16-days on the marina in Ponta Delgada, which is the capital of Sao Miguel. I was back to work so I worked remotely during the day and explored the island in the evenings and on the weekends. I hiked all corners of the island, swam in natural hot springs and ate dinner cooked in a pit in the ground by the volcanic steam. Of all the islands in the Azores, Sao Miguel probably has the most to offer from sandy beaches to lush green forest hikes in the volcanic mountains.

On my last weekend, I borrowed a tent and took the 3-hour ferry ride to the island of Santa Maria. This is the warmest of the Azores islands with the least rainfall and nicest beaches. I wanted to see this island for two reasons. Columbus on his return from finding the Caribbean in 1493 took shelter with his crew from a storm on Santa Maria. His ship was not given friendly treatment by the residents as they thought Columbus was a pirate. Some of his crew were captured and complex negotiations were undertaken to free them. On return of the crew a mass was held to celebrate in the small church in the village of Anjos. All that remains of the original chapel Columbus visited is a ruined ornate window arch. I stood by the window arch in the same place Columbus had stood over 500 years ago. We both made the same voyage across the Atlantic to the Caribbean and back to Europe via the Azores. My route closely followed his. My second reason for visiting Santa Maria was to see the location of Santa Maria Atlantic Air Traffic Control, which I had listened to, while crossing the Atlantic. It was a great weekend and I enjoyed sleeping in a tent again, after what must be 20 years. Time to get back to Ponta Delgada as the crew will be arriving soon for the final leg of the trip.

17th July 2018

It is departure day and the final leg of the Atlantic circuit. I am sailing with one crew member, Heather King, to mainland Portugal, 820 miles. I will have the boat lifted out of the water at Faro for the winter and finally end my 13-month adventure. With just two crew, for 6-days we will be on a 4-hour rotating watch system: 4 hours on duty and 4 hours off to relax and sleep. The weather forecast is for light winds initially. It is hot and sunny, which makes for pleasant sailing. I am back on holiday again for 10 days. I am looking forward to switching off the laptop and switching off from work.

On the first day, as we sailed along the coast off Sao Miguel, we came across a big sperm whale. It popped up just 200 metres from the boat so we cut the engine and watched it gracefully moving through the water. As we got nearer, the whale started to circle the boat. It was about 15 metres long, longer than the boat. At one stage it went vertical in the water with its head sticking upwards in the water. We are sure the whale was watching us. The whale spent 30 minutes with us and got very close but we never felt in danger. In the end it flipped its tail and dived down deep to the depths. It was gone with one impressive tail flick as a goodbye. This was my first close encounter with a whale and it was a stunning experience. They are such graceful creatures. This is their ocean and we are the visitors.

We saw seven turtles paddling by, all heading west. I wonder where they were going, do they even have a destination in mind? There is plenty of food out there for the turtles as they like to eat the Portuguese Man-of-War.

20th July 2019

On the HF radio, I heard NASA broadcasting a special radio message, as today is the 50th anniversary of the first moon landing. In real time they replayed the audio communications from 50 years ago of the moon landing. As we got closer to Europe, BBC Radio 4 could be heard. The news is that Boris Johnson is taking over as Prime Minister from Theresa May who seems to have made a mess of Brexit; a heatwave hits the UK tomorrow; and Iran has taken a UK registered oil tanker captive.

Phil who left the Azores a day before me, is now just 60 miles to the north of our position and we are in contact. We will soon diverge as he is heading north to Cascais, Lisbon. A cargo ship called the Vienna Express passes very close at just 1-mile heading for New York. It is getting busier as we approach Europe. An 800-foot cargo ship was closing in on us. When it did not alter course, I decided I better check they were not all asleep and that they could see Esperanza. I called the ship on the radio, he acknowledged and agreed to maintain separation. It was good to know they were awake.

The weather is very mixed on this trip. It was not all glorious sunshine but there were days of overcast skies, slack winds followed by strong 25 knot winds and rough seas. I am finding the watch system tiring; I can't seem to get enough rest. When I feel tired and I am about to drop off to sleep I need to get up for my watch and let Heather rest. The most important rule in sailing is never be late when coming on watch. I actually feel more tired with the two of us sailing than if I was sailing single-handed. When I am alone, I can manage the boat around my sleep patterns as there is no one waiting for you to come on watch. What works best for me on long voyages is to go single-handed or have a minimum of three people onboard.

Approaching Cape St. Vincent, we had to cross the shipping lanes where there is a traffic separation scheme around the south west coast of Portugal. Just like a motorway, ships going north and west stay in one lane while those going south and east stick to another lane. To cross the shipping lane we waited for a gap between the ships and motored across at right angles.

23rd July 2019

Land ahoy! On the horizon is the lighthouse on Cape Saint Vincent. We have 3G phone coverage so we are back in touch with the real world again. I am also back to work today so I am downloading emails at the navigation table while Heather sails. We arrived in Portimao, Portugal after 6.5-days, 840 miles and 88 hours of engine time.

We spent one night in Portimao's overpriced marina and then moved to the lovely anchorage by Ferragudo beach. Over the next few days we leisurely sailed up the coast to Faro. We anchored at Culatra Island, to explore Faro's island beaches before we motored up the mangrove channel to the Faro city anchorage. Heather flew home the next day.

27th July 2019

Esperanza was lifted out at Nave Pegos boatyard, Faro (known as Bruce's yard). My last week in Portugal was all about boat jobs, servicing the engine and waxing the Hallberg Rassy blue line on the hull. I am now in the aeroplane flying home to Dublin and below I can see the boatyard, which is Esperanza's new home until next year and the next adventure.

I completed my dream, a transatlantic single-handed sail to the Caribbean and back. It was 13 months ago, June 2nd, 2018, that I left my home port of Dun Laoghaire in Dublin, Ireland. In total I sailed 9,259 nautical miles or 17,145km. It has been an amazing adventure. I have seen so many new places, experienced many new things and more importantly met such interesting people. The boat lived up to its reputation as a truly seaworthy vessel – she looked after me. The trip has changed me, anything now seems possible. I look forward to spending more quality time with my family but I know I will soon start dreaming of the next adventure, destination unknown. To be continued.

Appendix

Books that inspired me

The below books inspired my adventure and provided information of what to expect:
- The Atlantic Sailor's Handbook, Alastair Buchan, 2009
- The Last Man Across the Atlantic, Paul Heiney 2005
- Where the Ocean Meets the Sky, Crispin Latymer 2009
- Single-handed Sailing, A. Evens, 2014
- World Cruising Club Rally Handbook, World Cruising Club 2017
- Sailing Alone Around the World, Joshua Slocum, 1900

Documents

Photocopy important documents such as passport, boat registration, sailing licence, insurance papers and credit cards and put them in the ditch bag. If I have to abandon ship, I have copies of all the important documents with me.

Money

I can't rely on my Visa debit card working on all the Caribbean islands or even my credit card so I will also bring cash. I decided to bring €1000 Euros and $3000 US Dollars in cash. This can be exchanged for local currency. The US dollar is widely accepted on many of the islands and the Euro is the currency on the French islands. That is a lot of cash to keep on the boat but cash is king and who knows it might buy my way out of trouble. On the boat there is a small safe where I will keep the cash. A good idea is to leave a decoy wallet in the boat. I kept a $100 dollars in a decoy wallet alongside an old passport, so if I was broken into hopefully, they see the wallet and passport, grab them and go.

Power

Start the engine in the evening to charge the batteries for night-time in order to support higher power use at night.

Fill the fridge to its maximum even if it means packing it with water bottles. A full fridge uses less power.

I estimate the boat power usage when sailing will be 230 amps over 24 hours. How I came to this calculation was to switch on each electrical item one at a time and note the power measurement from the boat battery monitor. I then made an estimate of how long each device would be switched on over a 24-hour period. It is surprising how many electrical items are in the boat.

To reduce power consumption at night, all the boat's many light bulbs were changed to low power LEDs. To supplement charging the batteries I will use solar cells, in the Caribbean there will be plenty of sunshine. I added to the existing 45-watt solar panel another 100 watts from the two new solar panels. These were mounted on the davits so they could be tilted towards the sun for maximum energy.

I could not afford to install a diesel generator in the boat so I bought a portable Honda EA10i petrol generator. It had a 16amp waterproof socket so all I had to do for power was plug my usual marina shore power lead from the boat directly into the generator. The generator supplies 220 volts and 900 watts of power to the boat's battery charger producing 30 amps/hour. The generator is the emergency backup. It gives me redundancy and self-sufficiency in the ability to power the boat systems and autopilot, which is crucial when single-handed.

Batteries

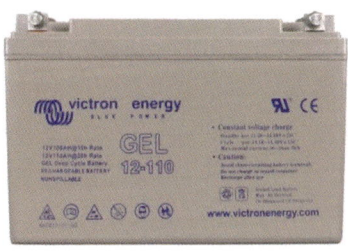

There are multiple battery options from common lead acid to deep cycle Gel or AGM batteries. Lithium batteries were very expensive so not an option. Gel batteries have the advantage that you can discharge them to a higher percentage than lead acid, which means they have a longer use time between charges. Decision made, I purchased four Gel deep cycle Victron batteries at a total cost of €1000 plus vat. There is peace of mind to start my voyage with a complete set of new batteries. Combined this will give a battery bank of 440 Amps of power. I will allow the batteries to discharge to no lower than 50% but no lower to maintain long battery life. When sailing I will recharge the batteries with the engine to 80%. Keeping the batteries between 50% and 80% gives a useful power 110 amps between charges.

The boat engine drives two separate alternators for redundancy. The first is the original alternator to charge the starting battery. The second is a more powerful Balmar alternator, which I added last year, to charge the four systems batteries. The Balmar alternator can produce up to 150 amps per hour. The maximum charge rate the batteries will accept is approximately 25% of total battery capacity. In my case the systems battery bank will accept up to 110 amps of charge per hour. To make up the 240 amps of power used over 24 hours, I will run the engine to charge the batteries twice per day, in the morning and again in the evening.

Weather & Routing

When planning a sailing trip, the actual distance sailed is likely to be 20% further, be prudent and allow for additional time, fuel, water and food.

The trade winds are the driving force when sailing across the Atlantic. These are permanent east to west winds in the equatorial region between latitude 30N and 30S. They are the winds used by sailing ships for centuries to cross the Atlantic. The trick is to find the trade winds as they move north and south depending on the time of year. The advice is to sail south to a latitude of around 20N where one should find the trade winds, then turn west and allow the trade winds to push the boat to the Caribbean. To follow the old sailing ship's advice, 'head south till the butter melts'.

It is tempting to try to sail directly to the Caribbean but by going south first has advantages: picking up the trade winds earlier; it gets warmer faster as every day you are 2 degrees of latitude further south; and the weather and sea conditions are usually more pleasant. The risk in taking a more direct route is that you sail into the Horse latitudes, located at about 30N. Here the winds are too light to sail and a horrible Atlantic swell rolls the boat side to side. Going too far south puts you into the Intertropical Convergence Zone (ITCZ), also known as the doldrums. Here cumulonimbus thunder clouds suck up all the wind, leaving no wind to sail with lightning and big squalls, an area to be avoided.

I used the Iridium GO satellite system which is fully integrated with the PredictWind Offshore App on my iPad. This allowed me to download GRIB files, weather routing, GMDSS text forecasts and satellite imagery offshore. For $150 per month I had unlimited data and could download weather as often as I liked.

Provisioning

- Remove all cardboard packaging as it can contain cockroach eggs. Instead put food in Ziploc bags and plastic containers. Write on the containers/bags what the food is.
- Wash fruit/veg before bringing onto the boat to remove any bugs, especially if purchased from a local market. I did not do this as my fruit/veg was purchased in the supermarket so assumed it was safe.
- Ziplock bags of various sizes are very useful, not just for food but I used them to organise the bits and pieces in the boat spares box.
- Kitchen Towel is essential for all sorts of clean up jobs including the skipper, bring plenty.
- Many items that we put in the fridge at home, don't need to be chilled on the boat: ketchup, mustard, jam, peanut butter, hard cheese, eggs, dried meats are all ok to store in a locker.
- Upgrading to a fast boiling kettle saves gas, especially when the kettle is on so often.
- Many sailors I met swear by using a pressure cooker as it cooks food quickly and uses little gas. I hemmed and hawed about the pressure cooker for weeks but never got one in the end due to the limited storage space onboard. Instead I purchased an Omnia Oven for cooking on the gas ring on the stove. This meant I did not have to heat the oven to bake bread.

Food ideas:
- Potatoes, onions, garlic, cabbage, apples, oranges, lemons, limes will last 3 weeks.
- Carrots, cucumber, pineapple, pears, grapefruit lasts 2 weeks.
- Iceberg lettuce, tomatoes, peppers, broccoli, bananas, melon lasts 1 week.
- Rice.
- UHT Long- life milk for breakfast cereal.
- Fried bacon at sea is amazing and as it is vacuum packed it should last weeks.
- Thai green curry sauces are popular with sailors, including myself.
- White cabbage lasts a long time and tastes as good raw when sprinkled with oil, salt and vinaigrette. A bottle of vinaigrette is a must.
- Pita bread is handy, just stuff in some cheese and ham and you have a quick sandwich.
- Tortilla wraps last a long time and are an ideal for sandwiches, as bread won't last more than a few days in the heat of the tropics. Whole Grain bread lasts the longest of all bread types.

- Eggs are great for lunch or dinner. But don't bring any cardboard egg boxes onboard, instead buy plastic egg boxes or wrap in bubble wrap. There is no need to wash or varnish eggs. Don't put eggs in the fridge, they are best kept in a cool dark locker for about 3 weeks. It is a good idea to test the eggs to check they are fresh. Place the egg in a cup of water. If it sinks to the bottom and lies flat on its side, it is a fresh egg. If they are older eggs but still good to eat, they'll stand on one end at the bottom of the cup. If they float to the surface, they're no longer fresh so throw overboard to the fish.
- Alcohol: A sundowner beer is also something to really look forward to during the day.
- Whiskey - I have it always onboard in case of shock or if you just need a little snifter.
- Cooking sauces, soya sauce for dinners.
- Tins of mushrooms, beans, carrots, sweetcorn, peas, beans, tomatoes.
- Flour for baking.
- Fruit - apples, bananas (they don't last long at all), oranges, tangerines.
- Salt and pepper.
- Fresh Garlic spices up any meal.
- Tea and coffee - I stick with instant coffee as it is too much hassle to be roasting real coffee on the stove and it is unlikely to be calm enough for a coffee pot.
- Cakes that are individually wrapped can last weeks, a nice treat to look forward to with a mug of tea in the evening.
- Butter, mayonnaise, olive oil, marmite, mustard.
- Jam, marmalade, peanut butter.
- Nuts, dried fruit and high energy snack bars.
- Biscuits - ginger biscuits are good to keep seasickness at bay. I found plain digestive biscuits are best. Chocolate biscuits just melt in the heat and make a mess.
- Yogurt/mousse - they will last 2 weeks in the fridge. They make a nice treat after any meal.

Water

Turn off the electric water pump for the Atlantic passage and only use the manual pump at the sink. This reduces consumption but also, in the event of a leak all fresh water won't be pumped away without you realising it.

The minimum water allowance per person per day is recommended at 3.5 litres but I don't think this is enough considering the heat of the tropics. The Atlantic Rally Cruise boats used on average 7 litres of water per person per day. I read other sailors were drinking 5 litres of water during the daytime and another

5 litres at night when they were near the equator as it was so hot and dehydrating. So that's 10 litres a day to keep hydrated, this seems a more realistic number to use. I don't want water anxiety so I will take lots of water. My boat does not have a water maker. The water maker is a clever gadget that takes in seawater and pushes it through a semipermeable membrane at high-pressure to filter out the salt and produce fresh water. With a water maker you are self-sufficient for drinking water at sea. For my next Atlantic trip I will certainly invest in a water maker.

Waste

What do I do with the rubbish and waste generated from 23 days at sea? Drink cans take 100-200 years to break down in the sea, tin cans 50 years; glass bottles 20-30 years; banana skins 3-4 weeks; orange peel 6 months; and paper towel 2-4 weeks. To reduce waste in the first place, I will remove as much cardboard and plastic packaging before anything goes on the boat. I will store waste plastic onboard as it takes 450 years to break down. Used plastic food packaging will be washed in sea water to prevent any smell and then stored in strong sacks on deck. Biodegradable waste will go overboard.

Amusement onboard

Blondie Hasler, a famous English ocean sailor would bring his ukulele to keep him entertained at sea. This is not for me as I don't play an instrument. Knitting was a tradition for seamen in bygone years but I have no urge to knit my way across the Atlantic. Books are my thing, actual books and audio books. I looked forward to reading each day when I had a break from running the boat. Books at sea seem much more vivid and engaging. I will download a few audio books as they help fill the silence of being alone, you feel the narrator is with you on the trip. Music is important to lift the inevitable low moods that occur when sailing alone. Netflix was a surprise hit for both my Atlantic crossings, giving me the opportunity of an hour or two each night to escape the boat and into a movie. I would not now be without Netflix on a long passage.

Sleep

It is easy to become complacent at sea, especially when you see an empty ocean day after day, but at some stage vessels will start to appear so be ready. There are many different views on how to manage sleep on a long voyage. Lack of sleep is dangerous, leading to silly mistakes and accidents. Being single-handed, it is even more crucial to get enough rest. The low point for human performance is 3-4am, when body temperature is at its lowest and decision

Appendix

making is impaired. To avoid any early morning decisions, I will rig the boat for the night-time and try to do as little as possible during night hours. This will help minimise mistakes.

Many single-handed sailors aim to have no more than 20 minutes' sleep at any one time. Every 20 minutes an alarm goes off and they get up to have a quick look around to check all is ok. Then back to sleep for another 20 minutes. Kitchen timers are popular but I have not found a kitchen timer loud enough to wake me up. The 20-minute routine was made famous by Ellen MacArthur who in 2005 broke the world record for the fastest solo circumnavigation of the globe in 71 days. I find this 20-minute sleep routine works well on coastal passages where there can be vessels around and where a regular look out is needed. I don't actually sleep but going below to lie down and close your eyes for 20 minutes is refreshing. The trouble with 20-minute sleep cycles is that you get very little actual sleep. I would not be able to maintain this for more than a couple of days.

My plan when sailing near the coast is to stick to the 20-minute naps on the starboard bunk where I can see the radar. The iPad will also be in the bunk beside me so I can immediately see the positions of nearby vessels and my own boat's speed/direction. The iPad will even show me if there is a collision risk and the closest my boat will be to another vessel. Once I get offshore and well away from the coast, I will switch to longer 90-minute sleep periods, the ocean is so vast that the collision risk is very small. Every 90 minutes my phone will alarm and will get up to have a look around. If I get four of these 90-minute sleep cycles during the night and a lunchtime nap I should be fine to make up near enough the 8 hours of recommended sleep per day.

What aids sleep is the comforting knowledge that I have the radar and AIS alarm set at 3 miles. The built-in alarm on the radar was a soft faint beep, which would never wake me, so I connected an external fire alarm siren. There was no way I could sleep through the piercing sound of this siren. A number of times crossing Biscay it alarmed and I awoke to find a ship on the horizon. I also have the AIS connected to the boat's HiFi speakers so the alarm is loud.

These electronic eyes make me feel safe, which sets the environment for a good night's sleep. This is how I meet rule 5 of the COLREGS (International Regulations for Preventing Collisions at Sea): "Every vessel shall at all times maintain a proper lookout by sight and hearing as well by all available means." My view is the electronic systems watching out for me are more vigilant than a crew member who is more than likely dozing in the cockpit. But all this electronic gadgetry won't alert me if I am about to hit a semi-submerged container or whale. Over 500 containers fall off ships each year. That's just the risk you have to take.

Safety

The big fear in sailing is falling overboard. I have a harness in my life jacket, which I can wear in rough weather or when working on deck at night, to attach myself to the boat at various secure points.

Breaking waves are the most dangerous waves for sailors. A breaking wave of the height of just third the boat length is considered dangerous and can roll the boat 90 degrees onto its side, this is called a knock down. For my 10.5 metre boat, it only requires a 3-metre breaking wave to hit the boat broadside and she would likely be knocked down onto her side with substantial damage. A breaking wave height equalling half the length of the boat, 5 metres in my case, is guaranteed to roll the boat under the water where most likely the mast will break. It is common for waves to reach 10 metres and more in the Atlantic. The key is not to let the boat get side-on to breaking waves, which are best taken bow-on. The danger is when the boat slows to a stop in the water, as then she is then at the mercy of the waves which can hit the boat broadside and knock her down.

What happens if the autopilot breaks down? I have a complete second system so I hope that eventuality is covered. But the autopilot needs power so as long as my batteries are charging all should be well. I have three separate ways to charge the batteries, using the boat engine, the petrol generator and solar power. Other Atlantic boats have installed a self-steering wind vane, which can steer the boat offshore for days on end, without the need of electrical power. I considered this but it required drilling more holes in the hull and it was awkward with the existing bathing platform at the stern. I felt comfortable with two separate electric autopilots which would get more use over the years as most sailing is costal sailing where a wind vane is not practical.

Seasickness

Seasickness and single-handed sailing is a real problem, as if the skipper is out of action who sails the boat? There are three stages of sea sickness: stage 1 you feel you are going to die; stage 2 you hope you are going to die; and stage 3 you are worried that you are not going to die! I am lucky that I do not suffer from seasickness. I am hoping my strong stomach keeps going across the Atlantic. I have noticed the first sign that someone is becoming seasick is uncontrollable yawning. What helps is to lie down flat for a while in the cabin or in the fresh air of the cockpit. It takes about 3-days to acclimatise to life at sea, what can help is to:

- avoid alcohol and fatty foods the day before departure;
- start anti sickness tablets 24 hours before departure;
- plan meals first few days at sea;

- dehydration can be a real problem in hot climates and long passages, drink plenty of water and have rehydration sachets onboard;
- sugar and salt helps (boiled sweets, salty crisps/biscuits, ginger biscuits), on my boat salty crackers are popular.

Hypothermia can follow from sea sickness, when the body's core temperature falls below 35°C. When crew are seasick, they often don't want to be in the cabin and stay on deck for too long, exposed to the elements and wind chill. Signs of hypothermia include confusion, loss of coordination, shivering stops, becoming rigid and sometimes curling into the foetal position. The action is to get the person down below into the cabin and out of the elements. Twice on my boat I have experienced crew showing these signs and it is a huge struggle to convince and cajole them to go below.

RNLI lifeboat recommendations for treating hypothermia is not to actively warm up a hypothermic person with warm drinks or a warm shower; don't give them whisky as alcohol lowers their core body temperature; remove any outer layers of wet clothing; and wrap them in blankets and cover their head. Hypothermia has not yet set in if you are still feeling cold and are shivering. If feeling cold act early, don't prolong exposure on deck or in the cockpit. Get below into the warm cabin for a break and have a warm drink. Too often crew are afraid to say they are feeling cold.

Heavy weather sailing

Squalls are a common feature crossing the Atlantic. A squall can be seen on the horizon in daytime so prepare immediately: reef mainsail and furl away jib. If necessary, start the engine to keep on route or turn the boat to run with squall if it is severe. A squall will only last 10-15mins.

I always stow the anchor in the bow locker for long ocean passages as then there is no risk of the anchor being pushed free out of the bow roller by a wave and punching a hole in the side of the boat. If the anchor became loose at the bow it would be risky to have to make my way up there in a storm to secure and manhandle a heavy anchor. For long sails I deflate the dinghy and tie it down on deck. An inflated dinghy on deck causes lots of windage and won't be long breaking free in a storm. Anything coming loose on deck in a storm is a real problem as it puts you at risk of injury or falling overboard when you have to leave the cockpit to secure the item.

John Kretschmer says the majority of sailing disasters occur from crews taking a passive approach to storms. Boats continue on route with the storm approaching, when they had time to sail further away from the storm centre and into less severe winds. We usually have at least 2-days' notice of the storm track, which could put you 200 plus miles further away from it and make all the difference between experiencing severe winds and seas to more moderate and forgiving conditions.

Esperanza's storm preparation plan:

1. Have the storm jib sail pre-rigged and hanked on inner forestay at the bow ready to launch.
2. Have the parachute anchor in the cockpit with its 100 metre of rope ready to deploy from the safety of the cockpit. The other end will already be secured at the bow.
3. Eat well before the storm and plan for easy food like sandwiches. Make a hot flask of coffee as it may be too rough to boil the kettle, which I encountered a few times in the Atlantic.
4. Don't allow fear to paralyze you, act, form a plan and stick to it.

The below are tried and tested storm tactics:

Heaving-to: to heave-to is to stop the boat. To do this you turn the boat as if you were to turn through the wind but don't let the jib sail off as you normally would. The jib sail backs to stop the boat. Trim the mainsail and adjust the rudder to keep the boat between 45-60 degrees off the wind. Heaving-to is the best strategy in most weather situations but maybe not so in a real storm. I can't heave-to with inner forestay connected at the bow as it is in the way. I would have to raise the storm jib instead. Drift will be about 2 knots so you do need sea room and to be well away from the coast.

Running: the best-known storm tactic, it is when you sail downwind with the wind and waves behind you with no sails up. Speeds can rise dangerously and if anything goes wrong there is lots of energy and something is going to break. Energy increases with the square of the speed, so going twice as fast down a wave will result in four times the energy as the boat impacts a wave. The autopilot may also not be able to handle a fast-downwind leg and trip out, so you really need someone outside in the cockpit ready to take the wheel. If single-handed this means you are at the mercy of the elements getting cold and wet and with no one to relieve you. It is exhausting, dangerous and cannot be sustained for long periods.

The advantage of running with the storm is the relative speed of the wind is reduced so it will feel calmer and more pleasant than if the boat was facing into the wind and waves. The disadvantage is that you are traveling with the storm, prolonging your exposure. When seas begin to break and you feel loss of steering

Appendix

control, you must slow the boat or abandon running. You could try to slow the boat down by launching from the stern a sea anchor or drogue trailing on a long rope. I bought a sea anchor for this purpose, which is a strong plastic cone to create drag and slow the boat down to safer speeds

Forereaching: requires a strong storm jib sail and a balanced mainsail reducing in size as the weather worsens. You keep sailing the boat at 2-3 knots, taking the waves 45-60 degrees off the bow, which is the strongest part of the boat. It is also better for the autopilot than running with the wind, which puts lots of force on the rudder. An advantage is that you can steer a course away from the centre of the storm, it might be slow but at least you are moving further from the storm and conditions should gradually improve. This is my preferred strategy as it is taking an active role to move away from the storm, which is a good idea as who knows how bad the low-pressure system could get.

Deploy parachute Sea Anchor from the bow: a popular option is to take all the sails down or furl them away, hide below and let the boat fend for itself. It has worked for many but there is a real possibility of being rolled and capsized by a breaking wave hitting the boat broadside. The better option is to first deploy a parachute anchor from the bow and then go below. For a severe storm this is my preferred method as hiding below in the safety of the warm cabin reduces the risk of injury and hypothermia form exposure to the elements. The parachute anchor should keep the boat head to wind, just like it is on a mooring so the waves are taken at the bow, the strongest point of the boat. It will be a wild rough ride in the cabin and would require plenty of Hail Mary's and a strong stomach to get through it. This is my strategy when forereaching becomes too much work.

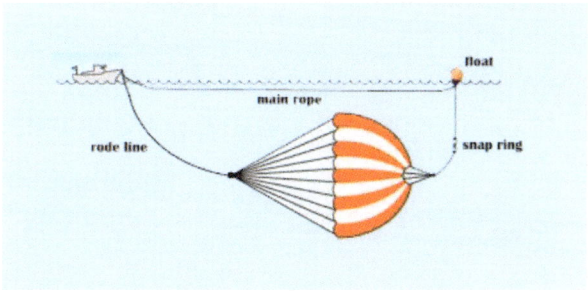

Hallberg Rassy 352

Hallberg-Rassy is a Swedish company, internationally known for producing high quality ocean-going sailing yachts, since 1943. The shipyard is located in Ellös on the island of Orust in Sweden. Hallberg Rassy yachts are known for their sturdy construction, superb craftsmanship and seaworthiness. Over 9,500 yachts have been built.

802 Hallberg-Rassy 352's were built between 1978 - 1991. From 1986 the skylight in the saloon was increased in size to give more natural light into the saloon and the hull was further raised, in order to get even better volume and headroom under deck.

Manufacturer: Hallberg Rassy, Ellös, Sweden.
Designers: Christoph Rassy & Olle Enderlein.
Category: Offshore cruising sailboat.
Type: Centre cockpit with Aft Cabin.
Construction: GRP (glass reinforced polyester).
Hull: Single skin fiberglass polyester; deck: Sandwich fiberglass polyester.
Hull length: 10.54 m / 34'9" feet.
Beam: 3.38 metre.
Draft: 1.7 metre.
Displacement: Empty: 6.7 tonnes; Esperanza fully loaded: 9 tonnes.
Keel: 3 tonne semi-full encapsulated steel in deep bilge.
Rudder: Single rudder on skeg.
Mast configuration: Keel stepped mast. Esperanza is the later tall rig with in-mast furling. The tall rig is easily recognised by the double spreaders.
Air draft: (tall rig) 15.6 m / 52 feet.
Engine: Esperanza re-engined with Yanmar 3JH4E engine, 39hp
Diesel: 250 litres (2 tanks).
Fresh water: 300 litres

Sailing Glossary

Port: facing forward, this is anything to the left of the boat.

Starboard: facing forward, this is anything to the right of the boat.

Bow/Stern: the bow is the front of the boat; the stern is the back.

Point of Sail: the boat's direction relative to the wind. If you're sailing into the wind, you are head-to-wind or on a beat, beating to windward. If the wind is blowing straight over the side of the boat, that's called sailing on a beam reach. You are downwind when the wind is blowing from behind the boat. When sailing between downwind and a beam reach this is a broad reach.

Helm: where you steer the boat, the wheel which controls the boat's rudder.

Keel: the keel is a long, heavy fin on the bottom of the boat that sticks down under the water. It provides stability and is the reason why yachts are difficult to capsize.

Heeling: this is the term for when a sailboat leans over in the water, pushed by the wind.

Sheet: a sheet is the name for any rope that is used to adjust the sails.

Lines: this is the nautical term for ropes that are not connected to the sails, for example shorelines are the ropes used to tie the boat to the shore or marina.

Halyard: a halyard is a rope that is used to hoist a sail up.

Tack/Tacking: to tack is to change direction by turning the bow of the boat through the wind. If the wind is blowing over the port side, you are on a port tack. If it's blowing over the starboard side, you're on starboard tack.

Jibe: a jibe is another way of changing direction, in which you bring the stern of the boat through the wind. It can be a dangerous manoeuvre as the boom flies across to the other side of the boat often violently. Watch your head!

Windward: the side of the boat closest to the wind. When heeling over, this will always be the high side.

Leeward: the side of the boat furthest from the wind. When heeling over, this will always be the low side.

Mainsail: the big triangular sail just behind the mast attached to the boom.

Jib: the jib sail is always forward of the mast, and unlike the mainsail, it does not have a boom.

Genoa: also called 'genny' is a larger size jib sail.

Furlex or furler: this is the jib/genoa furling system. It allows the jib/genoa sail to be pulled in or furled from the safety of the cockpit by pulling a rope which connects to the bottom of the Furlex drum system. This causes the drum and aluminium foil of the Furlex to rotate and the jib/genoa sail rolls up around the foil.

In-mast furling: the mainsail can be furled or rolled away into the mast. It allows full control of the amount of mainsail that is exposed to the wind.

Hank on jib: This is the older manual system; the jib sail has brass hanks which are clipped to a steel forestay wire. The jib is then pulled up the forestay to raise it. To lower the sail, you have to go to the bow and drop the sail down and pack away in a bag on deck.

Goose winged: a sail configuration where the jib/genoa sail is poled out on the opposite side to the mainsail when sailing downwind. It presents the largest possible area of sail to the wind and the boat is pushed along. It is an alternative to flying a spinnaker or cruising chute, easier to control though less efficient.

Spinnaker: a sail designed specifically for sailing off the wind from a beam reach (90° wind angle) to downwind (wind 180° off bow). The spinnaker fills with wind and balloons out in front of the boat when it is deployed. It is a lightweight nylon sail to capture light winds.

Cruising chute: cruising chute/symmetric spinnaker/gennaker are basically the same thing. They are made of the same nylon material as a spinnaker and used in light winds, up to a wind strength of Force 4. A cruising chute is easier to launch, setup and handle than a spinnaker, so it makes an ideal light wind sail for single-handed sailors. I opted to use this sail for the Atlantic passage and left my spinnaker at home to make more storage space on the boat.

Suffer: The snuffer is used with a spinnaker or cruising chute; it is a bucket-like device with a sail bag or sock attached. The bucket-like device is pulled down over the sail to snuff the air out of it, which collapses the sail into the sock or bag. Once in the sock bag the spinnaker can be lowered to the deck.

About the Author

Alan McMahon is 47 years of age with two teenage kids. He lives in Dublin, Ireland. He has worked for the last 20 years in a multinational company in marketing and I.T.

Sailing the Atlantic is his second adventure; in 2003 he flew 25,000 miles around the world in the single-engine light aircraft, crossing the Atlantic and Pacific oceans. Flying was his passion until he made a switch to sailing in 2007. A complete novice to sailing he built his experience in incremental steps, starting by learning to sail on a small day sailor boat, then buying a Westerly 25-foot yacht. After some years he took the next step and went bigger to 35-feet, buying Esperanza, a Hallberg Rassy 352.

Printed in Great Britain
by Amazon